A New Scottish History

Front cover
Standing stones at Callanish
(Crown copyright: Scottish
Development Department)

Back cover
Kilchurn Castle, Argyllshire
(Pictor International Limited)

Title-page
King James V
A wood carving in Stirling Castle
(Crown copyright: Scottish
Development Department)

Recreative drawings by
Jim Proudfoot

Book One

A New Scottish History

Eric Melvin
MA, MEd
Assistant Head Teacher
Tynecastle High School
Edinburgh

Ian Gould
MA
formerly Principal
Teacher of History
Broxburn High School

John Thompson
MA, PhD
formerly Rector
Madras College
St Andrews

John Murray

© E. Melvin, I. Gould and J. Thompson 1980

All rights reserved. No part of this publication may be reproduced, stored in a retrieval system, or transmitted, in any form or by any means, electronic, mechanical, photocopying, recording or otherwise, without the prior permission of John Murray (Publishers) Ltd, 50 Albemarle Street, London W1X 4BD

Set, printed and bound in Great Britain by
Butler & Tanner Ltd, Frome and London

0 7195 3638 3

Foreword

In 1957 the first book of *A Scottish History for Today* was published by John Murray. This present book is its successor and, to emphasise the extensive revision that has been made, the title is changed.

There can be few teachers of history working in Scotland today who have not been influenced by the original series—either as teachers or pupils! The strengths of the books have clearly stood the test of time and provide the foundations for the new series. The authors, Ian Gould and John Thompson—themselves practising teachers—sought to produce history books which presented Scotland's story against a wider background of international events. Each book was well illustrated with photographs and with line drawings which dovetailed neatly with the text. The text itself was clear and straightforward, and on occasions the narrative was reinforced with extracts from poems and contemporary sources. Indeed, the readability of the books was confirmed by the recent Bulletin 4 of the Scottish Central Committee for the Social Subjects.

Since the publication of the original series, however, there have been many developments—both in historical scholarship and in teaching methodology. There have been changes, too, in school organisation with the advent of comprehensive schools, a two-year common course and mixed ability teaching—however defined!

Teachers have responded to these challenges with a variety of approaches which has enabled history to grow and flourish in these changing climates. Publishers, too, have responded with a range of topic and source books to service the new methods. The authors of *A New Scottish History* are convinced, however, that a need exists for a chronological account of Scotland's story which represents both the best traditions of history teaching and the developments which have taken place since the original books were published. Such an approach is in keeping with the aims of history teaching established in Curriculum Paper 15 of the Consultative Committee on the Curriculum.

A New Scottish History has been written in two volumes, each corresponding to one year's work. Book One deals with the question of what history is and how historians work before looking at events up to the reign of Mary Queen of Scots. Book Two progresses from the reign of James VI and I and concludes with an examination of the historical origins of particular contemporary problems.

The original concept of placing Scottish events in a wider historical context has been maintained. So, too, has the extensive use of illustrations linked closely to the text. Now, however, photographs have almost completely replaced line drawings and it is hoped that Jim Proudfoot's evocative reconstructions will all the more dramatically help to fire the imagination of pupils. The increasing use of contemporary sources in S1 and S2 is reflected both in the text and in the assignments at the end of the major chapters.

Through their reading, writing and oral work pupils are encouraged to develop the important skills of inquiry, interpretation and reconstruction. Equally important, however, are the unique contributions which history can make to the development of empathy in pupils and to a growing awareness of the richness of their cultural heritage.

It is in this spirit that *A New Scottish History* has been written.

Eric Melvin

Acknowledgements

The identification and collection of the illustrations has been a major task. Help has been received from many sources. In particular the authors would like to express their thanks to the following:

Mr Stuart Maxwell and Dr David Clarke of the National Museum of Antiquities of Scotland; Mr Cameron of the Property Services Agency, Photographic Library, Argyle House; Mr Beacham of the Property Services Agency, Photographic Library, Hannibal House; Mr Gouldesbrough of the Scottish Record Office; Miss Whitehouse formerly of the Royal Scottish Museum; the staff of the Royal Commission on Ancient Monuments of Scotland.

The authors express their thanks to the following who have kindly permitted the reproduction of copyright photographs:

Ashmolean Museum, Oxford (p. 86 (bottom)); Barnaby's Picture Library (p. 171 (photo—Peter Larsen)); BBC Hulton Picture Library (pp. 43, 58 (top), 72, 145, 160 (top), 172 (bottom)); Bodleian Library, Oxford (p. 118); British Library (pp. 85, 86 (top), 87, 90, 105, 110, 113 (top), 114 (top), 119 (bottom), 120, 123, 125 (bottom, 126, 128, 130, 131, 144, 151 (top), 152, 154, 158, 161, 173, 180, 194); Trustees of the British Museum (pp. 29 (top), 34, 63, 84, 163 (top), 165, 205); British Tourist Authority (pp. 47 (bottom), 143); Cambridge University Collection (pp. 14 (bottom), 88, 106 (bottom)); Master and Fellows of Corpus Christi College, Cambridge (p. 139); Cambridge University Press (p. 157 (bottom)); Crown copyright: reproduced by permission of the Controller of H.M. Stationery Office (pp. 47 (top), 48, 49, 50 (top), 65 (photo—W. J. White), 140);Crown copyright: Royal Commission on Ancient Monuments, Scotland (pp. 51 (middle), 71, 124, 203); Crown copyright: reproduced by permission of the Scottish Development Department (pp. title-page, 2 (top), 19 (bottom), 20, 21, 51 (top and bottom), 67, 68, 78 (top), 102, 103, 109, 111, 112, 113 (bottom), 137, 151 (bottom), 187 (bottom), 206); Ray Delvert (p. 40); Director of Administration, East Lothian District Council (p. 119 (top)); Chief Librarian, City of Edinburgh District Council (p. 197 (top)); Edinburgh City Museums (p. 16 (photo—Len Cumming)); Mary Evans Picture Library (pp. 8 (bottom), 162, 166, 183); Florence National Museum (p. 172 (top)); Geneva Museum (p. 182 (top and bottom)); Governors of George Heriot's School (p. 164); Glasgow Art Gallery and Museum (p. 18); Griffith Institute, Ashmolean Museum, Oxford (p. 13); D. Henrie (pp. 9 (bottom), 11, 35 (bottom), 159, 197 (bottom), 198, 200 (top), 201 (bottom)); Dean and Chapter of Hereford Cathedral (p. 157 (top)); Hunterian Museum, University of Glasgow (p. 54 (bottom)); Keeper of the Records of Scotland (pp. 8 (top), 117 (photo by permission of the Duke of Buccleuch)); Lothians and Borders Police (p. 6); Mansell Collection (pp. 42, 44, 58 (bottom), 92, 94 (bottom), 97 (top), 170, 181, 187 (top)); Mansell Collection—Giraudon (pp. 93, 94 (top), 95, 96, 97 (bottom), 98, 99, 100, 104); Warden and Fellows of Merton College, Oxford (p. 115); National Portrait Gallery, London (p. 188 (top)); Trustees of the National Library of Scotland (pp. 91 (by permission of the Duke of Roxburghe), 176 (top)); National Monuments Record (p. 132); National Museum of Antiquities of Scotland (pp. 2 (bottom), 9 (top), 12 (bottom photo by permission of J. Close-Brooks), 19 (top), 23, 50 (bottom), 54 (top), 60, 74 (top), 78 (bottom), 81, 82, 107, 125 (top), 138 (top), 176 (bottom), 186 (top), 190, 204 (top and bottom), 208); National Trust for Scotland (pp. 7, 17, 135 (photo—Tom Scott), 200 (bottom), 201 (top)); Oriental Institute, University of Chicago (pp. 30 (top), 31); Popperfoto (pp. 3, 4, 27 (top), 33, 160 (bottom)); Public Record Office (p. 193); Royal Scottish Museum (pp. 27 (middle and bottom), 28, 29 (middle and bottom), 30 (bottom), 36, 177); Scottish National Portrait Gallery (pp. 101, 148, 150, 163 (bottom), 179, 186 (bottom), 188 (bottom), 191, 192 (top and bottom), 204 (middle)); Spanish National Tourist Office (p. 41); Trinity College, Cambridge (p. 114 (bottom)); Trinity College, Dublin (p. 70); Universitetets Oldsaksamling, Oslo (pp. 73, 74 (bottom)); Vindolanda Trust (p. 15); Yerbury Galleries (p. 10).

The picture of herbs on p. 159 appears by permission of D. Napier and Sons, Edinburgh.

Contents

Part one
Settlers, soldiers and saints

1	What is history?	2
2	How do we know what happened?	6
3	The work of the archaeologist	12
4	Skara Brae: An Orkney village of the Stone Age	18
5	The first farmers	24
6	Life in Ancient Egypt	26
7	Ancient Greece	33
8	The Roman Empire	37
9	Roman Britain	46
10	Caledonia	49
11	The break-up of the Roman world	57
12	England, Ireland and Scotland become Christian	65
13	The Vikings	72
14	Scotland becomes one country	81
15	England in the time of King Alfred	84

Part two
The forging of a nation

16	The Norman Conquest	92
17	Margaret, Queen and Saint	101
18	The Normans in Scotland	104
19	David the First and the Church	108
20	Life at Melrose Abbey	112
21	The Golden Age of Scotland: Life in the burghs	117
22	The Golden Age of Scotland: Life in the country	123
23	The War of Independence: The Hammer of the Scots	130
24	The War of Independence: The saving of Scotland	135
25	The story of the Auld Alliance	142
26	Stewart kings and unruly nobles	147

Part three
Explorers and reformers

27	Travel in the Middle Ages	156
28	The New Age	160

29	The great discoverers	167
30	James the Fourth	175
31	The Protestant and Catholic Reformations	180
32	Scottish rulers and the Scottish Church	186
33	Mary, Queen of Scots	190
34	The Lowlands in Queen Mary's time	196
35	The Highlands in Queen Mary's time	203
	Glossary	209
	Index	213

Note to Readers

You will find a number of important words in this book which have been printed in *italics* the first time they are used. The exact meaning of these words is explained in the Glossary at the end of the book, between pages 209 and 212.

PART ONE
Settlers, soldiers and saints

Pictish soldiers carved on a stone at Aberlemno in Angus

1 What is history?

Standing stones at Callanish, Isle of Lewis

What is history? Your dictionary will tell you that history is a study of the past. Those people who work full-time at the job of studying the past are called historians.

Many people get a lot of pleasure out of studying the past in their spare time, often in their holidays. These old stones at Callanish attract many visitors every year. Visits to castles, palaces and museums are also part of the fun of finding out about the past.

It seems that people have always been curious about the past: about their own families, old buildings and other old things they find or see. Here is a photograph of a hand axe from the Stone Age. Does it make you wonder about the man who made it, how he made it, what he used it for, what he looked like?

We all like good stories, and there are many good stories about people or events in the past. From early times there were special storytellers. Some told stories from the past to people gathered round a fire in the long dark winter evenings. Others wrote down what they had heard, seen or found out about past events.

A study of the past, then, gives us information about famous events and famous people. We can learn about what has taken place in our own country and in other countries too.

A study of the past can also tell us about important changes and developments which have taken place over many years. For example, what changes have there been in the ways houses are built, in the clothes people wear, in the food they eat? What changes have there been in transport, in the way people earn their living? What changes have there been in the ways people fight each other and in the ways they look after those who are ill? We shall be looking at these changes, and others.

Many changes can be seen in your own district, by studying local history. What was it like to live there fifty years ago? A hundred years ago? How many people lived in your town or village? What were their houses like? What jobs did they do? How much of that old district can you still see today? How would you start finding out about the history of your own district?

But many things happen outside our own district and outside Scotland. We live in a world faced with many problems which we read about in our newspapers or see on television every day. Many are difficult to understand. Why does a wall divide people living in Berlin? Why has there been fighting between Israel and the Arab countries?

Israeli tanks in the desert

Why is there trouble between people of different races in southern Africa? Why are these black youths rioting? Why has there been so much violence in Northern Ireland and why are there so many British troops there?

There are no easy answers, but studying history will at least help you to understand all these problems.

THINGS TO DO

1 What history did you study in your primary school? Copy the headings in this table into your notebook and write under each heading what you did in Primary 7. We have put in some examples of what you may have studied. If you are not sure where to put a topic ask your teacher for help.

Famous people	*Famous events*	*Important changes*	*Local history*	*A study of today*	*Anything else?*
Mary, Queen of Scots	The Great Fire of London	The history of flight	My district in Grand-dad's time	Life in the Soviet Union	A patch study on the Vikings

2 You probably know already how dates in history are written: AD 1066, 55 BC. We date each year from the birth of Christ.

AD is a short way of writing the Latin words 'Anno Domini', which mean 'in the year of our Lord'. So AD 1066 is another way of saying 1066 years after Jesus's date of birth.

BC simply means 'before Christ'. So the first invasion of Britain by Julius Caesar in 55 BC happened fifty-five years before Jesus was born—although of course the people living in 55 BC did not know this!

Copy this table in your notebook.

|⎯⎯⎯⎯⎯⎯⎯⎯⎯|⎯⎯⎯⎯⎯⎯⎯⎯⎯|⎯⎯⎯⎯⎯⎯⎯⎯⎯|⎯⎯⎯⎯⎯⎯⎯⎯⎯|⎯⎯⎯⎯⎯⎯⎯⎯⎯|
| 2000 BC | 1000 BC | *The birth of Christ* | AD 1000 | AD 2000 |

Now put these dates on the top line of the table in their correct order:
AD 1914   AD 563   10 BC   AD 1745   1339 BC   AD 1314   55 BC

Not all countries use this method of dating. Muslim countries such as Saudi Arabia date their years from the Hejira. This was the escape of their prophet Mohammed from Mecca, which took place in AD 622 by our reckoning. So Muslim years are 622 behind ours.

2 How do we know what happened?

If someone asked you the question 'How do we know about history, about what happened in the past?' you would probably answer 'By reading a history book'. Of course you would be right, for over the years historians have written thousands of history books for you to choose from.

But if you think about it, that is not a very good answer. How does a historian know what to put in a history book? How does he know that a man called William invaded England in 1066? How does he know that a battle was fought at Bannockburn in 1314 or that there was a great fire in London in 1666?

As we already know, however, studying history does not mean just learning dates of famous events. So we must ask more questions. Who was William? Where did he come from? Why did he invade England? Whom was he fighting against? Where was the battle fought? How was the battle fought? What happened after the battle? There are so many questions we can ask about each single event in history. Let us see how the historian finds out the answers.

The historian as a detective

Imagine that a crime has been committed and the police have been called in.

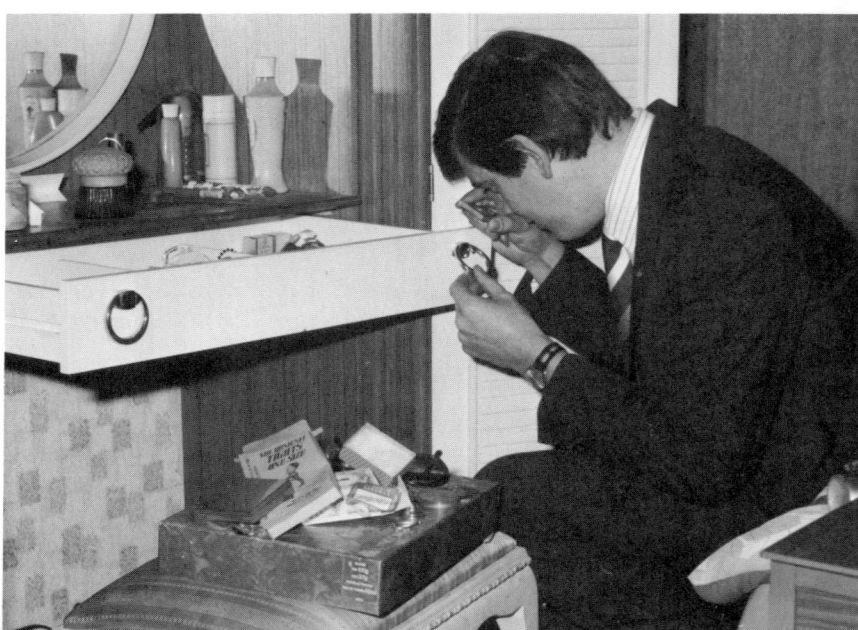

How does a detective get on with his job?

1 First of all he makes his inquiries. He asks a lot of questions, he takes statements from eye-witnesses and collects as much evidence as he can from the scene of the crime.

2 He then tries to explain the evidence he has collected. (We call this interpreting the evidence.) So he examines the statements of witnesses to try to find out what actually happened. He examines clues such as finger-prints to see if he can identify who was at the scene of the crime.

3 Finally he puts all his evidence together to try to reconstruct what actually happened when the crime was committed.

A historian goes about his job in much the same way. He inquires and collects his evidence, he interprets what he has collected and then tries to reconstruct what happened in the past to get possible answers to his questions.

Notice that we said 'possible answers'. Why is this? It is because historical detective work is different from police detective work. For one thing, most of our witnesses are dead! We can't interview William the Conqueror. Collecting historical evidence is rather like finding some pieces of a jigsaw puzzle. You do your best to put the puzzle together to make the complete picture, but there are always pieces of the jigsaw missing. Sometimes another piece is found, but you are never certain what the whole picture looks like. Historians are always looking out for more pieces of historical evidence—while they go on arguing about the evidence they already have!

The historical jigsaw

Let us look at some of the pieces of the historical jigsaw. This historical evidence can be anything that was built, used or written down during the event we are asking questions about.

Here are some examples of different types of historical evidence: different pieces of the historical jigsaw.

Buildings

The buildings left by our *ancestors* tell us a lot about them. Is there an old castle near your home or school? When was it built? How was it built? What sort of people lived, worked and played in such a castle? We do not build castles now, so why was it necessary to build them then?

Buildings from the past are not always as grand as castles. This is a photograph of a doocot at Phantassie in East Lothian, built about 300 years ago. It is really a kind of pigeon loft. Can you think why people kept so many pigeons in those days? Your answer should tell you something about what people ate and give you clues about what they could produce on their farms and buy at their markets.

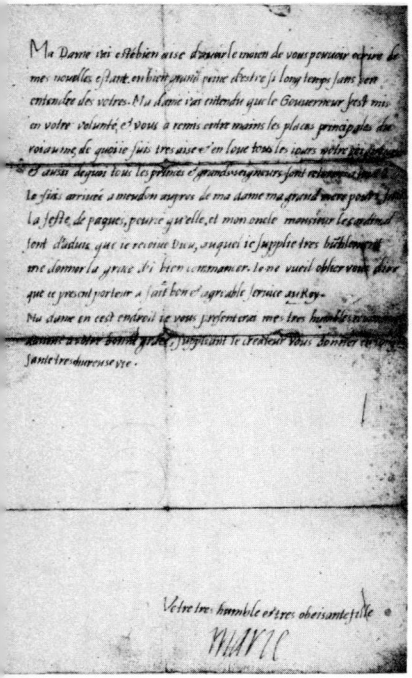

Documents

Look at this old piece of writing. It is called a *document*. (This is a letter written in French by Mary, Queen of Scots, when she was twelve years old.) From earliest times our ancestors made *laws* and *treaties* about what people could or could not do. The Ten Commandments in the Old Testament (Exodus 20) are followed in the Bible by a long list of laws (Exodus 21–5). Of course laws are still being made. It is a law of our *Parliament* that says you have to come to school! Many old documents still exist, even after hundreds of years, and these can still be examined by historians. Many old historical documents of Scotland are kept safely in Register House in Edinburgh.

Eye witness accounts

We have already said that a police detective tries to find and question eye-witnesses. But unless we are studying recent history (say, the Second World War, 1939–45) there are no eye-witnesses. We must use notes or diaries which eye-witnesses kept when they were alive. Perhaps you keep your own diary and have recorded events such as the Queen's Silver Jubilee? It is interesting to remember that you will be an eye-witness of that event for your own children and grandchildren.

What can old diaries tell us? Here, for example, is an *extract* from a famous diary kept by Samuel Pepys who lived in London about 300 years ago.

> Sunday September 2nd 1666
> We went to a little alehouse in Bankside and there stayed until it was dark almost, and saw the fire grow, and as it grew darker, appeared more and more. And in corners and upon steeples and between churches and houses as far as we could see up the hill of the City, in a most horrid, malicious, [here Pepys means 'cruel'] bloody flame not like the fine flame of an ordinary fire. It made me weep to see it.

This is a good description of the Great Fire of London. Thanks to Pepys we can get an idea of what it was like watching the terrible flames sweeping through the city. We can also feel how upsetting it was for Londoners like Pepys. We have no photographs of the Great Fire, of course, because the camera had not been invented.

Illustrations

For thousands of years our ancestors have recorded events in drawings and paintings. This picture of a bison was painted about 35 000 years ago.

We have only drawings and paintings until the 1840s when the first photographs were taken. Moving pictures were first taken in the

1880s and the first television pictures were made in the 1930s. So it is only for very recent history that we can examine photographs and films. Do you think it will be easier or harder for future historians to reconstruct our way of life?

Everyday articles

The everyday articles used by people in the past can give us a lot of information. Their clothes, tools, weapons, jewellery—even their pots and pans—all help us to reconstruct what their life was like.

Here is a Roman oil lamp about 2000 years old. We can see how it is made. We can find out how it works. We can think about why it was necessary for people of those days to use lamps like this. (Why did they not just switch on an electric light as we do?) We can try to imagine what it must have been like to have had only spluttering oil lamps to give light on long, dark, winter nights.

Look at these three articles from the time of the Second World War. They were given out to families in this country at the beginning of the war. Why do you think people needed a helmet, a gas mask and cooking leaflets from the Ministry of Food? (These have recipes using dried eggs and puddings made from potatoes.) Your answers should tell you something about what life must have been like for *civilians* during the war years. Perhaps your grandparents still have articles like these that they have kept. If so, ask if you may borrow them to show other members of the class.

THINGS TO DO

1 Look at the two photographs of Princes Street in Edinburgh. The one on the left was taken in 1859. We can learn quite a lot about life at that time if we look at it carefully.

Write these headings in your notebook:

        Clothing (1859)   Clothing (Now)

then, leaving a few lines:

        Transport (1859)   Transport (Now)

Describe the clothing and transport of 1859. Then do the same thing for the present day. Write down what you think are the three main differences between life then and now as shown in these photographs.

2 The everyday articles from the Second World War give us some clues about what life was like then. What else could tell us about that war? Write the heading 'Second World War Evidence' in your notebook. Then list as many things as you can think of which would help you to find out more about that war. (The headings on pages 7, 8 and 9 will help you.)

3 Talk to your parents and grandparents about some of the things they may remember: the Second World War (1939–45); the Coronation (1953); the first moon walk (1969).
Other interesting topics you could talk about are what kind of clothes they wore when they were your age, the sort of entertainment they enjoyed, and what their school was like.

11

3 The work of the archaeologist

In the last chapter we saw that the historian is like a detective. He uses the evidence of buildings, documents, eye-witness accounts, illustrations and everyday articles to try to reconstruct what happened in history.

Now let us look at the work of someone who provides the historian with a lot of this evidence. Your dictionary will tell you that an *archaeologist* makes a special study of the things people have left behind them. He is interested in the remains of their buildings, *tombs*, tools, weapons, jewellery, furniture; in everything that they used in their day-to-day life.

As we have seen, some old buildings are still standing: some have stood for thousands of years. Sometimes, things simply turn up by accident: you may have heard of people finding old coins or bits of pottery in fields or on beaches. Can you suggest why such evidence should turn up? A find like this is known as 'treasure trove'. If you come across anything you think is treasure trove then take it to your local museum. They will find out more about it for you.

But most of the archaeologist's evidence lies buried in the ground and has to be searched for. Why?

First, it may have been deliberately buried by the people at the time. On page 13 we can see the inside of the tomb of an Egyptian king, called a pharaoh, named Tutankhamen. We know that he died in 1339 BC when he was only eighteen years old. The Egyptians, like many other peoples, believed that there was another life after death. So it was very important that a person had his (or her) everyday things buried beside him to use in his next life. This is what Tutankhamen's tomb looked like when it was found by an English archaeologist, Howard Carter, in 1922.

Of course, very few people buried long ago had such a grand tomb as Tutankhamen. Here is a simple grave of a man who died about 3000 years ago, surrounded by his few precious possessions.

Secondly, archaeological evidence may be buried quite naturally with the passing of time. A building may be destroyed and just left to become a ruin. The stones are scattered (or used for new buildings) and the foundations are overgrown. After many years the land on which the building stood is covered with trees or used for farming.

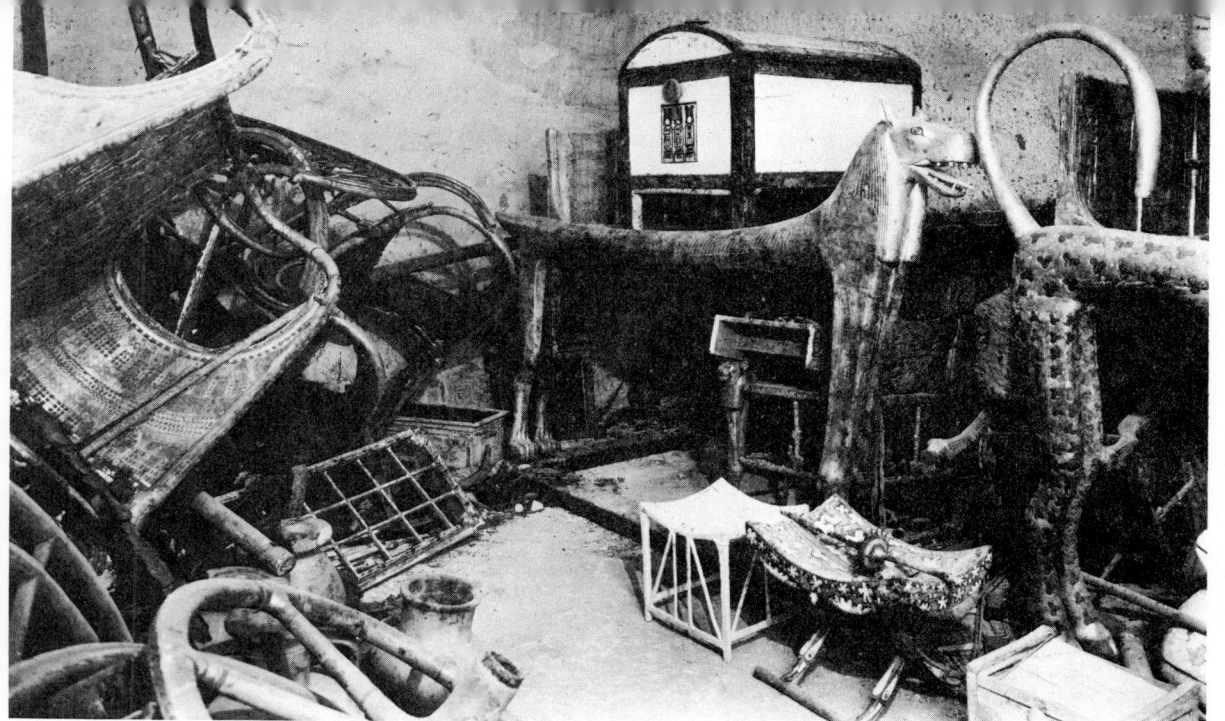

Years later, perhaps, new buildings are put up in the same place—and the old one is completely hidden and forgotten. (We shall find out later how the archaeologists can discover these lost and forgotten places.)

Thirdly, archaeological evidence may be buried by some terrible natural disaster such as an earthquake, a flood, or even a shipwreck at sea.

Perhaps the most famous disaster *site* is in southern Italy near the volcano Mount Vesuvius. In the year AD 79, on August 24th, the volcano erupted. Hot ash, lava (melted rock) and boiling mud gushed down the mountain completely covering two Roman towns, Pompeii and Herculaneum. Archaeologists have uncovered not only complete streets of Roman houses and shops but also the contents of these buildings, left exactly as they were at the moment the disaster struck. Even some of the victims have been found where they fell.

How do archaeologists find sites?

Until recently the archaeologist's work was rather like a series of treasure hunts: a likely spot was chosen and the digging began. Nowadays it is much more scientific.

One of the most interesting new methods of finding or locating sites is by using aerial photography. This was invented during the First World War, when the army used cameras in aircraft to search for enemy troops and guns. The archaeologist obviously is not interested in these, so what is he looking for?

First, he may be able to see the layout of a complete town or fort simply because a camera can look straight down from a great height.

Secondly, he may actually be able to see the remains of buildings even though they are completely buried! How does he do this? One way is by studying crop marks. Look at this diagram. It shows

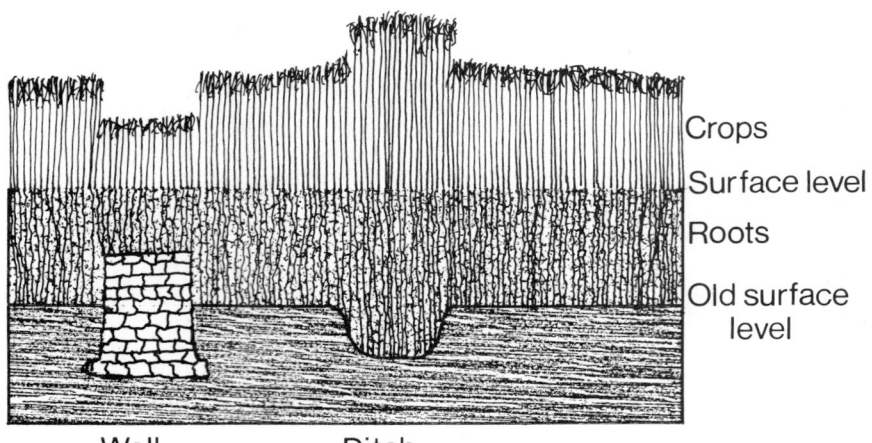

a cross-section of a field of grain growing over a buried wall and ditch. Those seeds planted over the wall will grow stunted while those planted in the ditch, where there is more moisture, will grow much taller than the rest. This is how it looks from the air. Can you see the outline of the walls and ditches of this Roman fort at Glenlochar in Perthshire? Thanks to aerial photography, archaeologists continue to find new sites which have been lost for hundreds, sometimes thousands, of years.

Excavating a site

When an important site has been found, the archaeologist and his team of helpers uncover the evidence, record what is found and identify it. This is known as an excavation. Each stage in an excavation or 'dig' is carefully recorded by drawings and photographs.

Here we can see a team of archaeologists at Vindolanda, a Roman settlement near Hadrian's Wall in Northumberland. How did they set about excavating this site?

This is how they did it.
1 The turf and topsoil were removed, using picks and shovels.
2 The earth was cleared from the walls with smaller hand tools.
3 The exposed walls were carefully cleared with small trowels and brushes.
4 The position of all objects, such as pottery and bones, was carefully noted.
5 These objects were then placed in labelled boxes, to be cleaned in the museum for identification and *restoration*. This means trying to name exactly what it is that has been dug up and trying to put it together again.

The identification and restoration may be very difficult. Some of these objects will be broken or rotted, which is not surprising when you remember that they may have been lying in damp soil for hundreds or even thousands of years! Many, many hours of painstaking and skilled work are needed before we can see the restored objects in our museums.

Rescue digs

It is a common sight nowadays to see huge excavators tearing up the ground for the building of a new motorway or tower block. These massive excavations often uncover previously unknown archaeological sites. What is to be done? The motorway cannot be rerouted to bypass the site, nor can the office block or flats be built somewhere else. Often the only thing that can be done is to call in archaeologists to do a quick 'rescue dig'. They uncover the site, record what is there and take away any objects they find. Then the site has to be covered up again, perhaps to be destroyed by the new development.

This site at Cramond, near Edinburgh, was more fortunate. When workmen were digging up the ground for a new car park, they discovered the remains of an old wall. Archaeologists were called in and they excavated this Roman bath house which is about 1800 years old.

Industrial archaeology

A new development in archaeology has been the *preservation* and restoration of old machines and places of work. This is known as industrial archaeology. Archaeologists argue that our ways of life and work have changed so rapidly during the past 200 years that many of the old methods of working are being forgotten, and the evidence

is being destroyed. So archaeologists and their helpers are trying to preserve and restore old machinery such as this water mill at Preston Mill in East Lothian.

The work of the archaeologist never stops. New sites are being discovered all the time and the evidence for historians increases. It is an interesting thought that every day someone, somewhere, adds to our knowledge of our ancestors.

THINGS TO DO

1   Imagine that some time in the future your house is destroyed by a Pompeii-type disaster. (It won't in fact happen: there are no active volcanoes in Scotland!) An archaeologist has excavated the house in the year 2500 and is preparing his report.

Put the heading 'Excavation Report' in your notebook and make up his report for him. Here are some questions the archaeologist is trying to answer, which you can use as subheadings.

(*a*) Where is the site (your house) located?
(*b*) How many rooms were there in the house?
(*c*) From the evidence, what was each room used for?
(*d*) What particularly interesting evidence has been found? (Perhaps what the people who lived there ate or did for entertainment.)

2   Draw a strip-cartoon of the main stages in an excavation, carefully labelling each of your pictures.

4 Skara Brae

The first settlers in Scotland

On page 8 we looked at a picture from Spain which was painted about 35 000 years ago. Why didn't we use a picture from Scotland?

The simple answer is that there were no people living in Scotland at that time. In fact, Scotland was one of the last places in Europe where people settled to live. Why was this?

Perhaps you have heard about the Ice Age and *glaciation* in your Primary School or in geography lessons. In the Ice Age Scotland was covered by a huge mass of ice hundreds of metres thick. It was not until about 8000 BC that our climate became warmer and the ice melted.

We think that the first visitors to Scotland came about 5000 BC. We call these people the strand-loopers. They hunted, fished, gathered shellfish and then moved on. Here you see a great pile of shellfish shells left behind at one of their camp sites on Oronsay.

All their tools and weapons were made of stone or bone and we call them Stone Age people. They did not know how to make things from metal.

About 4000 BC other people arrived in Scotland. They were still Stone Age people, but they knew how to farm as well as how to hunt. They brought cows, sheep and pigs in their boats and, probably, wheat and barley seed for planting.

When they found a place which suited them, they settled there. We shall now look at one of these settlements.

Skara Brae

On page 13 we mentioned Pompeii. You will remember that Pompeii is one of our most famous natural disaster sites. We have an archaeological natural disaster site here in Scotland too—perhaps not as grand as Pompeii, but nevertheless of great interest to archaeologists and historians.

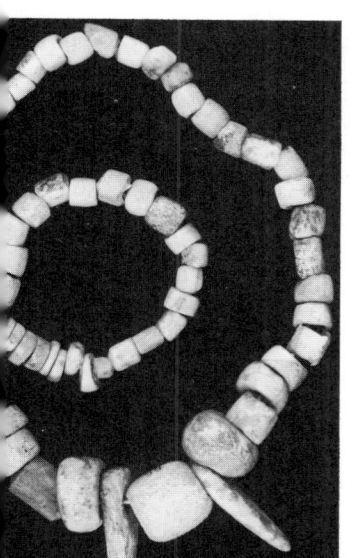

If you had been living in Orkney about 150 years ago you might have known a high dune called Skara Brae, but you probably would not have paid much attention to it. In the winter of 1850, however, a great storm swept the top of it away and laid bare some old buildings which had been buried in the sand. Now the sand has all been cleared away and we know quite a lot about the lives of these Orkney people who lived at least 4500 years ago.

The huts were found just as if the people had left the day before. They had left behind treasures such as necklaces and valuable tools. But clearly they had not been attacked, nor had their houses been robbed: nobody had been killed and their belongings were still there. They certainly were in a hurry to get away. As one woman squeezed through her narrow doorway, she broke this precious necklace and her beads fell as she ran, terror-stricken, from her house.

What happened? There was no volcano here as there was at Pompeii, but a great sandstorm must have swept sand from the dunes into and over the houses and forced the people to flee immediately. So everything was buried, too deeply for these poor folk to uncover, and remained hidden there until recently. Let us visit Skara Brae and have a look for ourselves.

Here is the Skara Brae site. We can see the remains of the seven huts that made up the village. These are roughly square in shape (the smallest 4 metres and the largest 6 metres square) and are connected by a covered passage. The huts were built on ground level and then buried in a *midden* heap of earth and rubbish to the tops of their walls. Why was this?

In Orkney there were no trees, so the huts were built of stone slabs, like a drystane dyke. The spaces between these slabs were packed with smaller stones and rubbish and the whole wall was covered with clay to keep out the wind. To make them warmer the huts were built in two lines, facing each other, but the wind would still find its way in. So round the huts was piled rubbish such as ash, broken bones and shells, all mixed together with sand to make a kind of mortar. This was packed right up to the top of the walls.

At first archaeologists thought that the rubbish was piled up as the people were finished with it. Now they think that the rubbish was stored in great heaps and left for many years before it was used. Can you think why?

The walls are about 2·3 metres high and slope inwards slightly, but no roofstones have been found. We think what the Skara Brae folk did was to make rafters of whalebone or wood that had been washed ashore. On top of the rafters they laid divots of turf or stretched skins. Can you guess why none of this has survived?

In between the two lines of huts ran a passage and the hut doors opened on to it. It was still draughty so they covered over this passageway with slabs and then covered them with rubbish too, right up to the hut walls on either side! All that a visitor to the 'village' would see was a big mound with an entrance hole in the side and several tent-like roofs standing out above it.

Let us go into the main passageway. The entrance is quite narrow, and after a few steps, we come to an even smaller doorway, only about 1·1 metres high and 0·6 metre wide. On each side of the doorway there is a hole for the long thin stone bar or bolt which used to secure the door. The bolt was pushed into the longer hole on the right when you wanted to open the door. To enter you just pushed aside the stone slab-door. A metre or two along the passage a narrower passage branches off. As we creep along it we should remember that it used to be a dark tunnel completely covered over. At the bottom of the passage we come to the entrance of the hut. The doorway is paved with stone slabs and there is the same kind of door and bolt as before.

The inside of one of the huts as it is today is shown opposite. In the centre of the hut is a fireplace made by placing some stones on the earth floor.

On the left and the right are 'boxes' made of thin stone slabs. These are the beds, which used to be lined with heather or bracken. At each end there were stone pillars to support a canopy. You can

20

see one of these stone pillars lying on the floor. In these beds the archaeologists discovered treasured necklaces that had been hidden for safety, and chop bones that had been gnawed the night before the great sandstorm. Above the beds are little open cupboards for personal belongings such as pots and axes. There were no chairs: the people sat on the edge of their beds.

On the end wall stands a piece of furniture you can easily recognise—the dresser. To the right of this are tanks let into the floor. They were carefully made watertight with clay and were probably used for storing shellfish used by the Skara Brae folk as fishing bait.

To the left is the entrance to a simple toilet—just a drain in the floor.

What sort of life did these folk lead? They left no written evidence so we have to rely on what the archaeologists have found. In addition to what the Skara Brae folk left in their huts, the archaeologists have found many interesting pieces of evidence in the middens surrounding their homes. From the bones and other bits of debris it is possible to reconstruct their way of life.

The people were both hunters and farmers. They do not seem to have grown any crops, but they have left bones of cattle, sheep, deer and dogs. They fished, using limpets for bait. There is no evidence that they knew how to weave clothes so they must have worn animal skins kept in place with bone pins like this. With stone scrapers they made wooden or bone tools which they used to clean the skins. We already know that they wore jewellery. The little pot contains the remains of red ochre which they used to paint themselves. Their water, milk and food were kept in animal skins or simple clay pots. They made ropes out of twisted heather.

Their tools were made from wood, bone or stone. Below is the shoulderblade of a cow which they may have used as a spade.

To sum up, the Skara Brae folk were what we call self-sufficient. This means that they produced all their own tools, food and clothes. There were no such things as shops in those days.

THINGS TO DO

1 Put the heading 'Skara Brae Comparisons' in your notebook. From what you have learnt about Skara Brae list six differences between a typical day in your life compared with a young person's day at Skara Brae.

2 Perhaps you mentioned 'going to school' as one of your differences. There were of course no schools at Skara Brae. The children, however, still had to be taught some things. Try to answer these questions in sentences in your notebook.

(a) Who do you think would do the teaching at Skara Brae?

(b) What sort of skills do you think boys would be taught?

(c) What sort of skills do you think girls would be taught?

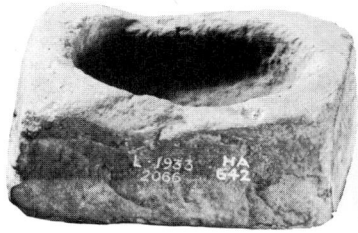

3 On page 20 are the measurements of a Skara Brae hut. Arrange the desks in the classroom to 'make' one of these huts. It is not very big, is it? Remember that a family lived, ate and slept in that one room.

4 Re-creative exercises

In a 're-creative' exercise you are asked to write about an event in the past as though you were there at the time. So you must remember to use the information that you have learned and also to use your imagination.

Imagine that you are a young person living at Skara Brae about 4500 years ago. Of course you would not be able to write, but pretend that you are sending a letter to a friend on the mainland telling about your way of life. Put the heading 'A Letter from Skara Brae' in your notebook and write to your friend.

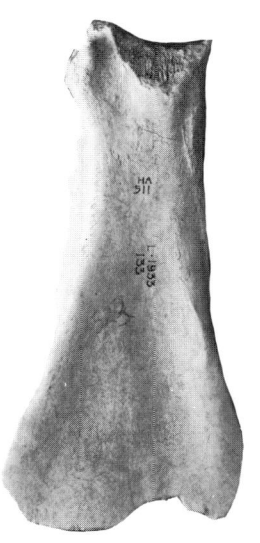

5 The first farmers

While Scotland was still covered by the huge glaciers of the Ice Age, men and women had been living in warmer parts of the world for thousands of years.

At first they were wanderers, hunters who had to follow the herds of wild animals to obtain their food. Later, they were able to settle down and make their homes in one place because they made two important discoveries.

First, they learned how to tame some of the wild animals they hunted. They became herdsmen, looking after cattle, sheep, goats and pigs.

Secondly, they learned how to grow the seeds of wild grasses and use the seeds, the grain, to make flour. They kept some of the seeds to plant for the next year's harvest.

Archaeologists think that man made these discoveries about 8000 BC, in the part of the world known as the Fertile Crescent, in the Middle East. Look at this map.

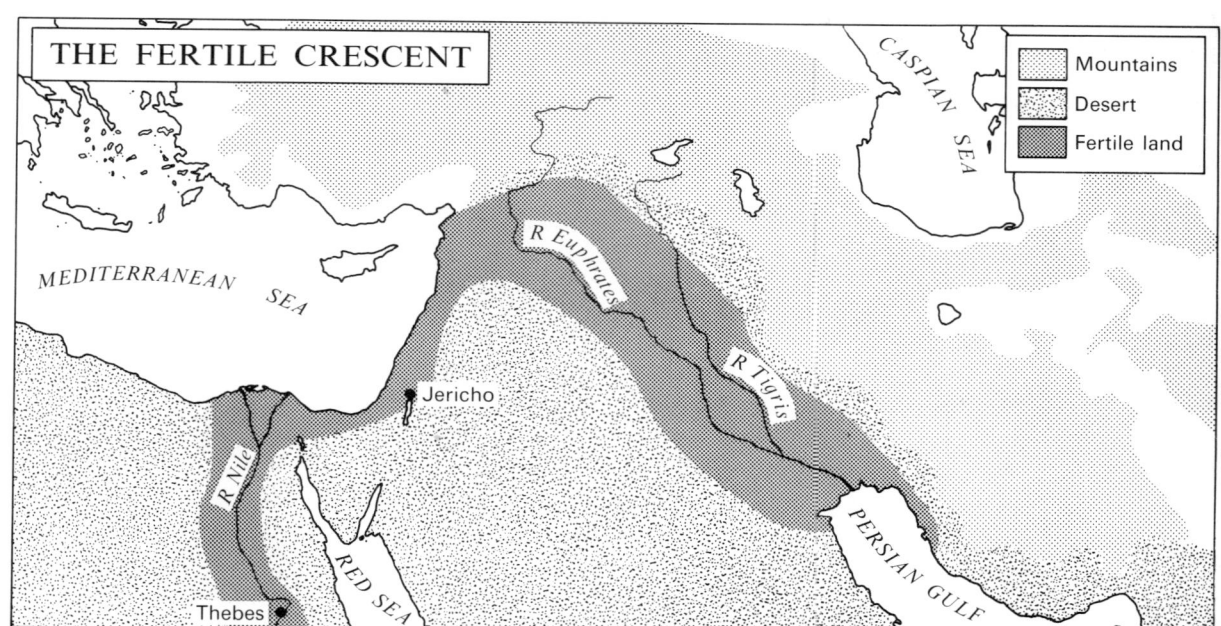

This is an area which has plenty of sunshine—and it was as important then as it is now for farmers to have enough sunshine, as well as water, to grow their crops and rear their animals. The water came from the great rivers flowing through these lands. Can you see the Nile, the Jordan, the Euphrates and the Tigris?

So it is not surprising that the first farmers lived in this part of the world, and came to live together in larger groups in such 'cities' as Jericho.

These 'cities' were very small compared with our cities today, but by 6000 BC perhaps as many as 3000 people were living in Jericho. They were protected by the famous walls you may have read about in the Old Testament. Parts of these walls have been excavated by archaeologists.

As the people of Jericho did not have to move about hunting for food, they had time to think about ways to improve their lives. They lived in houses made of bricks. They had learned to make pots of clay to hold their grain, water and milk, and had learned to spin and weave cloth.

Another of the most important discoveries made, perhaps actually in Jericho about 5000 BC, was the secret of making things out of metal. Men there learned how to melt copper. They would then pour it into a mould, rather like a present-day jelly mould. When it was cool, the metal could be shaped and sharpened more easily than stone. The first things they made were jewellery and ornaments, as copper is too soft for tools and weapons. But by about 3000 BC they had learned that if they mixed tin with copper the mixture—bronze—was hard enough.

So now people in the Fertile Crescent were living together in larger numbers. They were building better houses, making better tools and weapons, and improving their ways of farming. They also found that they needed laws, rules they all understood, to settle their quarrels. They also needed a judge-ruler to make sure the laws were obeyed. They were trying to live together in what we call a civilised way.

In the next chapter we shall study one of the most famous of these early civilisations, that of the Egyptians. We shall compare their way of life with what we know about life at Skara Brae.

6 Life in Ancient Egypt

The River Nile is more than 6400 kilometres long. It rises in the snow-covered mountains of Africa and runs northwards towards the Mediterranean Sea. For the last 1200 kilometres of its journey it flows through the flat desert lands of Egypt.

Each year, between the months of June and September, the river overflowed its banks and flooded the surrounding countryside for over 3 kilometres on each side. When the floodwaters went down, they left behind a layer of fresh, rich soil.

By 8000 BC people in Egypt had become settled farmers. In this fertile land they learned to feed their flocks and grow their crops. During the hot, dry months from March to May they learned to draw water from the river for their fields. We call this irrigation.

Gradually the number of people grew and, like the folk of Jericho, the Egyptians tried to improve their way of life. While most of them continued to farm the land, some began to specialise at different jobs. Some made tools, others made pots, others again made jewellery. Some discovered the secrets of making things in copper and, later, in bronze. When Egypt was ruled by a pharaoh, we read of doctors, lawyers, *architects* and *scribes*. We shall look at the work of a scribe later in this chapter.

At first the Egyptians did not use money to pay for the things these specialists made or did for them. How do you think you would have paid a metalworker if, say, you were a farmer?

The first settlements grew into towns with magnificent buildings. As in Jericho, people found they needed laws to keep the peace, and soldiers to protect the towns. So they paid taxes to a leader, a king, who made sure that laws were kept and towns protected. About 4000 BC Egypt was divided into two kingdoms, each ruled by a pharaoh. In 3250 BC the kingdoms of Upper and Lower Egypt were united under one pharaoh, a man named Mares. The people ruled by a pharaoh thought he was a god. He lived in a huge palace with hundreds of servants and court officials to help him.

The Ancient Egyptians believed in a life after death and great preparations were made for the funeral of a pharaoh. The pharaoh's body was buried inside a pyramid. The most famous pyramid they built is the Great Pyramid, which was completed in 2600 BC for the pharaoh Khufe.

The sides of this pyramid are more than two football pitches in length. It was built from 2 300 000 blocks of stone, each about $2\frac{1}{2}$ tonnes in weight and cut exactly to size. It took twenty years to build. A Greek traveller, Herodotus, visited Egypt about 500 BC. He described the Great Pyramid and marvelled at its size. He was told that 100 000 slaves had been needed to build it, but we know this was a 'traveller's tale' and that only about 4000 day-labourers were employed. Many of these were farmers who worked on the pyramid during the flood months from June to September when their fields were under water.

(Such people seem to have made the first recorded strike in history. We are told that in 1170 BC workers downed tools 'because the pharaoh had not paid them their wages of food for two months'.)

A pyramid had a splendid decorated burial room or chamber for the pharaoh deep inside it. (You can see Tutankhamen's burial chamber on page 13.) This chamber was filled with all the treasures the pharaoh would need in his next life. Sometimes there were even models of his servants ready to work for him.

The pharaoh's body was preserved by soaking it in a special liquid called natron for seventy days. The preserved body or mummy was then wrapped in bandages and placed in a painted coffin. Often a lucky charm known as a scarab was placed beside the body.

It was not only pharaohs who were buried in this way. Anyone who could afford it tried to prepare for the next life. Not only grown-ups, but also children and pets were mummified. Here we see the mummy of a young girl who died about 3000 years ago.

A scarab

Unfortunately grave robbers often broke into these burial chambers and stole the treasures. So later pharaohs were no longer buried in pyramids but in secret graves in a hidden valley known as the Valley of the Kings. Even here thieves were at work and archaeologists have often found tombs of pharaohs stripped of all their treasures. However, as we have already read, the great tomb of Tutankhamen was found untouched. From this evidence we can get some idea of the wealth and importance of the pharaohs.

But what was it like to live on an ordinary farm in Egypt about 2500 years ago?

Your home would be made of mud-bricks and beside it there might be a garden for flowers and vegetables. The house would have several rooms: a dining room, a living room, bedrooms, a kitchen and storage rooms. You would also have a bathroom and toilet. The furniture would be made of wood and your stool might have looked like this. Even your pillow would be a wooden headrest: you would find this very uncomfortable!

If your father could afford it you would have servants to do all the housework and you would enjoy collecting beautiful things such as jewellery. You would spend a lot of time on your make-up, using a make-up kit complete with little pots of coloured ointment for use as eye-shadow. You could then admire yourself in a bronze mirror. Indeed, men and boys wore make-up and jewellery too!

Your meals would consist of meat, bread, cakes, fruit, vegetables and even sweets, with milk, beer and wine to drink. Surprisingly, you would not eat any fish, as you would think it was unclean. Here you can actually see part of a meal prepared for a man of Ancient Egypt which was preserved in his tomb for thousands of years! It includes bread biscuits and fruit.

Your family would dress in loose, flowing, white linen robes like those this family is wearing. They are hunting wild birds, using special throwing-sticks, which was a very popular sport in those days. (Do you notice how small the wife and children have been painted compared with the husband? The Ancient Egyptians thought that the man was much the most important person in a family—they had not heard of Women's Lib!)

Children would play with toys you would recognise: a spinning top, for example, and a wooden mouse. There were no schools as we know them, but a few boys were trained as scribes. The Egyptians did not have an alphabet like ours. Instead they drew pictures known as hieroglyphics. Starting at the age of five, the boys were taught to copy the hieroglyphic characters with a writing set like this.

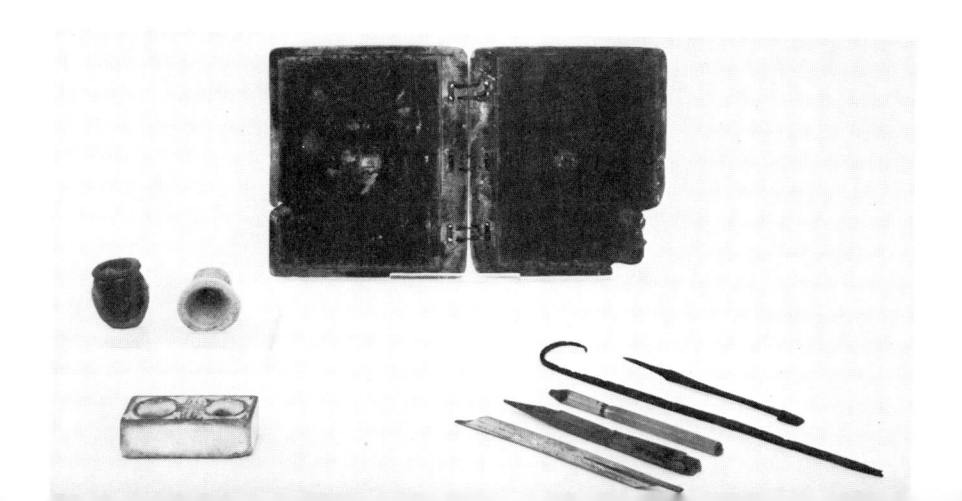

This is the back of the scarab shown on page 27. Here you see examples of hieroglyphics. Did you notice others on the mummy on page 27?

The schools for scribes must have been very strict. An old saying tells us that 'a youngster's ear is on his back—he listens when he is beaten'! After twelve years' training, the scribe started work. He had a very important job recording the business of pharaohs, nobles, doctors, architects, craftsmen and farmers. Much of the writing was done on papyrus, made from strips of dried reed pressed together, or on the walls of palaces and tombs.

These writings tell us a great deal about the way of life of the people of Ancient Egypt. We also learn about their discoveries and inventions. From their studies of the sun and the moon they made a calendar of twelve months of 365 days. They also divided the day into twenty-four hours and invented a water clock which kept accurate time. We are told that their doctors were the first to advise the use of castor oil for upset stomachs!

Sadly, this great civilisation disappeared and the hieroglyphic characters were forgotten. (In fact it was not until 1822 that a Frenchman named Champallion discovered how to translate them.)

The last ruler of Egypt was the famous Cleopatra. In 31 BC Egypt was conquered by the Romans and rather than submit to them she committed suicide. So Egypt became part of the Roman world.

THINGS TO DO

1 This is a copy of an Egyptian wall painting. Many of these paintings are very useful to us because they show scenes from day-to-day life in Ancient Egypt. As you can see, this shows a harvesting scene. Start at the bottom left-hand corner and work your way along to get the story of this harvest on the farm of Menna, an official of the pharaoh.

(a) Look at the people at the bottom left-hand corner. Which ones do you think are slaves?

(b) How is the grain cut?

(c) How is the grain carried?

(d) Look at the two girls in the cornfield. What do you think they are doing?

(e) What are the two men doing who are sitting under the tree?

(f) After the grain has been cut, it has to be threshed. This means separating the grain seeds from the stalk. How is this being done? (You should now be at the top right-hand picture and working along to the top left!)

(g) The next stage in harvesting is for the chaff, or husks, to be separated from the seed. How is this being done?

(h) How is the grain carried to the store house?

(i) What do you think the scribes are doing?

(j) Menna is busy watching the harvest being brought in. The last picture shows us how he got to the farm. What is it?

2 Comparison exercise

We are going to compare what we know about life in Ancient Egypt about 2500 years ago with what we know already about Skara Brae. Copy out the table below and complete the comparisons. Add two blank spaces to the bottom of your table and see if you can write down two other differences between life in Ancient Egypt and life at Skara Brae.

	Ancient Egypt	*Skara Brae*
(a) HOUSES		Very small; one-roomed, made with stones like a drystane dyke
(b) FURNITURE	Beautifully made with wood	
(c) CLOTHING		Animal skins—the Skara Brae folk did not know how to weave
(d) TOOLS	Made by specialist craftsmen from wood, stone and metal	
(e) GREAT MONUMENTS		None
(f) FARMING	Crops and animals kept; fields watered by irrigation	
(g) WRITING		Unknown to Skara Brae folk
(h) JEWELLERY	Beautifully made from precious stones and gold	

3 Imagine that you are a young person being trained as a scribe. Write a letter to a friend describing your home and what you do at the school for scribes.

7 Ancient Greece

Other great civilisations were also starting to grow as people learned the skills of farming and of making things from metal. Probably the most famous of these early civilisations was in Greece. From about 2000 BC the people of Ancient Greece made some remarkable discoveries which are still important to us today. Let us look quickly at some of them.

Government

We have already looked at the need for laws to keep the peace amongst groups of people.

If you look at a map of Greece you will see that much of the land is covered by high mountains. The Greeks settled in small groups which were cut off from each other by these mountains or by the sea.

As time passed these groups or communities grew into important cities, each controlling its own affairs with its own rulers. Some city-states, as they were called, were ruled by kings; others by powerful *nobles*. In Athens, however, the people elected their own rulers each year. We call this arrangement, where people vote for their leaders, democracy. Democracy comes from the Greek words 'demos' meaning 'people' and 'kratos' meaning 'strength' or—as we might say—'power to the people'. Many countries today, including our own, are democracies. You in turn—when you are 18—will have the chance to vote for our leaders or, indeed, stand for election as a leader.

Do you know what this shows?

The Olympic Games

You probably recognised the photograph. It is, of course, the opening ceremony of the Olympic Games. Our modern Games have only been held since 1896, but the first Games were held in Ancient Greece in 776 BC.

Every four years the city-states stopped any quarrelling or fighting that was going on and sent their best athletes to Olympia to compete in the Games. The winners of the events received only laurel wreaths as victors but brought great honour to their cities. Athletes still compete in the same events today. We still talk of the 'Olympic spirit', where arguments between countries are put to one side to let the Games go ahead.

There was another side to this, however. Can you think why it was important for a young man to be good at running, throwing a javelin or hurling a discus? Look closely at this Greek vase and you should get the answer.

Art

This vase (called an amphora) is just one example of the many hundreds of beautiful works of art which have survived. One statue, the Venus de Milo, has inspired artists for hundreds of years.

The Parthenon

Architecture

Many of you will recognise this place. It is one of the buildings known as the Acropolis in Athens. Unfortunately an explosion in 1687 caused a lot of damage, but even so we can get an idea of how magnificent they must have been. The Greek style of building, particularly the beautiful columns, has often been copied.

Look at this building in Edinburgh. Although it was built in the nineteenth century, about 2300 years after the Acropolis, the Greek style was used.

The Royal Scottish Academy building

Thinkers

All of us at some time ask questions about life. What do we mean when we talk about being good? How should we treat other people? What are the most important things in life? Ancient Greece gave us some of the world's greatest thinkers—or philosophers, to give them their proper name. The ideas of men such as Socrates, Plato and Aristotle are still considered important today. So too are the ideas of Greek scientists such as Archimedes and their mathematicians such as Euclid.

In the fifth century BC Greek civilisation was threatened by an invasion of the hostile Persians. The Greeks won great victories at Marathon and Salamis, so Greece was saved.

In 338 BC a new invader appeared. This was Philip of Macedon, who defeated the Greeks at the Battle of Chaeronea. Philip's son, Alexander the Great, conquered a huge empire which included Persia and Egypt and stretched as far as India. When he died—aged only thirty-two—his empire was divided among his generals.

Other conquerors soon followed. Like the Ancient Egyptians, the Greeks too became part of the Roman Empire.

A coin showing Alexander the Great

8 The Roman Empire

When Alexander the Great was making his empire in the east, Rome controlled an area of Italy no bigger than the Lothian Region. The rest of Italy was held by other people—Greeks in the south, Etruscans north of Rome, Latins and Gauls in the valley of the River Po. The history of Rome is the story of how the people who lived in the seven-hilled city by the River Tiber made themselves masters first of Italy, then of the lands round the Mediterranean, and finally of lands as far north as Britain.

To win this empire, the Romans had to fight many times. One of their most famous campaigns was against Carthage in North Africa. Carthage was a great trading nation with *colonies* in Sicily and Sardinia which were protected by a strong fleet of ships. War broke out in 264 BC.

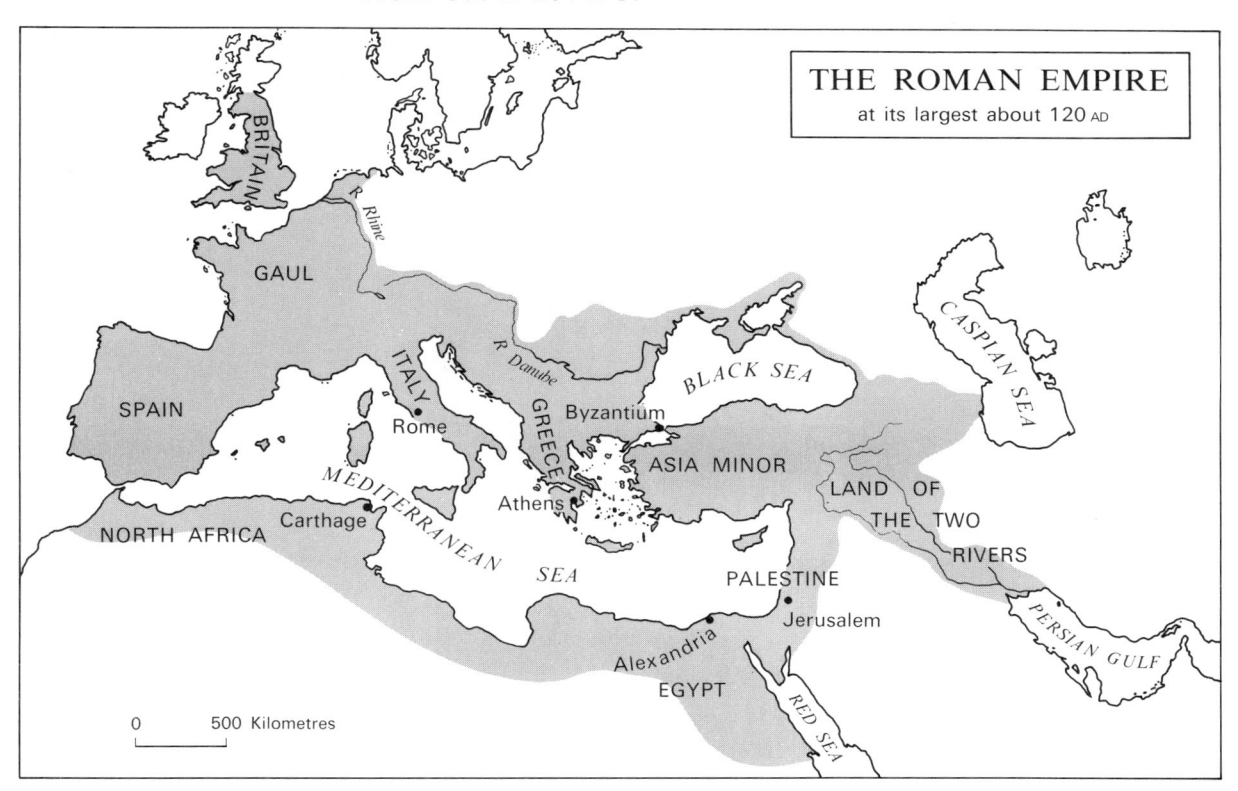

THE ROMAN EMPIRE at its largest about 120 AD

The Romans were unused to fighting at sea: they had to learn how to build ships and fight in them. At first, the Romans were victorious. But then a young soldier named Hannibal was given command of the Carthaginian army in Spain. He decided to attack Italy. This meant that he had to march his army, which even included elephants, over the icy Alps. He reached Italy and defeated the Romans at the Battle of Cannae in 216 BC. Despite this victory, Hannibal's army was not strong enough to capture Rome itself. The Romans recovered and carried the fight to North Africa. The Carthaginians were defeated at the Battle of Zama in 202 BC. The city of Carthage was destroyed by the Romans; Hannibal escaped but later committed suicide rather than surrender.

The Roman Empire lasted for 500 years. At its largest it covered an area of more than 5 million square kilometres with perhaps as many as 50 million people living under Roman rule. (How does this compare with the present population of Scotland?) This huge empire was divided into forty-three provinces. Each province was controlled by a *governor* helped by *civil servants* and of course the famous Roman legions. The empire was policed by twenty-seven of these legions, each of about 5000 men under the command of a *legate*. In each legion there were ten cohorts, made up of six centuries each commanded by a centurion. As the name tells you, a 'century' at one time had a hundred men in it, but by 120 there were only eighty men in a century.

Here you see a centurion with his vine staff, the symbol of his rank. Beside him stands the aquilifer, or chief standard-bearer, who carried the famous eagle standard of the legion. To lose this standard in battle was a terrible disgrace. (We shall find out more about the life of a legionary in the next chapter.)

One of the great Roman generals who made his name in these wars of conquest was Julius Caesar. His greatest campaign was the one he fought to conquer Gaul, the land we now call France. He wrote a full account of his battles from which we learn a great deal both about the Roman army and about the people he fought. In 55 BC and again in 54 BC he invaded the south of Britain to punish the Britons for helping their friends in Gaul, but he decided not to try to conquer the whole island.

Caesar was more than a soldier, though. By this time the old Roman democracy (or *republic*, as it was called) was breaking down. Greedy men were misgoverning both the conquered lands and even Rome itself. Many thought that a new kind of government was needed. Caesar was one of them. He marched his army back to Rome and tried to take over control of the state. For a time he succeeded, but he had made many enemies. In March, 44 BC, he was murdered in the Senate, the Roman Parliament.

After fourteen years of confused fighting, Caesar's nephew Octavian came to power. In 27 BC he took the title of Augustus and ruled as emperor. Emperors ruled Rome for the next 400 years. It was Augustus who defeated Cleopatra and it is the same Augustus who is mentioned in the New Testament: 'And it came to pass in those days that there went out a decree from Caesar Augustus, that all the world should be taxed. And all went to be taxed, everyone to his own city.'

Look again at the map on page 37. Palestine, or, as it is sometimes called, the Holy Land, was part of the Roman Empire when Jesus was born. As a young man training to be a carpenter, Jesus would have come into regular contact with Roman soldiers and officials. When Jesus began preaching he had dealings with the Romans. Do you remember the story of how he helped the centurion? Finally, it was the Roman governor of Jerusalem, Pontius Pilate, who ordered Jesus to be crucified. It was Roman soldiers who carried out this cruel execution.

Of course our story does not end there. Thanks to the work of the early followers of Jesus, called disciples, many Romans were converted to Christianity. They were forced to meet in secret places such as the catacombs (the ancient burial cellars under the city of Rome). These were dangerous times for Christians. Many hundreds were arrested. Some, like St Peter, were crucified; some, like St Paul, were executed. Some were burnt to death, while others died in the Roman arenas. Often they were torn to bits by wild animals. In 313, however, the Emperor Constantine made Christianity an official religion of the Empire. Christians could now worship freely.

If the Romans had been conquerors only, we would soon have forgotten them. We remember them, and their language—Latin—is still learned in our schools, because they were much more than conquerors. The Romans gave us our present-day alphabet as well as about one-third of the words we use in our English language. Our calendar is the one used by the Romans.

Wherever they went they took new ideas and new ways of doing things—making roads, bringing water into towns, building country houses and big town houses with central heating, building bridges. Below you can see the remains of a complete Roman town in North Africa, at Timgad in Algeria. You can see the well-laid-out streets, the tall columns and, in the background, the open-air theatre. This beautiful Roman aqueduct at Segovia in Spain is still used to carry water to the city. It is part of a system nearly 100 kilometres long which the Romans built to bring water from the mountain springs.

Above all, the Romans made laws. Even in Scotland—which they never conquered—our law today is based on Roman law.

In the Roman world you could travel easily along magnificent roads from one side of the empire to the other, so that merchants from North Africa sold their goods in Britain. The empire was linked by more than 300 major roads, 80 000 kilometres altogether.

A journey along a Roman road would give us a good idea of Roman life.

The road itself was usually very straight and well engineered: we might see part of it being built. First the soil is dug out, then a layer of concrete put down. On top of this the men roll layers of square stones and concrete. Then a top surface of big smooth stones is cambered to let water run off. Usually a kerb is built to separate the road from a footpath for pedestrians.

As we journey along the road we see soldiers marching under their centurions, heavy carts drawn by white oxen, merchants with pack-mules, light fast chariots drawn by a pair of horses, slaves carrying their owner in a chair with two handles, and the ordinary country-folk taking their butter or eggs to market in baskets. Perhaps the thing that seems strangest to you is the men's clothes. Trousers are not in fashion and most men wear some kind of flowing robes (called 'togas'), especially important men. Every 19 kilometres or so there is a relay station where government messengers can change their horses.

41

At the end of our journey we arrive at a town with a comfortable inn where we spend the night, near the market-place—called the Forum. If we want entertainment we go to see chariot races, or fights between *gladiators*, or between gladiators and wild beasts. (The Romans were bloodthirsty in their amusements.) We might go to a luxurious swimming-pool, where better-off people spend a good deal of their time.

A shop in the market place

We might be invited to dinner in the house of a well-to-do family, and we would find it very comfortable. The floors are made of *mosaic*, warm to the feet from the central-heating furnace. Instead of sitting down to table we lie on couches on three sides of the low table, while slaves bring the food and wine to the fourth side. Fingers and spoons take the place of knives and forks. There is probably too much to eat and some of the food looks very strange. It might include jellyfish and eggs, sea urchins with spices and honey, boiled ostrich with sweet sauce and dormice stuffed with pork! After the meal is over we are entertained by jugglers, musicians or dancers.

But you must not think that all Romans lived like this. Many men and women were slaves and the ordinary people were often very poor, living in one or two little rooms in a tenement, or in small cottages. Yet they all enjoyed the peace which the Roman Empire gave the world.

The centre of this empire was of course the city of Rome. By 120 there were a million people living in Rome: about the same as Glasgow today and about twice as many people as live in Edinburgh now. Many of the people here were very poor and lived in the city's 45 000 blocks of tenements.

Let's visit one of the busy streets thronged with people. Roman citizens doing their shopping mingle with tourists from the far corners of the empire. Some are going to visit one of the city's public baths, some are on their way to borrow a book from one of Rome's twenty-nine libraries. Others are going to buy slaves, recently captured in victorious campaigns.

Later in the day crowds of people will be on their way to the Circus Maximus to see the exciting chariot races, or to the Colosseum. Here is a photograph of the Colosseum today.

At the Colosseum 50 000 people push in to see bloodthirsty contests between gladiators and lions or other wild beasts. The mosaic below shows some of the most popular gladiators in action. People say that as many as 5000 animals are killed in a single day. And sometimes the arena is flooded for naval battles between boats manned by slaves or gladiators. Today, perhaps, Christians will be dying for their beliefs before the roaring crowds.

This, then, is the scene in the bustling heart of the Roman Empire.

THINGS TO DO

1 Using the map on page 37 and an atlas, write down the modern names of countries which were ruled by the Romans.

2 From what you have learned in this chapter, make a list of the reasons why you think the Roman Empire was important.

3 Prepare a poster advertising a programme of events at the Colosseum.

4 Imagine that you are a young person living in Gaul. Your father is a merchant, who has taken you on a journey to Rome, and you have arrived safely at your inn. Write a letter home describing your journey to Rome by road and your first impressions of the capital of the empire.

5 Put the heading 'The Invasion of Britain' in your notebook. This story is taken from a contemporary document. This means that it was written very soon after the events described and so it is a very important piece of evidence for us. Read the passage, then answer the questions using (i) the information in the passage, (ii) your textbook, (iii) your own guesswork and (iv) your teacher.

> Caesar decided to lead an expedition to Britain as the Britons had been helping the Gauls against him. He also wanted to find out more about the country—such as good landing-places, as only traders had been there.
>
> He sent Gaius Volusenus to spy out the land in a warship. When he had got as much information as he could, Caesar sailed from Gaul with eighty transports (enough to carry two legions) and, in addition, eighteen transports to carry his cavalry. The fleet sailed at sunset and arrived at the fourth hour of the day to find the armed forces of the enemy on the cliff-tops. It was easy for the enemy to hurl missiles from the cliffs so Caesar ordered the fleet to move farther round the coast to a point where the troops could land. The enemy pursued the fleet.
>
> The landing was very dangerous. The ships could not be run ashore because of their size and the troops had to disembark in deep water. They were weighed down by their armour and as they struggled to find their feet, the enemy attacked them with chariots and missiles. Seeing the danger, Caesar ordered his warships to bombard the enemy with stones and arrows to allow our men to get ashore but the troops still held back. However, the standard-bearer of the Tenth Legion cried 'Leap down soldiers, unless you want to betray your eagle to the enemy. I will do my duty to my country and my general.' With that he waded ashore and was soon followed by the rest of our men. After a fierce fight, the enemy were forced to retreat. [Adapted from 'The Gallic Wars IV' by Julius Caesar.]

(a) Why did Caesar decide to invade Britain?
(b) What is the modern name for Gaul?
(c) What sort of information would help Caesar? Where would he get it?
(d) How many men were in a legion?
(e) Why was the landing-place not suitable?
(f) What made the landing very difficult?
(g) How did Caesar help his men?
(h) How was the battle won?
(i) Imagine that you are the standard-bearer. Describe your job and your part in the landing in a letter home.

45

9 Roman Britain

The real invasion of Britain came in AD 43, when the emperor Claudius sent Aulus Plautius with four legions (the Second, Ninth, Fourteenth and Twentieth). This force of about 20 000 men swept aside the British resistance, led by Caractacus, and pushed inland. They were later joined by the emperor himself. The Romans were soon in control of southern Britain and, to celebrate the victory, Claudius named his baby son Britannicus.

Britain then was a country divided among Celtic tribes with names such as the Iceni, the Coritani and the Brigantes. Each tribe defended its own territory and was ruled by a king or chief.

These people were not simple savages wearing animal skins: they were warrior-farmers. They did not try to farm the valleys, which were marshy and thickly forested, but the drier, more open land on the slopes of the hills. In times of danger they retreated to hill-forts

Maiden Castle in Dorset

like this. They drove their farm animals inside the safety of the walls and prepared to defend themselves. They were also skilled craftsmen.

The Romans quickly made southern Britain into a Roman province, and then pushed northwards. As they went they built roads, forts and settlements which soon grew into towns. The Latin word for a fortified camp is 'castra'. Can you name any places in England with 'caster' or 'cester' in their names? They were originally Roman settlements. Four of these settlements, Glovum (Gloucester), Lindum (Lincoln), Eboracum (York) and Colchester, were used as places for retired soldiers to live with their families. They were known as 'coloniae'. Why do you think the Romans were keen to have former soldiers settling in newly conquered Britain?

There was resistance to the Romans, of course. In AD 61 Boadicea, Queen of the Iceni, led a rebellion which destroyed the Roman settlements of Colchester, Verulamium (St Albans) and London. Thousands of people were killed before the British were crushed by the Romans, led by Seutonius. Boadicea killed herself rather than surrender.

What was life like in Roman Britain? The forts and settlements soon grew into towns with fine public buildings, including baths and even *amphitheatres*. They were linked by the famous Roman roads. Some of our modern roads follow the routes taken by the Roman legionaries, and in other places you can still see the original road surface. This is part of the Roman road over Whealdale Moor in Yorkshire.

Many Britons dressed in togas like the Romans, learned Latin and tried to copy the Roman way of life. Hundreds of young men were recruited into the Roman army. People had to obey the Roman laws and pay the Roman taxes. Those who could afford it built beautiful Roman *villas*. Some of these villas were very grand, with hundreds of acres of farmland and scores of labourers and slaves.

Most of these villas were in the south of Britain. If you had travelled northwards along the Roman road known as Ermine Street you would have seen great changes. There would be fewer settlements of any size, far more soldiers on the road. Perhaps a troop of cavalry would gallop past you. About 112 kilometres north of Eboracum (York) you would see a wall before you, stretching to the east and west as far as your eye could see.

This was the most northern Roman frontier: the barrier which separated Roman Britain from the fierce tribes of Caledonia.

10 Caledonia

Try to imagine a wall built of stone, 117 kilometres long and 6.5 metres high, wide enough at the top for two people to walk side by side. About 6 metres to the north of the wall there is a wide and deep ditch; to the south a road runs from one end to the other.

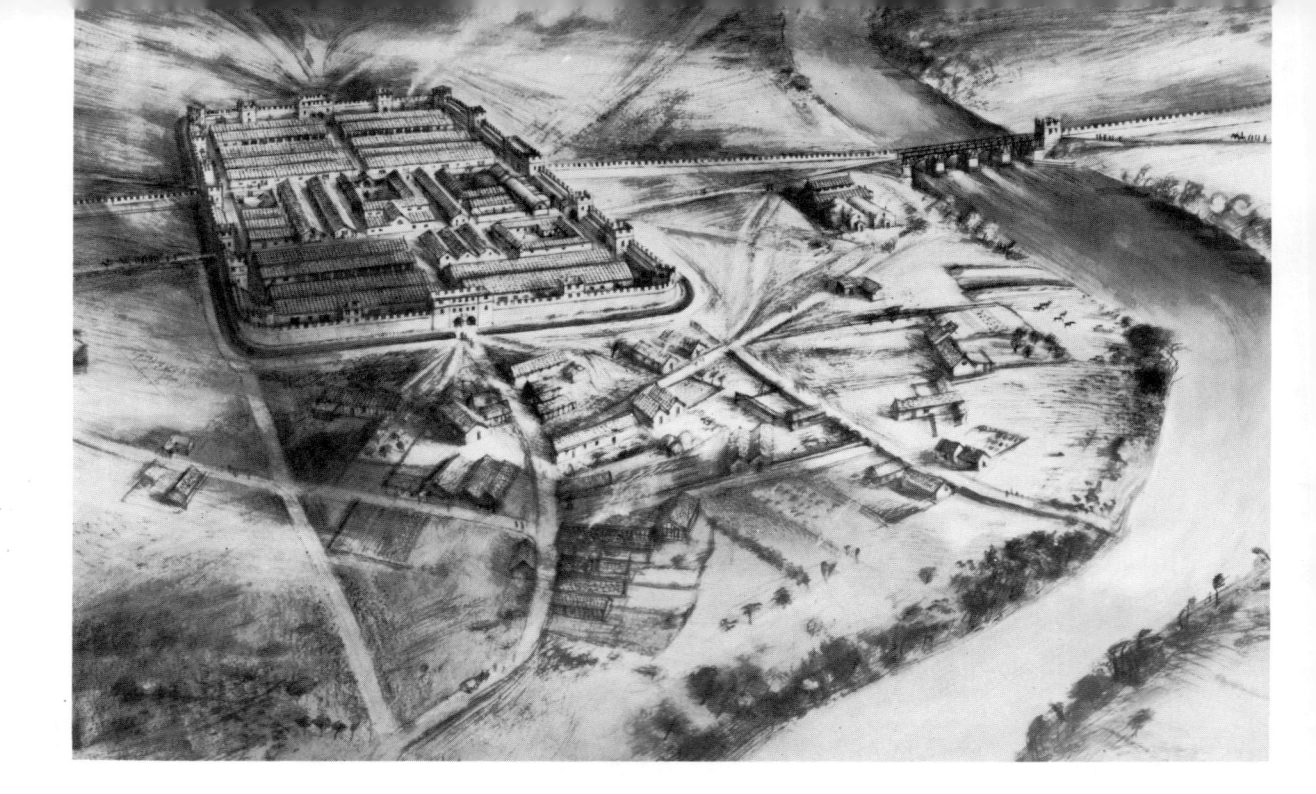

Almost every 8 kilometres along the wall stands a large fort. (Here you see Chester fort as it probably looked in about 150.) Altogether there are sixteen of these forts, each garrisoned by about 500 men. Between these large forts, every Roman mile (about 1500 metres) stands a smaller fort or 'mile-castle', manned by twenty to thirty legionaries. Then, between each pair of mile-castles there are two small watch-towers for sentries.

All this—the wall, the ditch, the road, the forts, the mile-castles, the lone sentries—was to protect Roman Britain from attack by the people of the north! This was Hadrian's Wall, built on the orders of emperor Hadrian when he visited Britain in 122. For nearly 300 years it was the barrier between Roman Britain and the Caledonians.

The Romans made three attempts to conquer the tribes of the north. The first attempt was made by Agricola, the governor of Britain, in AD 80. He gathered together a large army and crossed the River Tweed into Caledonia.

He invaded a country occupied by different tribes. The Votadini controlled the Lothians area, the Vencones lived in what we call Fife and the Damnonii held the Clyde Valley. Farther to the north and west were other tribes such as the Lugi ('the raven folk') in Sutherland and the Cerones ('the folk of the rough land') in Argyllshire. These tribesmen were warriors and farmers ruled by a chief—but they were not simple savages. They were very skilled metalworkers. They could also make beautiful jewellery.

50

The tribesmen fought either on foot with spears and long swords, or from small chariots drawn by two ponies. These were dangerous times, for the tribes not only fought the Romans but each other. To protect themselves, some of the tribes built forts on hills known as 'duns'. Two of the most famous were at Dumbarton and Duneiden (now, of course, Edinburgh). Can you name any other places in Scotland beginning with Dun? They also built curious forts known as 'brochs'. This is one at Mousa in the Shetlands: as you see, they look rather like cooling towers at a modern power station. In times of danger, the people stayed in rooms built between the inner and outer walls. Brochs are found only in Scotland.

Each tribe had meeting-places known as 'oppida'. Here they held markets to exchange their goods and to listen to the news from travellers. Some were built on hill-tops, where they could be defended from attack. The largest was on Traprain Law near Haddington in East Lothian, and was the capital of the Votadini tribe. A stone wall enclosed a space of 13 hectares, the area of a fair-sized field.

These people were not always at war! At Traprain and other places archaeologists have found Roman pottery (which probably held wine), Roman glass and Roman coins. So they must have traded with the Romans when they were not fighting them.

The Romans called these people Caledonians, a name which covered all the tribes. Later, they called them Picts, probably meaning 'the painted people', because they liked to tattoo their bodies with patterns. The Picts were good artists and have left us many stones carved in beautiful patterns, perhaps similar patterns to the ones they painted on themselves. This stone stands in Aberlemno churchyard near Forfar. Although we cannot understand Pictish writing, we know something about these Caledonians from the writings of Tacitus, the son-in-law of Agricola.

51

What were the feelings of the legionaries as they prepared to move into Caledonia? Let us try to imagine how they felt.

As you buckle on your armour ready to march you have a last check on your equipment. No wonder your nickname is 'Marius's mule'! You remember asking whether old General Marius had added to the load a poor legionary has to carry.

You carry two javelins, more than 2 metres long, a short sword called a 'gladius' and a dagger. On your back you carry a tool-kit with a saw, axe, sickle, chain and rope. You need these tools because, at the end of each day's march in every country, you have to build defences round your camp. You also carry two wooden stakes to help with the defences. In your bag are your bronze dish and pan, your food ration and your spare clothes. Altogether you have to carry more than 60 kilos on your back.

On the march you share a tent at night with the seven other legionaries who live in your barrack-room.

When you joined the legion you signed on for twenty-five years. Each pay-day you give some money to your standard-bearer who keeps the savings bank. If you survive the twenty-five years you could use the savings to start up as farmer on the small plot of land given to you when you retire. You might even open a shop in one of the 'coloniae' and stay in Britain.

You just hope you will survive—it would be a pity if all those savings were simply used to pay for your funeral! You and your friends think a lot about the painted people, and how fierce they are supposed to be. You also talk about your home-country, perhaps Spain or North Africa: warmer than Caledonia! (The legionaries who served in Britain came from all over the empire. Can you think why?)

For five years Agricola campaigned in Caledonia. Some tribes, such as the Votadini, surrendered to the Romans and learned to live with them. Other tribes retreated into the forests and mountains, attacking the Romans when they could. The map opposite shows the Roman progress. Notice how Agricola kept to the Lowlands. Can you think why? As the Romans advanced they built roads and forts. Two of the most important forts were at Ardoch and Inchtuthil in Perthshire. These forts guarded the entrances into the glens in the mountains. Agricola built a fort and a harbour at Cramond, near Edinburgh, so that he could get help from the Roman fleet. In AD 84 this fleet sailed right round Caledonia, proving to the Romans that Britain was an island.

As the legionaries moved northwards they must have kept looking to the mountains on their left, to the west. This, they knew, was where danger lay.

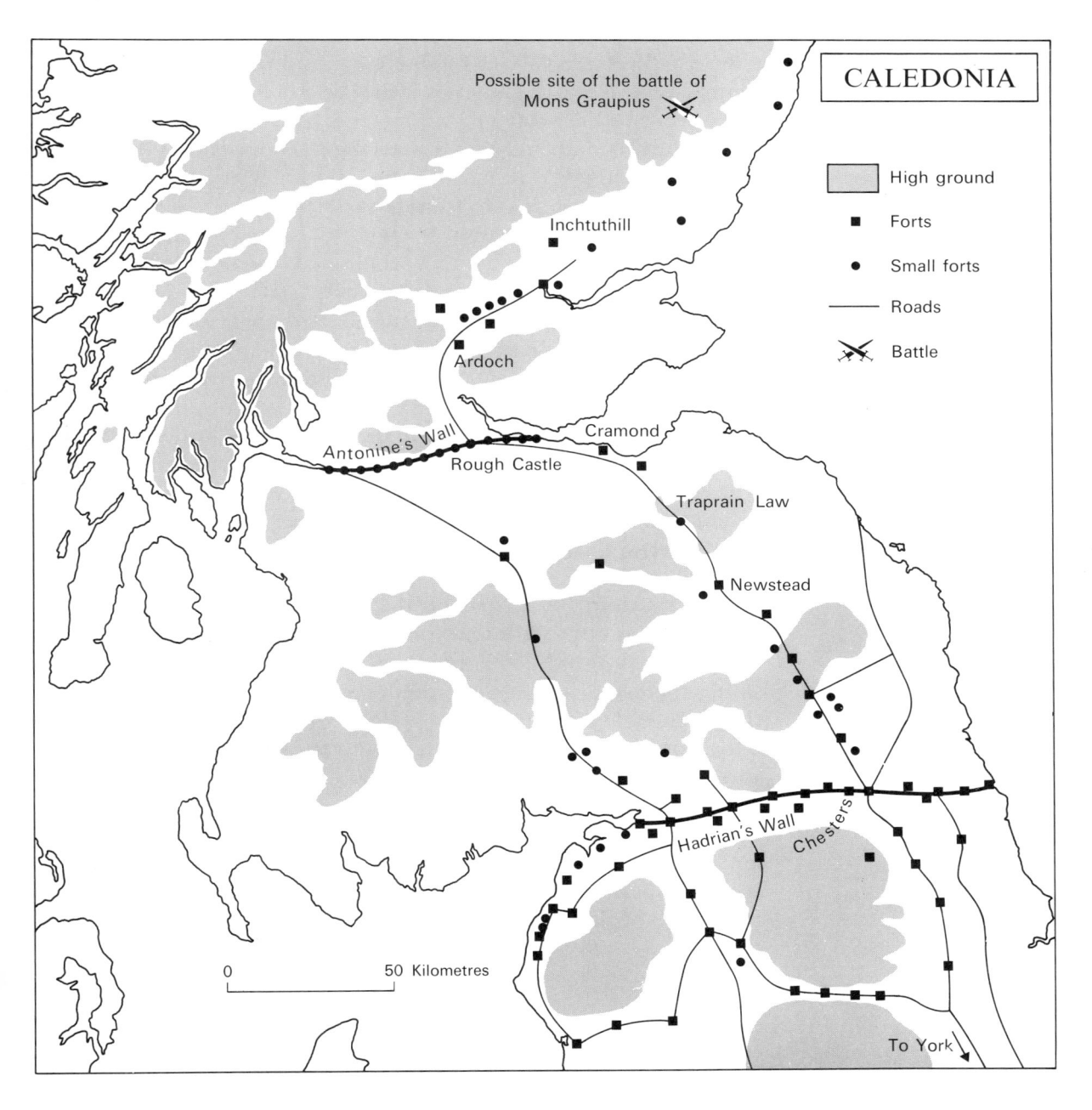

Tacitus tells us that in AD 84 a great battle was fought at Mons Graupius. We do not know exactly where this is, but it is probably in Kincardineshire. The Caledonians, led by Calgacus ('the Swordsman'), attacked the Romans. The battle was very hard fought, but the Romans, with their better weapons and armour, won the day. Ten thousand Caledonians were killed and only 367 Romans. At least that is what Tacitus tells us and we do not have the Caledonian side of the story! The surviving Caledonians retreated to the mountains but continued *guerrilla* raids on the Roman forts.

In AD 85 Agricola was suddenly recalled to Rome by Emperor Domitian and the legionaries were withdrawn from Caledonia. They seem to have left in a hurry, and tried to destroy their forts so that the Caledonians could not use them. At Inchtuthil they buried more than 750 000 iron nails—some 10 tonnes in all. Why do you think they took great care to hide these from the Caledonians?

In 142 began the second attempt to conquer Caledonia. The emperor sent a new governor, Lollius Urbicus, to Britain. He decided to invade Caledonia to teach the tribes a lesson. Perhaps they had been attacking Hadrian's Wall. Perhaps it was something to do with the terrible disaster that seems to have happened to the Ninth Legion. After 120 the legion simply disappears from the records. Maybe it was destroyed in battle; maybe it was broken up because the legionaries had run away from the enemy. We just do not know.

Unfortunately there was no Tacitus to tell us about this invasion. One Roman historian, however, tells us that 'Antonius [the emperor] subdued the Britons through Lollius Urbicus and after driving back the *barbarians* erected another wall made of turf'. This was 'Antonine's Wall' but little of it remains. It stretched for about 60 kilometres from Bridgeness on the Forth to Old Kilpatrick on the Clyde. It was built with turfs on a stone base and stood more than 6 metres high. Just like Hadrian's Wall about 130 kilometres to the south, there was a protective ditch and a military road running all the way beside the wall. Every 3 kilometres along the wall there was a fort and, between each fort, look-out towers. A network of forts and roads linked it with Hadrian's Wall.

The soldiers who built the wall put up distance slabs like the one below to show who had done the work. Look carefully at the wreath and you will see how we know this was put up by legionaries from the Twentieth Legion. Underneath there is a carving of a wild boar, the badge of their legion.

From the safety of their forts the soldiers were sent out on patrol. The sentries were constantly on the look-out for raiders or for signs of smoke from a watch-tower further along the wall. Life must have been hard for the legionaries posted to Antonine's Wall. Yet they still had some luxuries: many of the forts had small bath-houses, for example. At Carriden, at the east end of the wall, there is evidence of a settlement where wives and children lived, close to the protection of the wall. Here, too, traders from the south came with pottery, glass and wine.

Antonine's Wall held back the Caledonians only for about forty-five years. Indeed, there is evidence that parts of it were destroyed at least once and rebuilt. By 186 the Romans abandoned the wall and retreated to Hadrian's Wall.

The last attempt to conquer Caledonia came in 209, when Emperor Severus marched north. As before, the Caledonians seem to have retreated to the safety of the woods and mountains. This short campaign ended in 211, when Severus died after returning south to York.

There were no more attempts to invade Caledonia. From now on the Romans were hard-pressed even to defend Hadrian's Wall. Indeed, the whole Roman Empire was being threatened by invaders.

Source extract

This is how Tacitus described the battle at Mons Graupius. The Caledonians have attacked the Romans beside the hill:

> Higher up the hill were masses of Britons who had not yet joined in the fight. Now they began to descend to take the Romans in the rear. Agricola saw this and ordered his cavalry reserves to block this move. The trumpets sounded, the auxiliary horsemen—gripping their lances—hurled themselves forward. Their forward gallop broke the Caledonian ranks. It was the critical moment. The Caledonians, split up into groups by the cavalry, began to waver and then scatter. The Roman discipline triumphed. While the enemy were in disorder the Roman troops kept their fighting formation. Agricola now sent his cavalry to take the enemy in the rear as they broke and ran. The legions did not move in pursuit, for now it was a cavalryman's battle. The Caledonians tried to rally in the nearby woods, the cavalry ringed it while others dismounted and flushed them out. Leaderless and broken, the Caledonians fled—leaving 10 000 dead on the field. The Romans lost only 367.

THINGS TO DO

1 Imagine that you are a legionary in the Twentieth Legion. You are doing sentry duty on Antonine's Wall. Write a letter to your younger brother telling him about your life in the legion. Try to persuade him to join up as a legionary too.

2 The Romans had no newspapers as we know them. But let us imagine you are a reporter for the 'Rome News'. Here are three headlines for your newspaper:

> CALEDONIANS DEFEATED AT MONS GRAUPIUS (From our reporter on the battlefield)
> HOW A ROMAN ROAD IS BUILT (Readers' questions answered)
> GLADIATOR MARCUS KILLED AT THE GAMES (From our Sports Reporter)

Write stories for each of these headlines, and include pictures if they will help your story. Try to arrange your stories on a double page of your notebook, like a newspaper. If you have spaces between your stories, make up some Roman advertisements to fill them.

11 The break-up of the Roman world

The Europe we live in dates from the break-up of the Roman Empire. Several tribes from the north and east burst into the empire and set up their own rulers in such countries as Spain, France, Romania, Belgium and England.

What had gone wrong with the Roman Empire?

One answer is that the empire was sometimes not so strong as it seemed to be. From 180 onwards rival generals often fought for the title of emperor. While they were fighting it was possible for the northern peoples to invade the empire. So when the general Magnus Maximus took the army from Britain to Gaul to try to make himself emperor, the Picts from the north broke through Hadrian's Wall and raided southern Britain. In fact, Hadrian's Wall was twice over-run by the Picts when the Roman legions were away fighting other Romans.

Even after one general had won the title of emperor, the ordinary people were worse off. The new emperor had to impose heavy taxes to pay his soldiers and bribe his enemies. More money was spent bribing the chiefs of the tribes so that they would not attack the empire.

Besides, many Romans had begun to dislike soldiering very much and the Roman armies contained a very large number of men who were not Romans at all. Indeed by 350 more than half the army was made up of Franks, Goths and Vandals (tribesmen from outside the empire whom the Romans called 'barbarians'). There were two reasons for this. First, fewer Romans were prepared to leave their homes to go and fight hundreds of miles away defending the frontiers of the empire. Secondly, by 350 the frontiers were so long—16 000 kilometres in all—that they needed 400 000 soldiers to guard them. The cost of keeping this army was enormous and often the soldiers were not paid. Do you think the barbarian legionaries would be as reliable as Romans?

Far away, on the other side of Asia, things were happening that were to drive other tribes westwards. The Chinese Empire had become very strong and a great wall had been built to keep out the Huns, tribesmen from central Asia. These Huns were finding that the rainfall was no longer sufficient to produce the grass their animals needed. They could not get beyond the Great Wall of China and so they began to look for fresh pastures in the west.

In 375 the Huns crossed the River Volga and swarmed over the steppes of south Russia. They moved in great bands mounted on horses or ponies, living in round black tents and moving from place to place in search of good pasture. They were magnificent mounted soldiers and ugly enough to make people frightened, with flat noses, slit-eyes, big heads and shrill voices. At first men wondered if they were apes or devils. St Jerome, writing at the time, said: 'The Roman army is terrified by the very sight of them.'

THE WANDERINGS OF THE PEOPLES

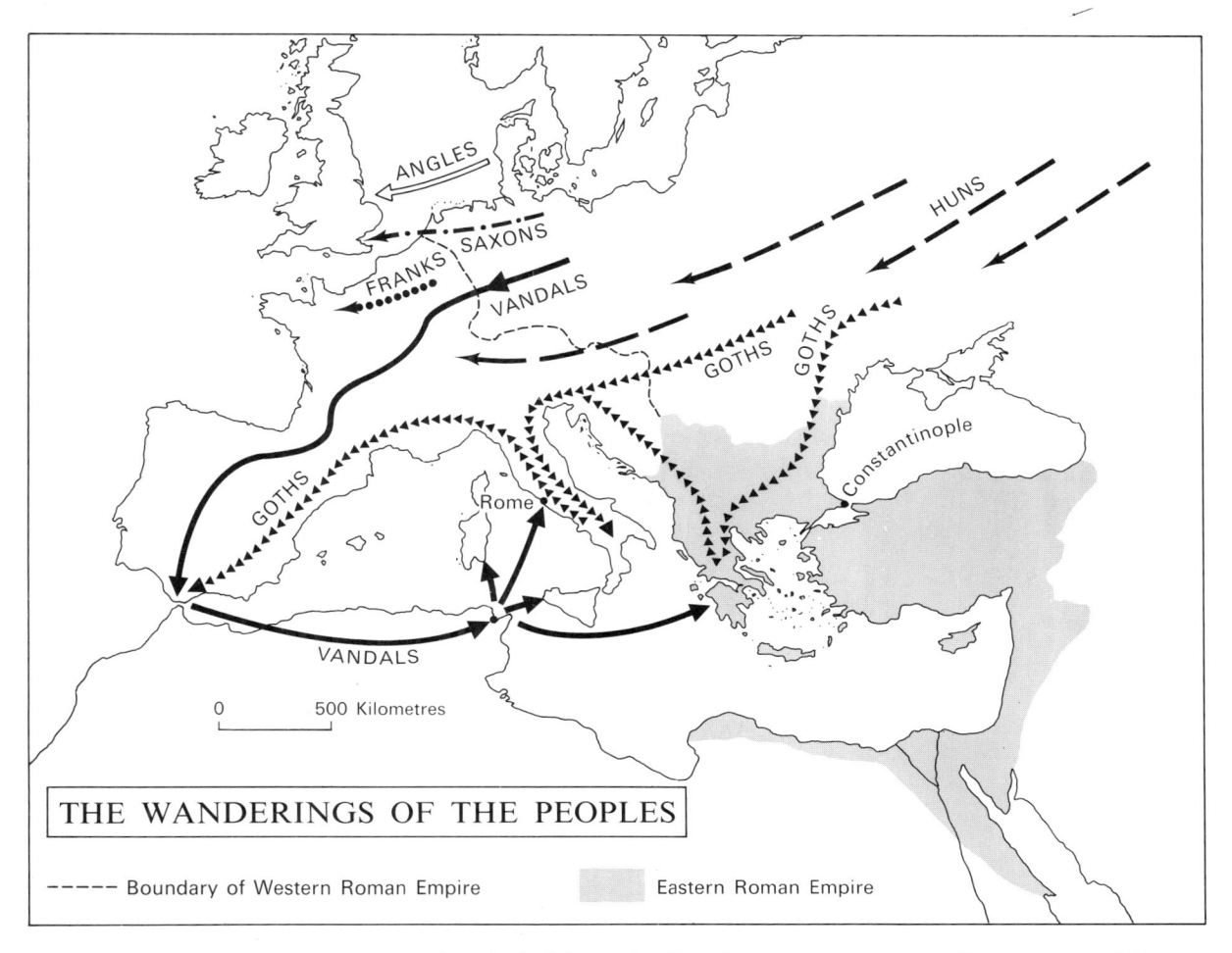

- - - - - Boundary of Western Roman Empire   Eastern Roman Empire

Under their king, Attila, the Huns over-ran Europe, reaching as far as eastern Gaul, before they were stopped at a great battle near Châlons in 451.

As the Huns spread westwards, other tribes had fled before them, each pushing on the tribe in front of it like a train of goods wagons being shunted. In 376 some Goths were given permission to settle in the Roman Empire; soon others followed without asking leave. There was no great wall to keep these people out, as there was in north Britain. The River Rhine was a natural barrier which could be defended, but in 406 it froze over. The barbarians crossed it and overwhelmed the defenders. Eight Roman cities, including Rheims and Boulogne in Gaul, were destroyed. The rush had begun and many different peoples came pouring into the empire, conquering all before them.

Pope Gregory, who witnessed these events, wrote: 'The cities are devastated, myriads [very large numbers] of people are killed, the earth is soaked with blood, and a foreign people is running through the land as if it were theirs.'

Indeed, it was now theirs. The Goths, led by Alaric, captured Rome in 410. At one time he had been an ally of the Romans and so refused to allow his followers to destroy the city. Other Goths occupied Spain; the Franks took over the Roman province of Gaul; the Vandals marched through Spain to conquer North Africa. In 476 the last Roman emperor in Rome was *deposed* and the barbarians were masters even of Italy.

But, as we already know, many Roman ways survived.

In 330 the emperor Constantine had built a new capital at the entrance to the Black Sea called, after him, Constantinople. This remained a great centre of Greek and Roman life for another thousand years.

In the west, most of the invaders learned Roman ways. In what are now France, Spain, Portugal, Italy and parts of Switzerland and Belgium the tribes began to speak the language of the people they had conquered. They began to use Roman law, to live in Roman towns and to accept the Christian faith of Rome. The languages people speak in these lands today are called Romance languages because they are based on the Roman language, Latin.

What happened to Roman Britain?

Even before the Romans left, raiders from Germany and Denmark had attacked the shores of Britain. These Angles, Saxons and Jutes crossed the sea in large open rowing boats, each carrying thirty to forty warriors. The Romans built a number of forts, known as the defences of the Saxon shore, to protect Britain.

In 410 the emperor Honorius called all the legions back to defend Rome. Britain was defenceless and the raiders took the chance to come looking for treasure. One of these raiding parties buried their loot on Traprain Law, near Haddington in East Lothian. They had stolen a lot of silver plates, cups and spoons, probably from a Roman home. Most of the loot had been cut into little pieces ready to be shared out amongst the raiders. We know the people they stole from were Christians: this spoon from Traprain has the early Christian chi ro sign.

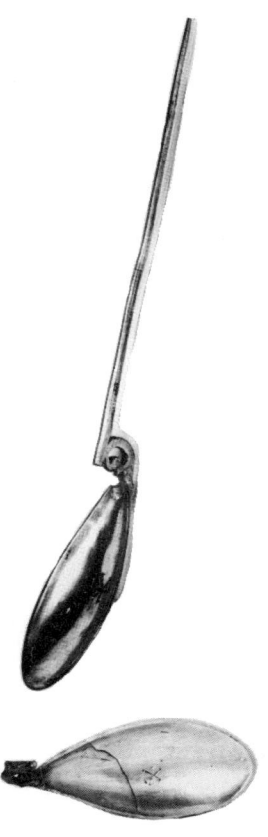

The Britons pleaded with the Romans to come back. We are told they sent a message: 'The barbarians drive us to the sea; the sea drives us to the barbarians; between these two ways of death, we are either massacred or drowned.' But no help ever came.

Try to imagine what an Anglo-Saxon raid must have been like. Here are the boats creeping up a British east-coast estuary in the morning mist. You see the raiders tie up under cover, send out scouts and wait anxiously for their return. You can feel their excitement when the scouts hurry back with the news that a Roman-British village lies up the river.

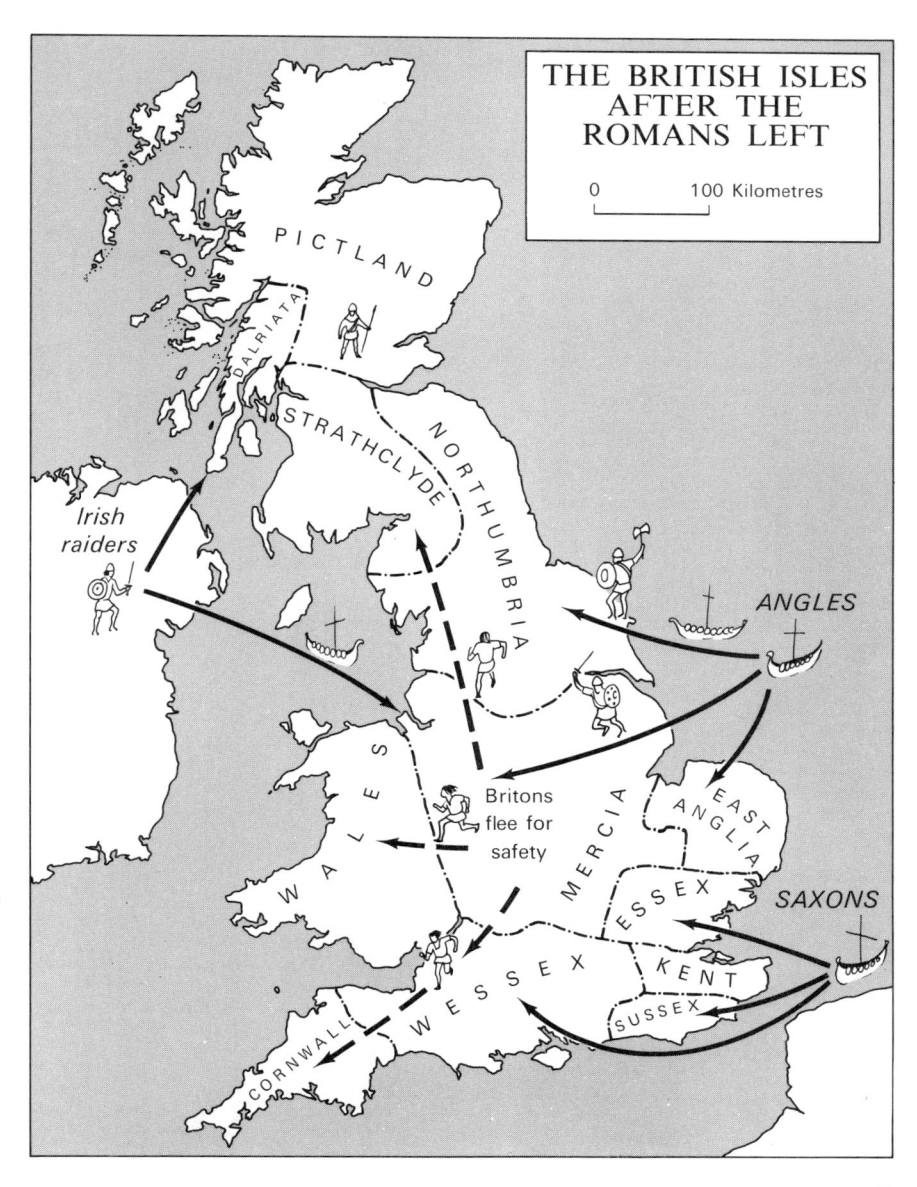

THE BRITISH ISLES AFTER THE ROMANS LEFT

0   100 Kilometres

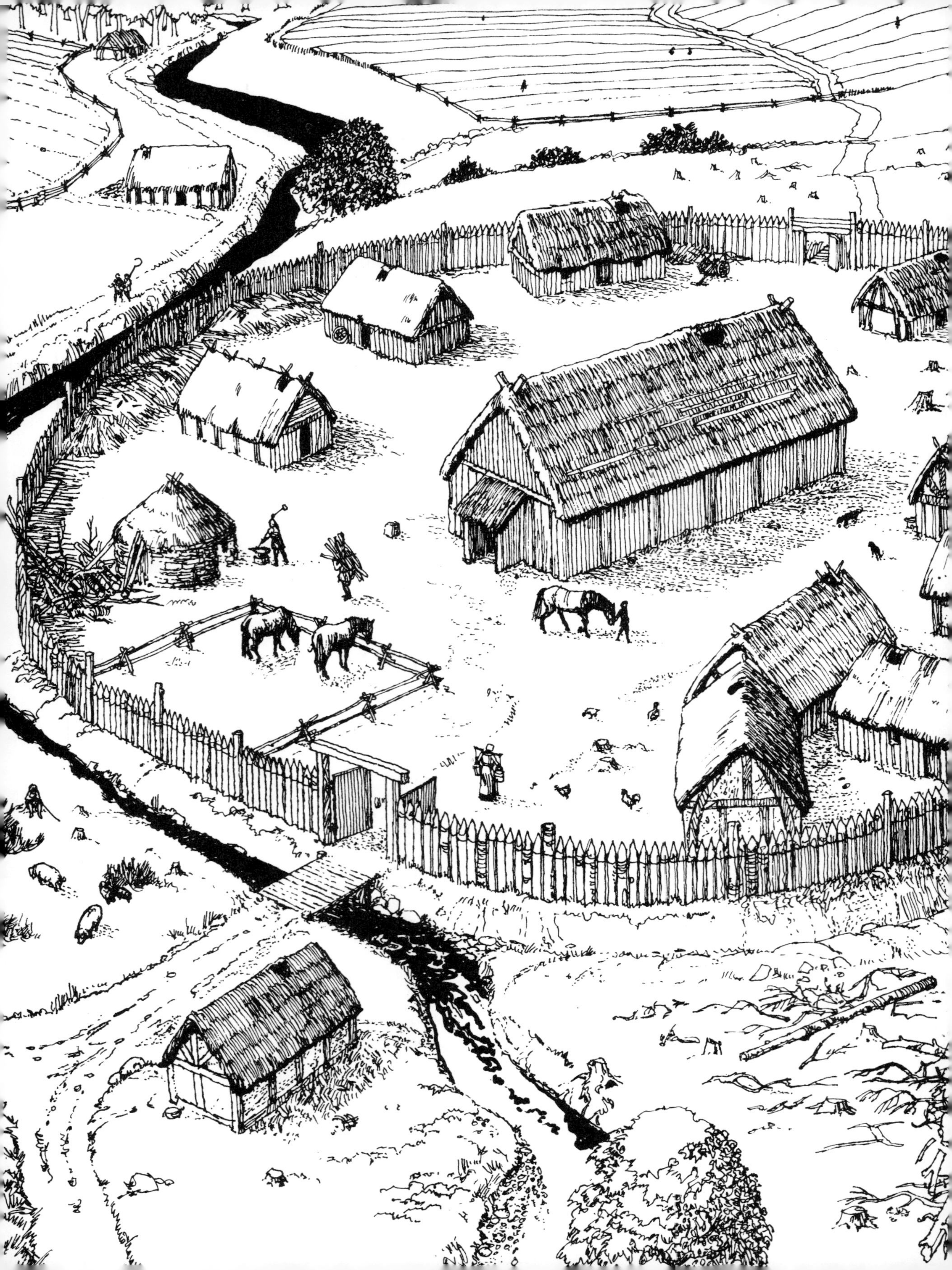

Then you see the preparations for attack at first light the next day, the warriors falling on the sleeping village, killing and taking slaves and plunder. Months later you see them come upstream again, landing, clearing some forest, building a village, growing crops, sending over to Germany for their families; making a new home in a new land which is soon to be called after them Angle-land or England.

The British are enslaved, killed, or driven westwards. Soon the Roman towns and villas are all deserted and the buildings fall down, because the Anglo-Saxons prefer to live in their own settlements. The Anglo-Saxon language replaces Latin.

The invaders were not just destroyers, however. In 1939 archaeologists discovered a burial ship at Sutton Hoo in Suffolk. It must have belonged to a Saxon chieftain who died about 650. He was probably killed fighting somewhere else because no body was found in the boat. Like the Ancient Egyptians, his followers placed all the man's treasures in this unusual grave. He must have been a very rich man —as you can see from his belt-buckle, made of solid gold. Some of his treasures came from as far away as Egypt.

All over northern Europe the invaders made themselves at home. By 700 England was divided into the seven kingdoms shown on the map. Elsewhere, on the ruins of the Roman Empire, they began to build new states which have lasted to the present day. By 800 the ruler of the Franks, Charlemagne, was powerful enough to be crowned emperor by the Pope. On his coins he had himself shown looking like a Roman emperor. So, although the great Roman Empire had been destroyed, in many ways Roman ideas and the Roman way of life survived.

THINGS TO DO

1 Put the heading 'The End of the Roman Empire' in your notebook. Try to make a list of the reasons why the Roman Empire was destroyed.

2 Write a report of an Anglo-Saxon raid as if you were living in a British village which was attacked.

3 Imagine you are a new settler just arrived in England and you are going to live in the village shown on page 62. Write a letter home, describing the village. Use the information in the picture to help you.

4 Here is an extract from a book written by the Roman historian Herodian. He is giving reasons why the Roman legionaries were not such good soldiers as they used to be. Read it carefully, then answer the questions in sentences. First, however, make sure you know what all the words mean.

> Emperor Septimus Severus granted the soldiers many privileges which they did not previously have. He was the first to increase their grain ration and permitted them to wear gold rings and to live with their wives ... all of which used to be considered unsuitable for soldiers when making preparations for war. He was the first to undermine their famous vigour ... teaching them to covet money and making them think of luxurious living.

(*a*) Who introduced the changes described by Herodian?

(*b*) What three privileges did he give to the soldiers?

(*c*) Can you suggest why he might have given these privileges?

(*d*) What effect did the privileges have on the soldiers?

(*e*) What happened to the man who introduced these changes? (This is a revision question: see page 55 if necessary.)

12 England, Ireland and Scotland become Christian

The Romans first brought Christianity to Britain. Here you can see a Christian mosaic from a Roman villa in Sussex.

You will remember how Christianity survived after the death of Jesus. The early Christians met in secret in the catacombs under the city of Rome and ran the risk of being executed or of being condemned to a horrible death in the arena. Both St Peter and St Paul were executed in Rome. But the new religion could not be stamped out. It taught about loving one's neighbour and that all people are equal in the eyes of God.

The Christian message of faith, hope and charity was far more attractive than the other religions of the empire. Christians believed in one god; in other religions there were hundreds to choose from. Christians had a simple communion service to remind them of Jesus's last supper; in other religions there were often horrible sacrifices which were supposed to please their gods. Gradually the number of Christians grew and soon they were worshipping quite openly. You remember how the emperor Constantine allowed Christians to worship freely. Then the leader of the Church became known as the Pope (which simply means 'father').

Christianity lived on after the Roman Empire was destroyed. Indeed Alaric the Goth, who captured Rome in 410, was a Christian himself. Most of the 'barbarians', however, did not know of Christianity and worshipped gods such as Odin and Thor. And so the Christians in the Church set out to convert the conquerors.

In England the Christian Church was destroyed by the *heathen* Anglo-Saxons who, as we have seen, invaded after the Romans left. They burned the churches and drove the priests into the west, so that soon Christians were to be found only in Wales in the west and among the Picts of the north.

But while England was suffering under the Anglo-Saxons and Christianity was being wiped out there, in Ireland things were much better. A young Briton, named Patrick, had been carried there as a slave. He escaped and became a monk. In 432 he went back to Ireland as a missionary and began his life-work of converting the Irish to Christianity. Soon Ireland was to become the chief centre of the faith in western Europe and to send out many missionaries. One of these, St Columba, set up a monastery on Iona, a little island off Mull. We shall read more about St Columba and Iona later in this chapter.

In 597, the year that St Columba died, Pope Gregory the Great sent St Augustine as the first Christian missionary to the King of Kent. St Augustine made use of an old Christian church in Canterbury, the Church of St Martin, and became the first *Archbishop* of Canterbury.

At first all seemed to be going well. The daughter of the King of Kent married Edwin, King of Northumbria, and took north with her a missionary named Paulinus. But soon Penda, the heathen King of Mercia, killed Edwin and once more Northumbria became heathen. When Christianity came back to Northumbria it was from Iona, brought by St Aidan, not from Canterbury.

From the north, missionaries went to convert the Midlands and the east of England. Finally in 681 St Wilfrid made Sussex Christian and we can say that all England was converted.

Unfortunately the two kinds of missionaries, those from Rome and those from Iona, disagreed about some things, especially about the date of Easter and even the shape of the tonsure, the way in which monks shaved their heads. The quarrel became so serious that in 663 King Oswy of Northumbria called a meeting of the leaders of the two churches to Whitby. This meeting was called the Synod of Whitby. There was much argument between the two sides, but in the end Oswy decided that he and his people would follow the Roman way. So England became part of the Roman Catholic world after 664, but in Scotland the change was to take longer. Now let us see how Scotland became Christian.

The first missionary to come to Scotland was St Ninian, a man from the Solway region, who may have lived in Rome. He came north in 397 and set up the first church in Scotland at Whithorn, a little church called in Latin 'Candida Casa' (The White Hut). There he worked, preaching to the Picts around him and training missionaries to carry the teachings of Jesus, the 'gospel', to the surrounding people after his death.

Some of these missionaries worked as far north as Aberdeenshire, at least, leaving their names and some stones carved as crosses as proof. St Serf, St Kentigern or Mungo (the patron saint of Glasgow), St Enoch and St Drostan—these were a few of the people who carried on St Ninian's work.

But St Ninian's missionaries do not seem to have had much to do with the people of the west. To them came a missionary from Ireland in 563: St Columba, who set up a church and monastery on Iona. Here is the abbey at Iona today.

Columba was a war-loving Irish prince. However, at the age of twenty-two, he gave up fighting and devoted the rest of his life to God. We are told that he did this to make amends for a cruel war he had started. He took the name Collum Cille (or Columba), which means 'Dove of the Church'. For twenty years he preached to the Irish people, then he decided to come to Scotland.

Why Scotland? You will remember that the Romans called our country Caledonia. At that time, the Scots lived in Ireland. Once the Romans had gone, they too attacked Britain and then came to settle here. About 500, a large number of Scots led by their king Fergus Mór settled in Dalriata, the land we call Argyllshire. So Columba really came to see his own countrymen.

He sailed across with a few followers in a small skin-covered boat, called a curragh, until he came to Iona. There he landed, destroyed his boat and set about his work. We know a lot about the early years of Iona from a history of St Columba written by Adamnan, who became *abbot* in 679.

From Iona, Columba soon converted the surrounding people. Then he tried to convert the Picts of the north, travelling to Inverness to try to persuade King Brude to become Christian. St Columba himself crowned Aedán King of the Scots of Dalriata. Columba became one of the king's closest advisers.

If St Columba and his followers had done no more than convert the west of Scotland to Christianity, we should still remember them. But they did much more.

In 617 the Anglo-Saxon King of Northumbria was killed in battle and his son Oswald came to Iona for safety. When Oswald went back to Northumbria in 635 he sent to Iona for Scottish missionaries to convert his people. The best-known of these missionaries was St Aidan. He founded a church at Lindisfarne (Holy Island), began to preach to the people of Northumbria and gathered round himself a band of followers. One of the best-known Christians of those years was St Cuthbert, a shepherd from the Lammermuirs.

Within a few years Northumbria was Christian and missionaries from there had converted many other parts of England.

Try to imagine what life was like in one of these early Christian centres. There would be a number of wooden or stone huts, earth-floored, grouped near the church. A little way off would be a barn for grain and a stable and byre for the beasts. The church itself would be roughly built of stone, heather-thatched maybe.

Nothing remains of the first settlement on Iona. The huts would probably have looked like this monk's cell on Eilach an Naomh, an island in the Firth of Lorne.

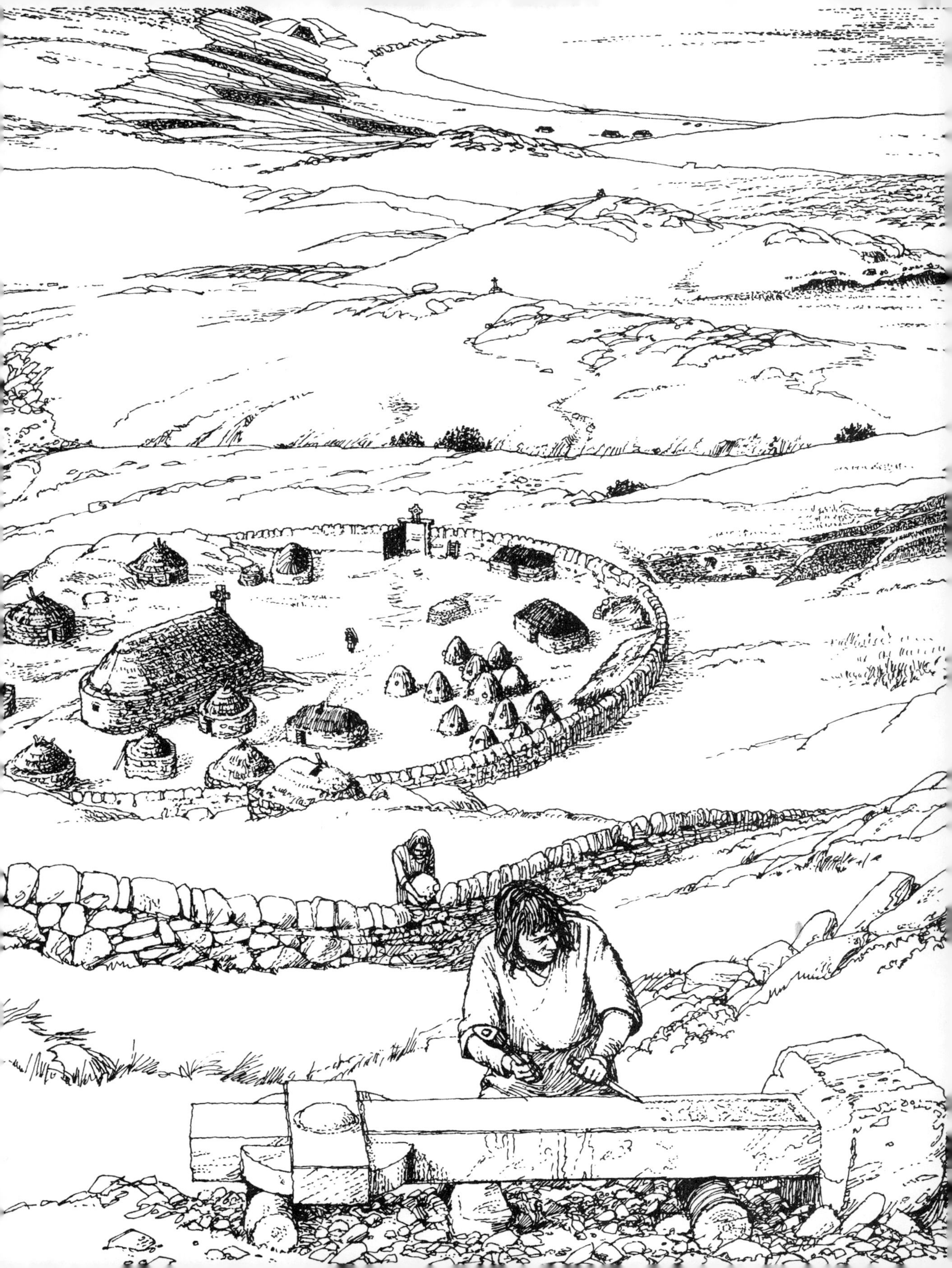

Round the buildings would be a strong drystane dyke to keep out intruders, with little fields stretching beyond it. The monks who lived there, ruled over by an abbot, gave up their lives to prayer, teaching, work in the fields, or copying books by hand.

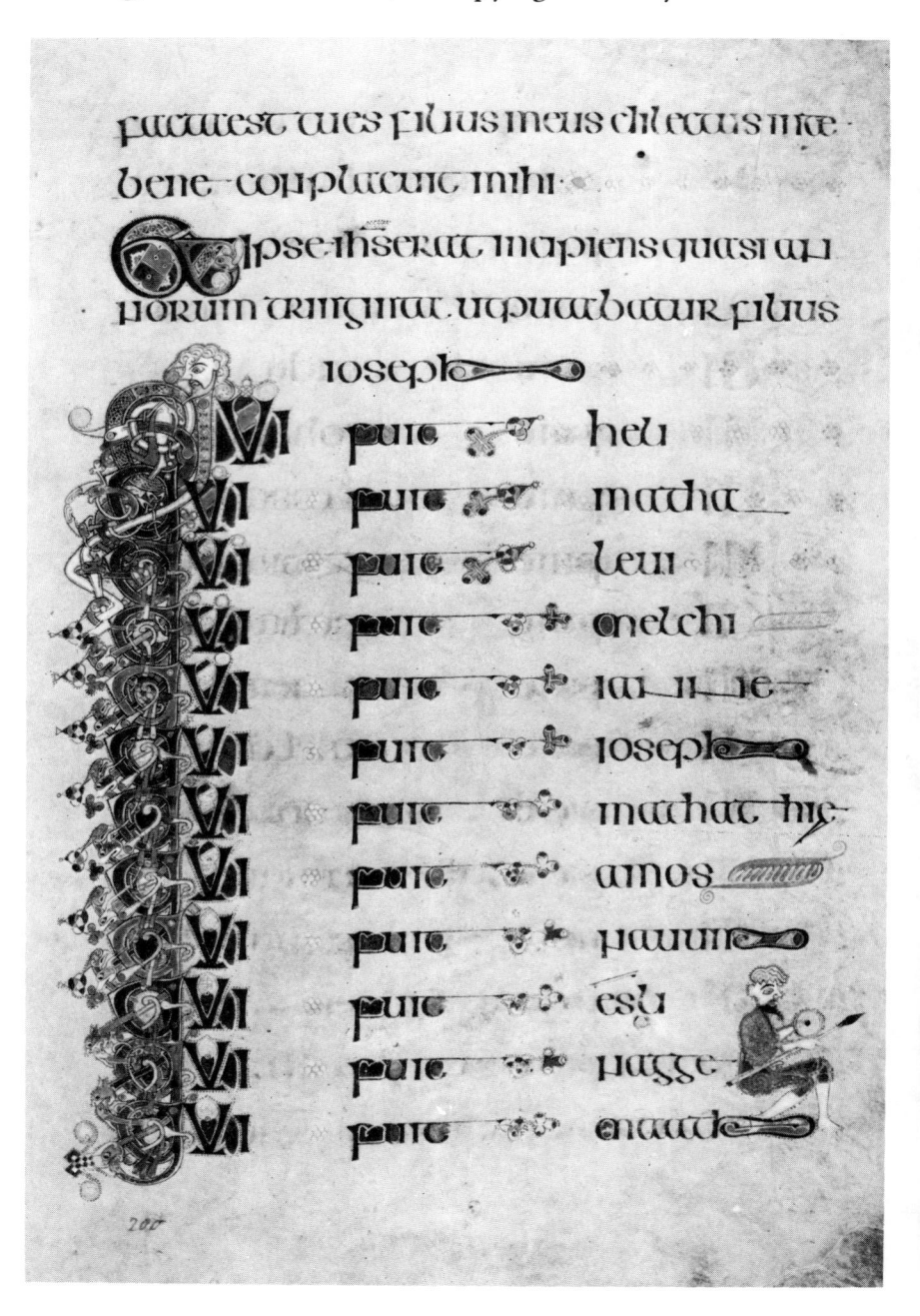

This is an illustration from the famous Book of Kells, started in Iona about 700.

Other monks were skilled carvers. At one time more than 360 of these beautiful stone crosses covered the island, but now only a handful remain.

The monks dressed very simply in a long rough robe of undyed wool, with a loose coat over it. On their feet they wore leather sandals or skin brogues. In church the priest wore a white surplice over his robe.

Their lives were hard. Adamnan tells us that Columba 'slept not except with his side against the bare earth, with nothing under his head but a pillar of stone for a pillow'. Their work was rewarded, however. For several hundred years Iona was the centre of Christianity in Scotland. More than sixty kings of Ireland, Norway and Scotland, including Kenneth MacAlpin (who we will read about later), are buried there.

St Columba died in 597, sadly mourned by his followers. His life throughout had been an inspiration to many people. Even today, about 1400 years after his death, thousands of people visit Iona, the isle of Columba.

THINGS TO DO

1 Imagine you are visitor to Iona in Columba's day. Write a letter home, describing the settlement there. Use the drawing on page 69 to help you.

2 When a famous person dies, you often read an obituary in the papers or hear it on television. An obituary is a brief account of a person's life, reminding us why he or she should be remembered.

Write an obituary of St Columba in your own words. Begin: 'Today we heard of the death at Iona of the good monk Columba. He was born in Ireland and as a young man....'

3 There are many interesting stories about St Columba in the book written by Adamnan—including the first mention of a monster in Loch Ness! Try to borrow this book from your local library and read some of these stories.

13 The Vikings

> AD 787. And in his [King Beorhtric's] days came for the first time three ships of Norwegians from Hordaland, and then the king's reeve [official] rode to them and asked them to go with him to the royal manor [court house] for he did not know who or what they were, and with that they killed him.

This is an extract from a book known as the Anglo-Saxon Chronicle, a kind of annual diary kept by monks in England. It describes the first recorded raid made by people we know as Vikings. They do not seem to have done much damage, but they were soon back again. In 793 they destroyed the monastery at Lindisfarne and the next year the monastery at Jarrow. In 802 they attacked Iona and about eighty monks were killed. Can you think why monasteries such as Iona were the first to be attacked by the raiders? (You should find a clue if you look at the map on page 61.)

Perhaps you are wondering why these fighters came at all. To understand why, we must look at their homeland in Scandinavia—the lands we now know as Norway, Sweden and Denmark. If you look at a map of Norway you will see that much of the land is mountainous and so it is difficult to grow enough food for a great number of people. Look again at the map. The coasts of Norway are made up of countless inlets called fiords or, as these people called them, 'viks'. So the men living in these coastal lands naturally became sailors and fishermen.

By the eighth century it seems that the population had increased. There was just not enough land for everyone. Also, the law at that time said that only the oldest son could inherit land from his father. What were the other sons to do? Many looked for a life of adventure, with the chance of rich plunder. These are the Vikings we are thinking about.

Being seafaring folk, they were able to build ships which could carry them safely on voyages of hundreds of kilometres. These were the famous longships. This is one known as the Godstad ship. It was deliberately buried by Vikings with the body of their 'jarl' (chief) inside.

The ship is 22·3 metres long and 5·25 metres wide, made of wooden planks which overlap each other. (This is known as clinker-built.) Notice how shallow the ship is. It could be run very close inshore and could be sailed many kilometres up rivers to carry out surprise raids. It has benches for twenty rowers, but you can also see what is left of the mast, which carried a woollen sail. The ship was steered by a large wooden paddle or steer-board on the right-hand side. Did you realise this is where the word 'starboard' comes from?

There would be a crew of about thirty men. Each man carried a sea-chest holding food and his personal possessions. His weapons—an axe, sword and spear—were wrapped in oiled skins to protect them from the salt water. He was dressed in a homespun woollen tunic and trousers, with a cloak or fur-skin to keep him warm. In battle he was protected by a leather jerkin or, if he could afford it, a coat of chain mail made of rings of metal sewn together. He wore a leather cap or a metal helmet and carried a wooden shield.

Vikings were fierce fighters. Sometimes, we are told, they dressed in wolf- or bear-skins and went berserk—like wild bears. They ran about howling and shrieking, even biting their shields to work themselves into a frenzy. Here is an ivory chessman, found on the island of Lewis, doing just that.

These Vikings had curious names. A man's surname often described his appearance (Harold Fairhair, Ketel Flatneb, Olaf the Fat) or showed that he was a great warrior (Bjorn Ironside, Eric Bloodaxe). If you were the son of a famous father, you showed it in your surname—Olaf Haraldson or Leif Ericsson. Many Scandinavian people today have such surnames—and, of course, so have many of you!

The Vikings were not Christians but had a religion of their own. They believed in several gods whose names you use every day! The list on page 79 may surprise you.

Their gods, they believed, lived in a place called Asgard. Odin was the chief god and in his palace there was a huge hall, Valhalla. The Vikings believed that Odin sent twelve young girls, the Valkyries, to keep watch over battles on land and sea. When a brave warrior was killed, they carried him off on his shield to the home of the gods. The one thing a Viking feared was to die in his bed.

Sometimes, to avoid this, an old Viking chief was given a sea burial. The old man was placed in his ship with his weapons and armour which he would need in the hall of the gods. The sail was hoisted and the ship pushed from the shore. At the last minute a firebundle was thrown in and the blazing ship carried the old hero to Valhalla.

This ceremony is still remembered in Shetland (one of these Viking settlements) where the people hold a festival called Up-Helly-A. In January every year a longship is set on fire by people dressed as Vikings.

Iona was only one of the many places all over Europe where the Vikings fought and plundered. In 845 they captured Paris, in 851 London, and in 860 they even attacked Constantinople with a fleet of 200 ships. It must have seemed that nowhere in Europe was safe from them.

A Frenchman named Ementarius wrote: 'The number of their ships increases, the endless flood of Vikings never ceases to grow bigger. Everywhere Christ's people are the victims of massacre, burning and plunder. The Vikings over-run all that lies before them and none can withstand them.' People prayed to God for help: 'From the fury of the Vikings, good Lord, deliver us.' How they must have dreaded the sight of Viking longships on the horizon, with their fearsome dragon-head prows!

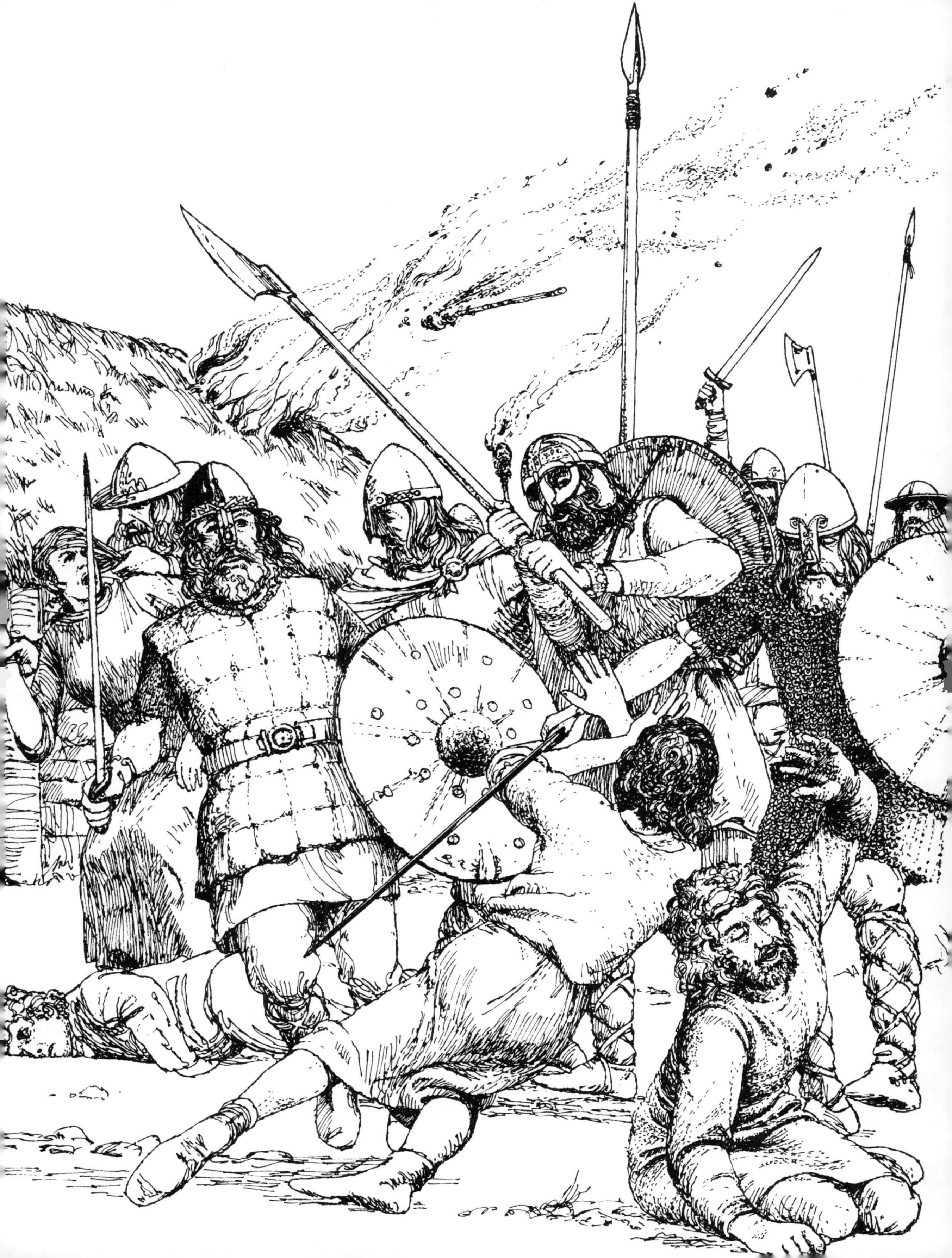

VIKING VOYAGES

→ The Westernway
--→ The Easternway

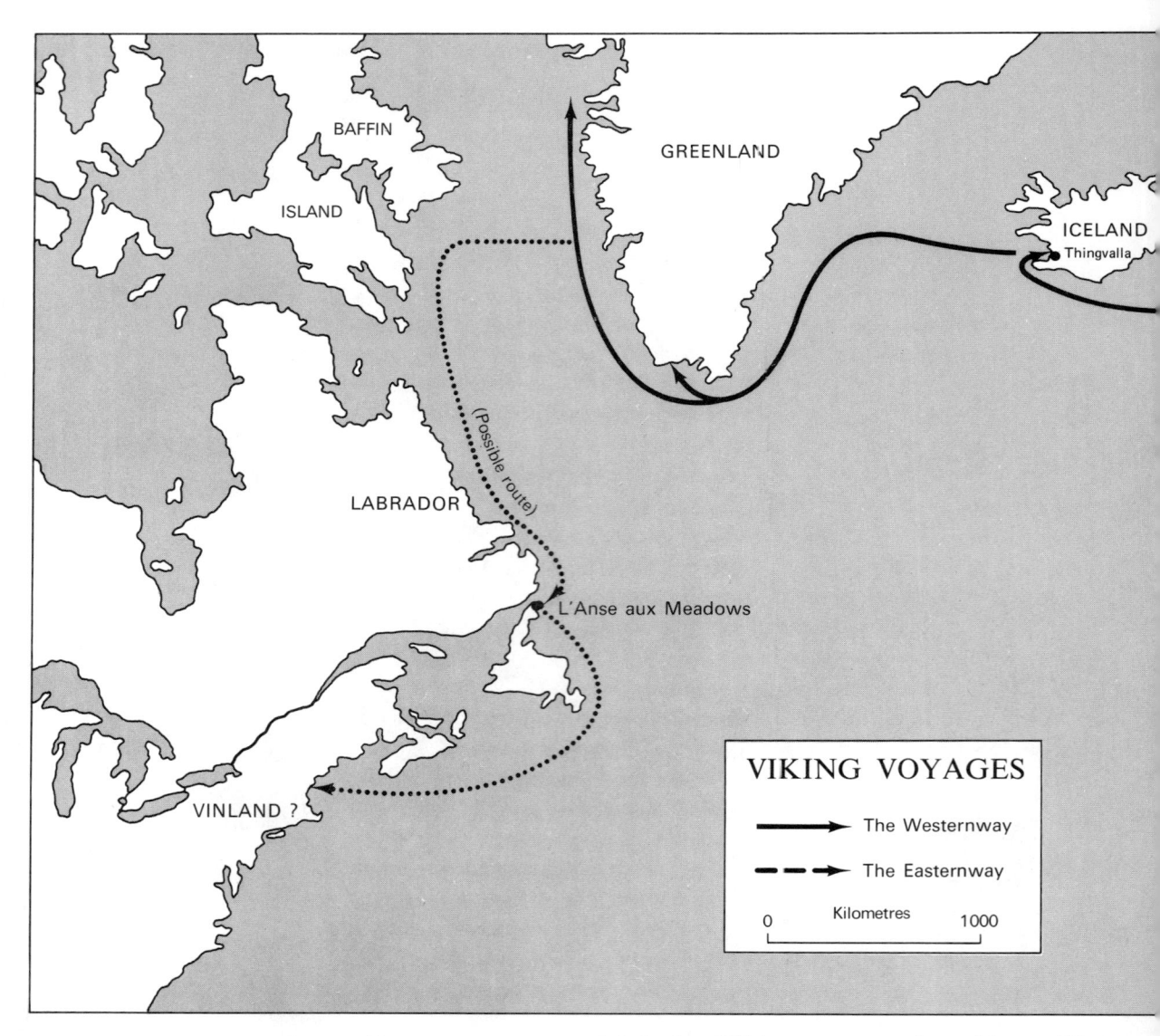

0 — Kilometres — 1000

But you must not think the Vikings were only robbers. They were wonderful explorers and great traders. In their tiny ships they followed what they called the Western-way to the Mediterranean Sea and on to Constantinople—and even crossed the Atlantic Ocean to land on the coast of North America. Others followed the Eastern-way, sailed down the rivers Volga and Dnieper and began the Russian cities of Kiev and Novgorod. These traders carried furs, ropes, timber, slaves (often captured on raids) and honey. (Honey was very important as sugar-cane had not yet been discovered.) On their return voyage they took back silks, spices, wines, gold, silver and precious stones. Archaeologists have found in Scandinavia more than 60 000 Arabic coins of this time. This shows how successful the Vikings were—either as traders or as raiders!

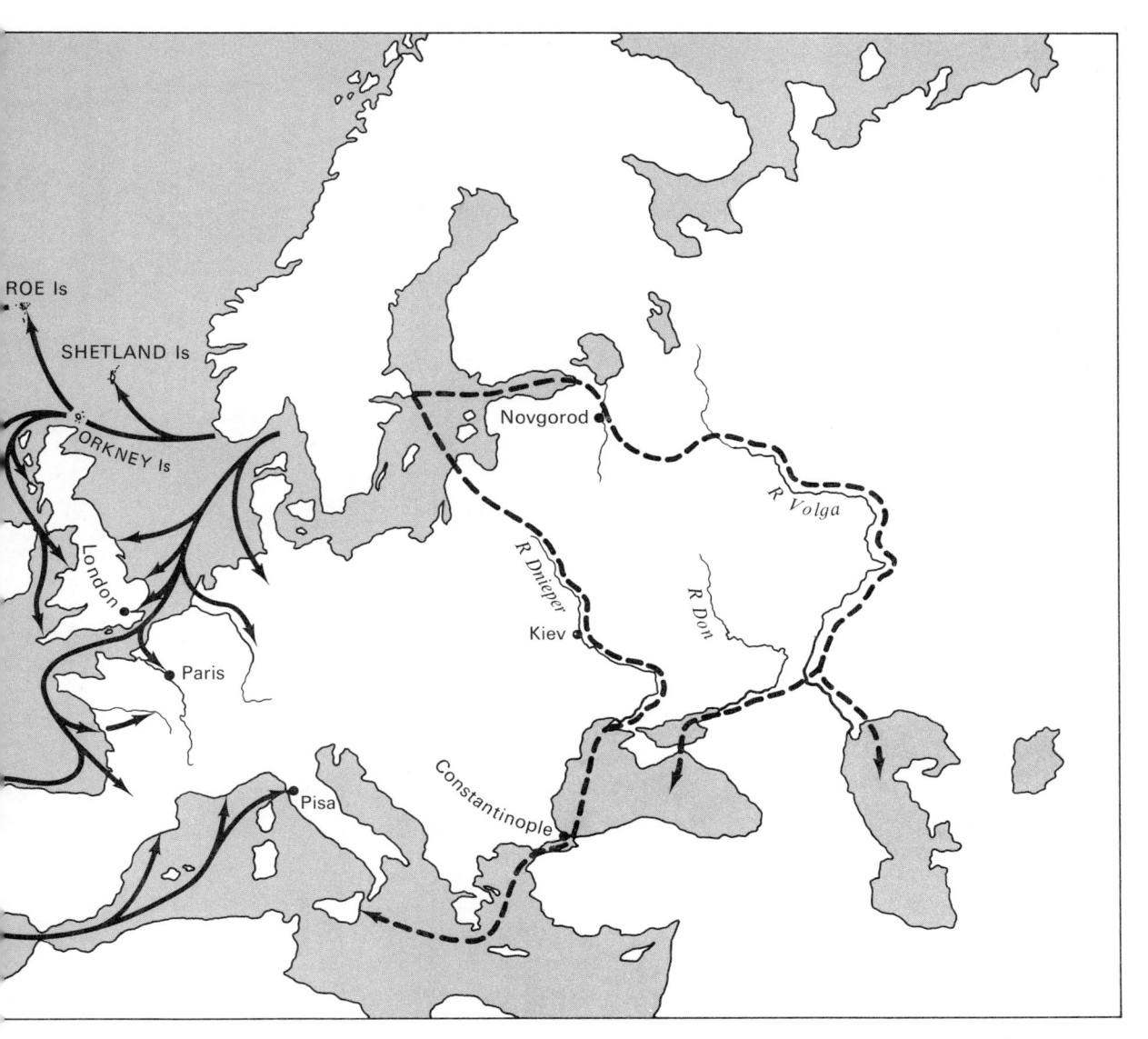

The Vikings were great settlers too. Larger ships, known as 'knorrs', carried families and their possessions, including farm animals, to new homes in other lands. One important settlement was in northern France. In 911 (as a bribe to stop him attacking Paris) a Viking leader named Rollo was given this land, which later became known as Normandy, the home of the Norsemen. We shall read about one of Rollo's famous descendants in Chapter 16.

Other Vikings settled in Scotland: in the Orkneys and Shetlands, in the Western Isles, in Caithness and Sutherland ('the land to the south') and in scattered places farther south. These settlers were farmers, fishermen and hunters.

77

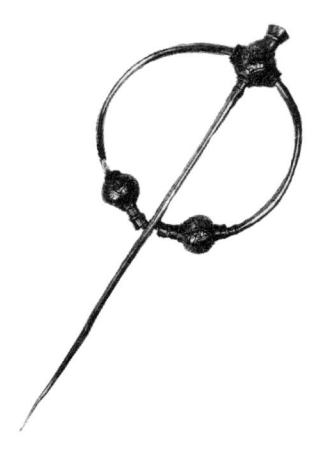

At Jarlshof in Shetland archaeologists have excavated the foundations of a large stone farmhouse. It had two rooms—a large living room and a smaller kitchen. In the centre of the living room was a large open fireplace and round the walls there would have been wooden benches for sitting and sleeping. Other buildings have been uncovered too—sheds, byres, a smithy, and one which archaeologists think may have been a sauna bath.

The Jarlshof folk grew barley and oats. They kept cattle, sheep, goats, horses and bees, and they hunted and fished. ('Lax' was the Viking word for a salmon. Is there anywhere near you with this word as part of a place-name?) The women wove homespun cloth which would be traded for luxuries, such as jewellery, when a trader's ship called at the settlement. Here is a piece of jewellery found at Skaill, in the Orkney Isles, and which may have been bartered for in this way.

The Vikings were great storytellers too. Nowadays we are used to being able to switch on the television or go out to the pictures. There were no such entertainments in those days. Imagine the scene inside the Jarlshof farmhouse on a dark winter's night. The family sit on the benches round the blazing fire. Outside the wind howls and makes the wooden rafters crack. All this adds atmosphere to the storyteller's tales of heroes, stories known as sagas. At first these were not written down, but learned by heart.

These sagas are much more than adventure stories. The Greenland Saga and Eric's Saga tell of the exploration and settlement of what the Vikings called Vinland.

Bjarní Herjolfsson is said to have been the first Viking to see North America, when his ship was blown off course about 980. There was an important Viking settlement on Greenland which, as you can see from the map on page 76, is only about 950 kilometres from Baffin Island off the coast of Labrador. The Vikings reckoned on being able to sail 150 kilometres a day, so it was quite easy for them to explore these lands to the west. Lief Ericsson was the first to land on North America about the year 1000. He called part of what he saw Markland, 'the land of woods', and another part Vinland, 'the land of grapes'. Other Vikings followed Leif and began to settle there. But they were attacked by the native people whom they called 'skralings' (wretches) and the settlements were abandoned. Archaeologists have excavated a site at L'Anse aux Meadows in Newfoundland, which is almost certainly one of these Viking settlements. If this is so, then Europeans lived in America about 500 years before Christopher Columbus!

The Vikings, then, were brave warriors, skilful shipbuilders, daring seamen-explorers, great traders—and they have made their mark on Scotland too. The Hebrides belonged to descendants of the Vikings until 1263. Orkney and Shetland did not become part of Scotland until 1469. (They were given to King James III of Scotland as a wedding present when he married Princess Margaret of Denmark.) Indeed, many of you reading this book must have Viking ancestors. That's something to think about!

Days of the Week

WEEKDAY	HOW DID IT GET ITS NAME?	
Tuesday	Tiu's day	Tiu was the god who put hatred in the hearts of men
Wednesday	Woden's day	Woden (or Odin) was the king of the gods, both for the Vikings and the Anglo-Saxons
Thursday	Thor's day	Thor was the god who sent thunder to the world
Friday	Freya's day	Freya was the wife of Odin

THINGS TO DO

1 This is an extract from King Harald's Saga. It tells the story of King Harald Hardraada, one of the most famous Vikings. He fought in Russia, Turkey, Italy, Germany and Scandinavia. He was killed in England in 1066: we shall be looking at his last adventure later.

This is part of a poem describing a raid made by Harald's men on a Danish village.

Bright flame burned in a village
Not far south of Roskilde
Tirelessly, King Harald,
Your fires devoured the buildings
Many Danes lay fallen
Death cut off their freedom
In silent grief the others
Crept to hide in forests.

Stumbling, the survivors
Scattered from the carnage
Sorrowing, they fled to safety
Leaving their women captured
Maidens were dragged in shackles
To your triumphant longships
Women wept as bright chains
Cruelly bit their soft flesh.

In your notebook print the heading 'King Harald's Raid'. Try to illustrate the scene described in the poem in one drawing, or the story of the raid in a series of pictures, like a strip-cartoon.

2 The Vikings are important for many reasons—not just their raids. Write down in your notebook as many reasons as you can think of.

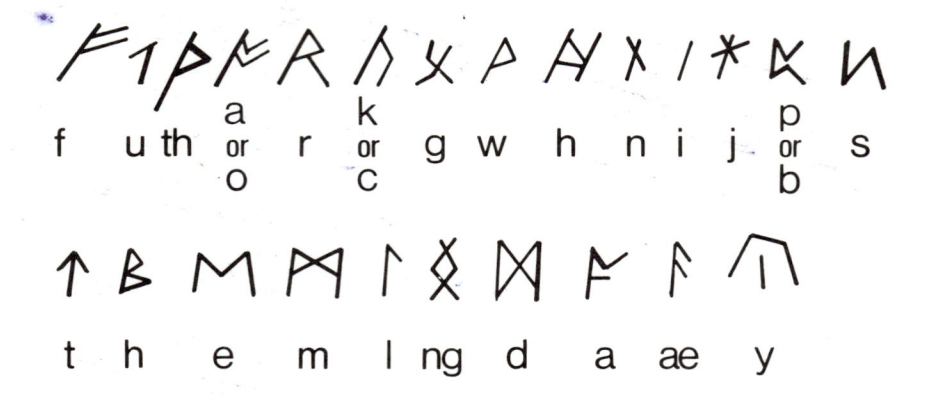

3 These are the letters of the Viking alphabet, known as 'futhark' or 'runes', with our own equivalent letters written underneath. The Viking alphabet was not written down in books or on parchment but was carved in wood or stone.

(a) Why do you think this alphabet is known as 'futhark'?
(b) Why do you think there are so few curved lines in the letters?
(c) What would be used to carve these letters?
(d) Where would you expect to find examples of Viking runes?
(e) Write your own name in runes.

14 Scotland becomes one country

At the time of the Viking raids there were several different peoples living in Scotland—Picts, Britons, Scots and Angles. The map overleaf shows where they lived—but remember that the boundaries between them were not as exact as they are shown on the map.

North of the River Forth was Pictland, divided in two by the great range of hills called the Mounth. The capital of one part was Inverness, the capital of the other part probably Forteviot or Abernethy.

You will remember from Chapter 10 that we know very little about these Picts, not even what language they spoke. Perhaps it was like Gaelic, perhaps like Welsh, perhaps it was different from both. There are no Pictish books. All we have are some stones with lines carved on them. These lines are known as ogham letters, but we just do not know what the words mean.

Until about 500 the Picts had shared Scotland with the Britons, who had two separate kingdoms. South of the Clyde, stretching into England as far south as Lancashire, was the kingdom of Strathclyde with its capital at Dumbarton. The other British kingdom, known as Goddodin, was in the Lothians. From 500 onwards the Picts and the Britons had to fight against two separate invaders.

We have already read in Chapter 12 how the Scots crossed over from Ireland and set up their kingdom of Dalriata in what is now Argyllshire. In 637 the Scottish king Domnell Brec lost his lands in Ireland. The Scots could not go back to their old homeland so they fought to make Dalriata bigger. They were not always successful. Domnell Brec himself was killed in Strathclyde. An old British poem tells us that '... the head of Domnell Brec, ravens gnawed it'.

On the other side of Scotland, in the Lothians and the Tweed valley, was the kingdom of Northumbria where the Angles now lived. Like Strathclyde, it stretched south into England. These Angles had invaded the east coast of Britain from their homes on the German coast and settled as far north as the Forth, as we saw in Chapter 11. In 638 the Angles captured Duneiden, later renamed Edinburgh. This was the end of the kingdom of Goddodin.

After this the Angles of Northumbria tried to conquer lands to the north of the Forth, but they were defeated by the Picts at Nectansmere, near Forfar, and had to turn back. But they remained in the Lothians and the Tweed valley and from their speech our Lowland Scottish language was formed.

These, then, were the peoples who had to be joined together before Scotland could become a nation.

Pict drinking from a horn

The first lasting union was made in 843 when Kenneth MacAlpin, King of the Scots, became King of the Picts too. In other words, he made Scotland north of the Forth and the Clyde into one kingdom. We are not sure how this union happened, but two things are certain.

First, the Picts as a separate race disappear. This does not mean that they were massacred by the Scots. They would live and work together—and would have to fight together. For the second thing we are sure of is that all the peoples in Scotland had to face the attacks of the Vikings. In 849 the headquarters of the Church in Scotland were moved from Iona to Dunkeld—as far away from Viking attacks as possible.

The next piece of land to be added was the Lothians. In 1018 Malcolm II, King of the Picts and the Scots, defeated the English at Carham and kept all the Lothians after the war was over. Malcolm's grandson Duncan already ruled Strathclyde, so when he became king he added Strathclyde to Scotland.

THE PEOPLES OF SCOTLAND

Viking settlers

Inverness

PICTLAND

Dunkeld
Battle of Nectansmere

IONA

DALRIATA

Forteviot
Abernethy

Dumbarton   Dunedin

GODDODIN
LINDISFARNE
Battle of Carham

STRATHCLYDE

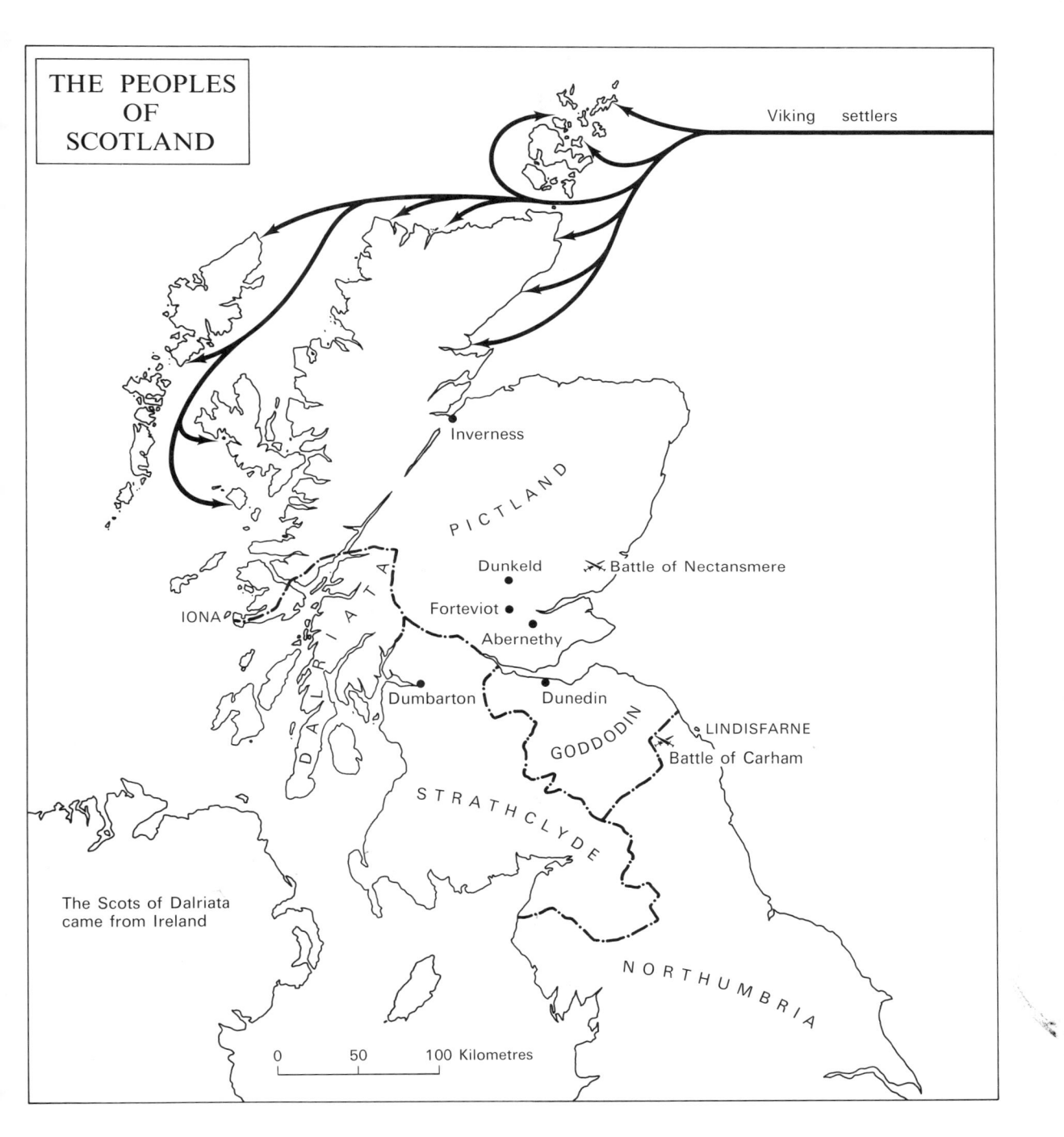

The Scots of Dalriata came from Ireland

NORTHUMBRIA

0   50   100 Kilometres

The four main parts of Scotland were at last under one king and could begin to come together to make one nation.
Unfortunately we know very little about these kings and the life and work of their people. However, we know much more about England at this time.

15 England in the time of King Alfred

In Chapter 11 we read how the Angles, Saxons and Jutes conquered England after the Romans left. Look again at the map on page 61 and you will see that England, like Scotland, was divided up into several separate kingdoms.

The men of these English kingdoms, like the men of Scotland, had to meet the attacks of the Vikings. For England, with many rich monasteries and farms, was a popular target for these fierce raiders from Scandinavia. Again and again, the Anglo-Saxon Chronicle tells us of the ravages of 'the host'—that is, the Vikings or Danes as they were also called. In the year 865, for example, 'a heathen host remained in Thanet and made peace with the Kentishmen, and the Kentishmen promised them money in return for the peace. And under cover of the peace and the promise of the money, the host went secretly inland by night and devastated all the eastern part of Kent.'

The Vikings were so successful that it seemed that the whole of England would be conquered by them. By 870 only Wessex—the kingdom of the West Saxons—stood against them. Then, in 871, a young man only twenty-two years old became King of Wessex. This was Alfred, the only King of England or Scotland who has been given the title 'the Great'. Probably he had never expected to be king, for he had three older brothers. Each of them was king for a short while, but they all died young—perhaps from wounds they suffered in fighting 'the host'.

When Alfred was only four years of age, his father sent him on a visit to Rome. When he was seven he went again, this time with his father, King Ethelwulf. When you think how hard and dangerous travelling was in those days, you will realise that these journeys must have been real adventures for a young boy.

As a young man Alfred was trained for warfare and his spare time was spent in hunting. He did not go to school, but he taught himself English and Latin. When he was older he regretted his own lack of education and (as we shall see later) he did a lot to improve education in England.

The young King of Wessex soon had to face the challenge of the Vikings. Like the Kentishmen we read about, he tried to buy himself some time by paying them money to stay away. This sort of payment was known as Danegeld. It worked for a while, but in 875 the Danes, led by King Guthrum, returned in force. In January 878 Alfred's army was taken by surprise and he only just managed to escape. With only a few followers he retreated to the Isle of Athelney protected by its swamps and marshes. These were dark days for Alfred. From this time we get the story of the burning of the cakes—but we do not know if this actually happened.

Gradually recruits joined Alfred's army and he was soon strong enough to take Guthrum by surprise. In the summer of 878 the Vikings were defeated at the Battle of Edington. The survivors were besieged by the Saxons in their camp at Chippenham and after two weeks they surrendered. Guthrum promised to leave Wessex alone and agreed to become a Christian to show that he meant to keep that promise. In return, the Vikings were allowed to settle in East Anglia. Later, in 886, Alfred made a treaty with Guthrum which gave the Danes control over a large part of eastern England. This territory came to be known as the Danelaw. Can you guess why?

Guthrum kept his word, but Alfred knew there would be attacks from other Vikings. He set about improving his defences.

First, he reorganised his army. Very few of his men were properly trained soldiers. Most of them were farmworkers who were called out to fight when the king needed them. This army of part-time fighting men was known as the 'fyrd'. They were often poorly equipped with only farm weapons to fight with—no match for the Vikings! Most of the fighting was done during the spring and summer months. (Can you think why?) So, as the men of the fyrd worried about missing their harvest, Alfred divided the fyrd into two. On this shift basis, half of them ready for fighting and half working on the farms, each man could spend at least some time getting in the harvest.

Secondly, Alfred ordered ships to be built to his own design. The Anglo-Saxon Chronicle tells us about this: 'Then King Alfred ordered warships to be built to meet the Danish ships; they were almost twice as long as the others, some had sixty oars, some more; they were both swifter, steadier, and with more freeboard than the others; they were built neither after the Frisian design nor after the Danish, but as it seemed to himself that they could be most serviceable.' This was really the beginning of our Royal Navy.

Thirdly, Alfred ordered the building of fortified townships known as 'burhs'. In these the local people had more chance of holding off a Viking attack until the fyrd arrived. People were attracted to these places to live and work and many of them later grew into towns.

There were other attacks from the Danes during Alfred's reign, but always his defences held. Alfred, then, deserves the title of 'Great' for saving his kingdom from invasion. He was much more than just a soldier, however.

We have already read that he educated himself. He translated several books from Latin into English so that (in his own words) 'all the youth of free men now among the English people may be set to study until the time they are able to read English writing well'. He also began the Anglo-Saxon Chronicle to provide a history of his time.

But he did even more. He encouraged works of art. This beautiful jewel, known as the Alfred Jewel, was found at Athelney about 800 years after it was made. Round the edge are the words in Anglo-Saxon (the English of the time) AELFRED MEC HEHT GENYRGAN, which means 'Alfred had me made'. Alfred also encouraged churches as centres of worship and learning. As he explained in a letter: 'I also remembered how before it was all ravaged and burnt I had seen how the Churches throughout England stood filled with treasures and books.' He also invented a candle which took four hours to burn so that people could tell the time of day or night.

Finally, King Alfred made important laws to keep the peace and he himself acted as judge at trials of serious offenders. Here we see an Anglo-Saxon king and his advisers giving judgement—and a criminal being executed.

How was the country governed? There was no Parliament as we know it. The king himself was the lawmaker. He was helped by his council, called the Witan, made up of the most powerful men in the land. The country was divided into shires controlled by ealdormen and thanes for the king. They carried out the law, collected taxes and organised the men of the fyrd when required. They were helped by officials known as reeves. These shire reeves of course became our present-day sheriffs. Each shire was divided into hundreds—originally made up of a hundred families. Each hundred had its small local court to deal with complaints.

Almost everybody lived and worked on the land. Important people owned large estates which were farmed by tenants known as cottagers or ceorls. People had special jobs to do on these estates. A tenth-century estate book describes the work to be done by the sowers, oxherd, cowherd, shepherd, goatherd, cheesemaker, beekeeper, granary-keeper and forester. Beneath the ceorls were slaves—often captives. The estate book gives details of what should be given to female slaves each year:

> Concerning women's provisions: For a female slave, eight pounds of corn for food, one sheep or threepence for water supplies, one sester [container] of beans for Lenten supplies [food for Lent, a church festival], whey in summer or one penny. All serfs [slaves] ought to have Christmas supplies and Easter supplies, one acre for the plough and a 'handful of harvest'. [What do you think this last item would be?]

The estate would be made up of small open fields. It would have looked rather like the one in the photo here. There would have been areas for animals to graze and of course forests for timber. The estate owner lived in a large hall and the other folk in simple timber huts.

Open fields at Laxton in Nottinghamshire

Times were very hard. A bad harvest could mean starvation. If you were ill or had an accident there were no doctors or nurses as we know them to go to for help. People had to find their own cures. Some of these can still be read in a tenth-century book called 'Bold's Leechbook'. They make very strange reading to us.

> For a very old headache, take salt and rue and bunches of ivy berries; pound all together, put into honey, and with it anoint the temples and the forehead and on the top of the head.

There were cures for all sorts of things. How about this?

> Against a woman's chatter, eat a radish at night, while fasting [going without food]; that day the chatter cannot harm you.

King Alfred died in 899. He was succeeded in turn by his son and grandsons. They were able to resist the continued Viking attacks and to expand their territory. In 934 his grandson Athelstan led the first English invasion of Scotland. By the reign of Edgar (959–75), the kings of Wessex were accepted as kings of all England. Edgar was succeeded by his thirteen-year-old son Edward, who was cruelly murdered in 978 and was succeeded in turn by Ethelred.

Ethelred was a weak man surrounded by poor advisers. He was known as 'the Redeless', which means 'poorly advised' or 'unready'. The country was swamped by a fresh wave of Viking attacks. Ethelred tried to buy off their king, Swein, with Danegeld, but their attacks continued. What resistance there was, was often poorly led. In 1009 the Anglo-Saxon Chronicle commented:

> ... And when the enemy was in the east, then our levies [the fyrd] were mustered in the west, and when they were in the south, then our levies were in the north....

We can get some idea of how bad things were from the Chronicle entry for 1011:

> All these misfortunes befell us by reason of bad policy in that tribute [Danegeld] was not offered them in time or resistance made; but when they had done their worst, then it was that peace was made with them. And notwithstanding all this truce and peace and tribute, they went about everywhere in bands and robbed and slew our unhappy people.

Poor Ethelred died in 1016. His eldest son Edmund also died that year and another son, Edward, fled to Normandy for safety. Cnut, the son of King Swein, now became King of England. For nearly thirty years, England was part of a Danish Empire that included Norway and Sweden as well. Cnut died in 1036 and was followed by his two sons, Harold and Harthacnut. In 1042, Edward returned from his long exile in Normandy to be crowned king.

THINGS TO DO

1 Write an obituary for King Alfred the Great.

2 From the information on pages 87–89 describe a visit to an English estate. You could perhaps describe the jobs mentioned in the estate book.

3 Put the heading 'English Costume' in your notebook. Sketch or trace two examples of dress from some of the pictures in the chapter.

4 The extract from the Anglo-Saxon Chronicle on page 89 tells of 'our unhappy people'. Write a short paragraph stating why you think the English were 'unhappy' during the reign of King Ethelred.

King Cnut and his wife Queen Aelgyfu present a cross to Newminster Abbey, Winchester

PART TWO
The forging of a nation

King David I (left)
with his grandson,
who became King Malcolm IV

16 The Norman Conquest

> In this year King Edward passed away and was buried on Epiphany [January 6th] in the newly *consecrated* abbey Church of Westminster.

This is how the death of King Edward in 1066 is recorded in the Anglo-Saxon Chronicle. Another very important source for the events of that year is the Bayeux Tapestry. Here you can see the funeral of King Edward as it is shown in the Tapestry. What are the men walking beside the procession carrying?

The Bayeux Tapestry is really a strip-cartoon in needlework. It was sewn on to coarse linen in strips 50 centimetres wide which were then joined together. Who actually did the needlework? This is rather a puzzle and historians still disagree about the answer. But, by looking closely at the pictures, two clues have been found. First, Odo, Bishop of Bayeux and half-brother to Duke William of Normandy, appears quite often in the pictures. Secondly, some of the Latin words describing the pictures are written in a special English way. So we think that Odo ordered the making of the Tapestry and that English women—who were famous for their sewing—actually made it.

In addition to the main story of the conquest of England, the borders of the Tapestry are embroidered with animals, hunting scenes and farming scenes.

King Edward had no children. The question was: who was going to succeed him?

Harold Godwinson, the Earl of Wessex, was the strongest leader in England, and a popular commander. His sister had been married to Edward—and Edward had probably promised him the throne. At least, that is what the Anglo-Saxon Chronicle tells us.

But William, Duke of Normandy, could claim the English throne for three reasons. First, he was descended from a member of the English royal family (although others had better claims than he had). Secondly, King Edward might have promised him the throne too! This is quite possible, for Edward had spent many years of *exile* in Normandy. Thirdly, the Normans claimed that Harold himself had promised to support William's claim to the throne (but the Anglo-Saxon Chronicle says nothing about this).

According to the Bayeux Tapestry and other Norman sources, Harold's ship was blown off course by a storm in the English Channel and he was taken prisoner by the Count of Ponthieu. He was sent to Duke William, who (according to the Normans, anyway!) treated him very well. William even took him on an expedition against the castle of Dinon in Brittany and Harold took part in the siege, dressed as a Norman knight. Here you see the defenders of the castle surrendering, by holding out the keys on the tip of a lance.

On their return to Normandy, Harold made a solemn promise that he would support William as King of England. The Tapestry shows Harold making the oath while touching caskets holding holy relics—probably the bones of a saint. Harold was then allowed to return home.

We do not know what really happened. Perhaps Harold was tricked and did not know about the holy relics. Perhaps he was threatened with torture. Perhaps.... What do you think?

If Harold did make such a promise he certainly did not keep it. Immediately after the death of Edward he was chosen as king by the Witan and crowned. Then he prepared to meet the threat of an invasion from Normandy. All through that spring and summer his army watched and waited. His ships patrolled the Channel. But there was no sign of the Normans and by September Harold must have thought that the danger was past.

What was William doing? He spent months carefully gathering together an invading force. Boats had to be built; men had to be recruited, equipped and trained; weapons and armour got ready. Here you see Norman weapons being taken down to the boats: notice how the armour is being carried. At last, when all the preparations were complete, strong winds prevented the army from sailing. Like Harold, William had to watch and wait.

Then about September 18th messengers rushed news to Harold that an invading army had attacked England. But it was not the Normans! It was a force of Norwegian Vikings, led by Harald Hadraada—and helped by King Harold's own brother Tostig. With all possible speed, Harold marched his army north.

Meanwhile, the Vikings won an easy victory over the local fyrd and relaxed—thinking King Harold was on the south coast, watching for the Normans. They arranged to meet the local people at Stamford Bridge near York on September 25th to receive their surrender. King Harald's Saga tells us that the Vikings even left their armour behind in their ships.

The English army took them by surprise. After a terrible battle with heavy casualties on both sides, the English won. Harald Hadraada and Tostig were both killed. We are told that the Vikings arrived in a great fleet of three hundred ships, but only twenty-four were needed to carry away the survivors. Harold's battle-weary soldiers were resting when news came that the Normans had landed. Here you see their ships approaching England's coast.

What was Harold to do? He could not telephone or radio to see if the message was true and how many Normans there were: he had to rely on word of mouth. He could not order up lorries or aircraft to transport his troops: his army could travel only on foot, horseback or ship—mostly on foot.

He decided to march south as quickly as possible. He force-marched his weary troops 300 kilometres to London, gathering more men as he went. On they marched another 80 kilometres to Senlac Hill, near Hastings on the south coast of England. As dawn broke on October 14th he prepared to battle for his kingdom. It was less than three weeks since the awful battle at Stamford Bridge 400 kilometres away.

Why did Harold move so quickly to fight? There is no doubt that, if he had taken more time, his army would have been larger and in a better shape to fight. Perhaps he was overconfident. Perhaps reports of what the Normans were doing spurred him to action.

William had landed at Pevensey on September 28th. Immediately he gave orders for a castle to be built at Hastings and for soldiers to be sent out to scout the surrounding countryside. Then he sent out his troops to destroy that countryside: to burn the houses and crops, to kill the people. Why do you think he gave these orders?

On the morning of October 14th his army moved out from Hastings to meet the English at Senlac Hill. Let us look at these two armies.

Most of the English army were members of the fyrd: about 6000 strong, poorly armed and no match for the Normans. Then there were 2000 'housecarls', formed by King Cnut: full-time soldiers who were the royal bodyguard. They wore long coats of chain-mail known as 'hauberks', woollen trousers bound with leather thongs, and sandals. Their heads were protected by steel caps with nosepieces. They fought on foot and their favourite weapon was the long Danish battleaxe—which could cut down a horse and rider with one blow.

All the Normans were full-time soldiers, properly kitted out for war. The most important were the 2000 cavalry, who were supported by men-at-arms and archers. Altogether the Norman army was about 7500 strong.

The English army had taken up position on Senlac Hill with the housecarls in the centre, protecting the king. The Normans attacked several times but were beaten back by the English. Then, it seems, some of the fyrd broke ranks and excitedly chased after the Norman cavalry. They were soon cut down, and the Normans returned to the attack.

A rumour went round that William had been killed. The Tapestry shows us William riding about the battlefield with his helmet pushed back, showing himself to his troops. His standard-bearer points him out: 'Hic est Dux Wilem', 'Here is Duke William!' William now ordered his archers to fire into the air; King Harold was wounded in the eye. By this time it was the middle of the afternoon and the English were beginning to tire. The Norman cavalry broke through, killed Harold and pursued the few survivors into the forests. The battle was won.

With their king dead, the English people offered little resistance. London surrendered without a fight and William was crowned king on Christmas Day. The new king immediately shared out lands in England amongst his chief supporters. These were unhappy days for the English. The Chronicle tells us that 'They [the Normans] built castles far and wide throughout the lands, oppressing [treating badly] the unhappy people, and things went ever from bad to worse'.

King William reigned until his death in 1087. Shortly before he died, he decided to find out more about the country he had conquered. So he sent officials to every village and every farm to ask how many people lived there, how many animals there were and how much rent was paid. The Chronicle did not think much of this: '... it is shameful to record it, but it did not seem shameful to him to do—not even one ox, nor one cow, nor one pig escaped notice in his survey.' This survey was known as the Domesday Book and (as you can see from the questions asked) it tells us a lot about life in England at this time.

The Norman Conquest brought many changes to England. There was a new king; there were new landowners with their new castles; and there was a new language—French—which replaced the English of Alfred the Great. For most of the ordinary people, however, life went on much as it did before. They worked their fields, paid their taxes, and spoke the English of their parents.

THINGS TO DO

1 Write the heading 'The Bayeux Tapestry' in your notebook. Use the information on page 92 to help you to write a paragraph explaining why the Tapestry is such an important source for historians.

2 Imagine you are Duke William. Draw up a list of the preparations you will need to make to carry out your invasion of England.

3 The story in the Tapestry ends with the flight of the English survivors from the battlefield. Try to draw the final scene of the Tapestry where William is crowned King of the English. The pictures from the Tapestry in this chapter will help you with such things as clothing, armour, etc. Write the Latin heading 'Hic residet Rex Anglorum' (Here sits the King of the English) above your drawing.

4 Write an eye-witness account of the Battle of Hastings as either an English housecarl or a Norman knight.

17 Margaret, Queen and Saint

In the next chapter we shall look at some of the ways in which the Norman Conquest of England affected Scotland. First, we are going to look at someone who fled from William the Conqueror.

After the defeat at Hastings, many English refugees fled to Scotland. Among them was the princess Margaret, the sister of the Saxon *heir* to the English throne. We know her today as St Margaret and think of her as one of the great people in Scottish history. She came to Scotland humbly, landing from a little ship in the Firth of Forth at St. Margaret's Hope, just east of where Rosyth Dockyard now stands.

She made her way to Dunfermline where King Malcolm III, known as Malcolm Canmore, had his capital. Although Malcolm spoke Gaelic, the language of the Scots, he had lived for some time in England and understood English. Margaret and he were married soon after she landed, and it was as Queen of Scots that she was able to do the work for which we remember her.

After her death the story of her life was written by Turgot, the *Bishop* of St Andrews, in Latin. He tells us of her kindness to the poor.

'When she went out of doors, either on foot or on horseback, crowds of poor people, orphans and widows flocked to her, as they would have done to a very loving mother, and none of them left her without being comforted.'

'She ordered that nine little orphans who were very poor should be brought to her at the first hour of the day, and that some soft food such as children at that tender age like, should be got ready for them every day. When the little ones were brought to her she did not think it beneath her to take them on her knee, and to get their food ready for them; and this she put in their mouths with the spoon she used herself.'

Turgot tells us too how she tried to make the court of Malcolm III more civilised.

'It was at her urging that the people of Scotland bought from traders clothing of various colours, with ornaments to wear. She brought so much state into the royal palace, that not only was it brightened by the many colours of the clothes worn in it, but the whole dwelling blazed with gold and silver.'

Above all she worked for the Church, living a life that was an example to all. She had the great abbey at Dunfermline begun. She and her women sewed the richly embroidered altar cloths for the church and the robes for the priests.

She had a ferry-service over the Forth begun to help pilgrims going to St Andrews. Pilgrims were people who travelled to holy places in search of a cure for sickness or to seek forgiveness for some wrong they had committed. Because they were religious folk they were thought to be under the protection of God. This usually gave them a safe passage from the many thieves and robbers who roamed the countryside. Today many Christians still go on pilgrimages to Jerusalem, Bethlehem, Lourdes and other holy places.

Margaret had long arguments with the priests of the Celtic Church of St Columba, with her husband acting as interpreter. She was able to convince them that the Roman way was better, and after her time we hear little more about the Celtic Church.

In spite of her goodness, her life ended in tragedy. In 1093 her son brought the news that her husband Malcolm had been killed on a raid on England. She died that year in Edinburgh Castle—where her tiny chapel still stands to remind us of her.

St Margarets Chapel at Edinburgh Castle seen from both outside and inside

18 The Normans in Scotland

St Margaret had come to Scotland to escape from the Norman conquerors of England. Her sons, however, brought the Normans into Scotland to help them rule the land. For the Normans were useful people to have. They were skilful in the new kind of fighting on horseback; they were good governors and, because they were foreigners, they were not likely to side with the king's Scottish subjects if there was a rebellion.

Men like these were badly needed in the days after King Malcolm III was killed fighting against the English at Alnwick in 1093. Civil war broke out between those who wanted to keep the old Celtic ways of Scotland and those who wanted to go on making it more like England. This struggle continued for four years.

While it was going on, the Scottish king Duncan II was crowned by the Celtic chiefs 'on the condition that he should never again introduce English or French into the land'. Why do you think the 'English or French' were unpopular? But it was the danger from the Celtic chiefs which made Malcolm's sons, Edgar, Alexander and David (who one after the other became kings of Scotland) try to get Norman help.

David I came to the throne in 1124, when he was forty-four years old. He had spent many years in England at the Norman court. He had been impressed by the ways used by the Normans to control England. David himself had been made Earl of Northampton and been given control of lands in Huntingdon.

When David returned to Scotland he brought many Norman nobles with him. He gave lands to Norman families, many of whom had been tenants on his English estates. Others were adventurers eager to seek fame and fortune in Scotland. Among the newcomers were the families of Bruce, Balliol, Stewart, Comyn and Melville—all to become famous names in Scotland's history. We can judge how large the grants of lands were: the Bruces, for example, were granted 200 000 acres in the south-west of Scotland.

Why did the Normans come into this land? Perhaps we can answer that best by seeing what advantages they had from living, or owning land, in Scotland. Hunting was one great attraction. The forests of Scotland in the twelfth century were full of wild animals—elk, caribou, lynx, bear, wolf, as well as deer of all sorts. The rivers were full of salmon and the Normans probably brought the rabbit with them.

Another great attraction was power, the power that comes from owning land and having many armed men at your command. Still another was wealth, for many of these Normans were quite humble men before they came to Britain. Other Normans were humble men even in Scotland. They were tradesmen and took their names from the work they did—Fletchers (arrow-makers), Falconers, Foresters, Lorimers (bridle-makers) and Baxters (bakers).

You will notice that we do not say that the Normans were 'given' land: we say that they were 'granted' land. The land was not a present: they had to pay rent for it. But it was a peculiar kind of rent, paid not in money but in service. Each great landholder was required to come to the king's help with a certain number of armed men whenever the king needed him for his wars. The Bruce family were given their lands in Annandale in return for the service of ten knights.

In the same way, when each great landholder divided up his lands among his knights he made them promise to come to his help when he needed them. In short, this way of holding land was a way of keeping up an army for the defence of the country. It is called the 'feudal system'. There was one great danger, though—the landholder might grow too powerful and be able to oppose the king.

The Normans built castles to control their new lands. At first they were built quickly of wood, like the one put up at Hastings by Duke William. Probably the local folk were made to help with the work.

What were these first Norman castles like?

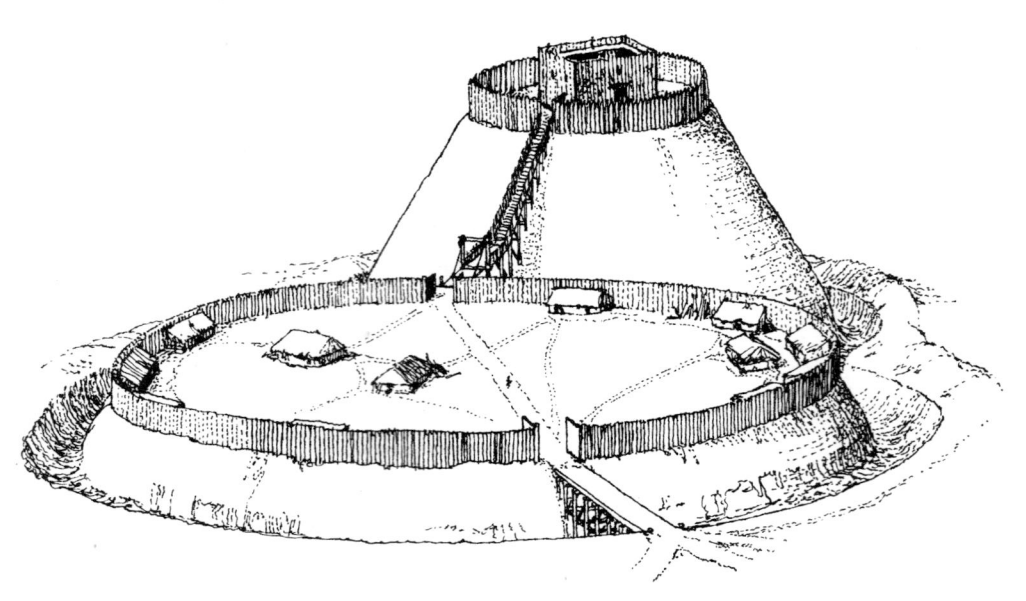

They were really built in two parts. The first part was called the 'motte'. This was the small hill or mound of earth on which the 'keep' was built. The keep was the tower where the lord, his family and his servants lived. In the keep were living quarters, a hall for feasts, store rooms and a prison or pit. The keep was protected by a wooden stockade and a ditch.

Below the motte was the second part, the 'bailey'. This was an open area with huts for the soldiers, store rooms, stables and a smithy. In times of danger, farm animals were kept in the bailey for safety. The bailey was protected by another wooden stockade and a deep ditch. Sometimes the ditch was filled with water but was always crossed by a drawbridge, which could be raised or lowered.

You can still see many examples of Norman castles in Scotland. Here—at Motte of Urr in Kirkcudbrightshire—you can make out the main features of a motte and bailey castle. Later, of course, stone was used instead of wood. Castle Sween in Argyll, built during King David's reign, was one of the first Norman castles to be built of stone.

The kings, too, built castles over most of the country. These royal castles became the headquarters of the sheriffs, the king's officials, each of whom ruled over a district about the size of a modern county.

They collected the king's taxes. Perhaps they were paid with silver pennies like this. The sheriffs also kept records of lands and their owners, made sure that the district was defended, and acted as the king's judges. In other words, the sheriffs acted for the king when he was in a different part of the country. Remember that there was not a fixed capital. David I stayed often at Roxburgh, but most of the time he was travelling about the country, seeing that justice was done and keeping law and order. Only the wilder parts of the Highlands were outside the king's control.

In another way the Normans helped Scotland: they were used to town life and knew the best way to run towns. We shall be looking at life in one of these towns (or 'burghs' as they were called) in Chapter 21.

The skill of the Norman knights was useful to Scotland in yet another way. They acted like a tank corps in the wars against England. They were able to move quickly and, protected by their armour, they could ride down enemy footsoldiers.

And there was fighting to do. King David made war on the north of England to try to make his niece Matilda Queen of England. In 1138 the Scots army was beaten at Northallerton, near York. This battle became known as the Battle of the Standard because the English fought round a wagon carrying the standards of their saints.

David's grandson, William the Lion, was also often at war with England. (William is said to have been the first Scots king to use the rampant lion as his badge.) He was taken prisoner at Alnwick and made to surrender all his lands to the King of England. But shortly afterwards King Richard Lionheart of England was needing money and sold back to the Scots their freedom for 10 000 merks. (The merk was a coin worth about 65p.)

To sum up, we can say that the Normans helped Scotland to become an efficient state, well governed, strong in war, with towns as the centres of trade and industry. We will look more closely at this Scotland in the next few chapters.

THINGS TO DO

1 Imagine you are King David. You are trying to persuade some of your advisers that it would be a good idea to bring the Normans to Scotland. Prepare a short speech (to give to the rest of the class) giving as many reasons as possible why the Normans should come.

2 We are very fortunate in Scotland to have so many castles still standing. Many of these are looked after by the Department of the Environment on behalf of everyone in Scotland. If there is a castle near you, try to visit it. Write a short report about your visit, describing the castle.

3 Make a drawing of a Norman castle, carefully labelling each part.

19 David the First and the Church

It was not only Norman nobles whom David and his brothers invited to Scotland. They wanted Norman bishops, priests and monks to come too.

The old Scottish or Celtic Church still had many followers. It already had bishops and monks, and they were not particularly bad men. But today we do not really know exactly what their duties were. There were Celtic monks called Culdees, with communities at St Andrews, Lochleven, Monymusk, Brechin, Abernethy and Iona. But their rules were not very strict and their work was not well organised.

King David wanted to change all this. He wanted to bring in more bishops and monks of the Roman Church as his mother Margaret had begun to do. These men were very hard-working and followed very strict rules.

The first man to draw up rules for monasteries was St Benedict. By the time he died in 543, monasteries obeying his rules had been set up in many lands. However, it was more than 500 years before the first one was set up in Scotland. Benedict taught that it was not enough for a monk to study religious books and take part in church services: he wanted his monks to do hard work just as Jesus's disciples did. His monks had to take vows (strict promises) of poverty, chastity and obedience: that is they had to remain poor, never marry and obey Benedict's rules. Their whole lives were to be devoted to the service of God.

Benedict was not the only man to make rules for monks. Others who had different ideas were St Augustine (not the St Augustine who went to Kent as a missionary) and St Bernard of Clairvaux in France. So there grew up three great Orders of monks as they were called: the Benedictines, the Augustinians and the Cistercians.

David I brought monks of all three Orders to Scotland. He granted them land and rents from land to provide money for their work. They built many beautiful abbeys: during the twelfth century, great abbeys were built at St Andrews, Holyrood, Cambuskenneth, Lochleven, Melrose, Newbattle, Dundrennan and Kinloss. This is what

Dundrennan Abbey may have looked like then. As we shall see, the monks in these and other abbeys did a lot of good work for David's Scotland.

But there was a danger. David and other kings and barons gave the Church so much land that it became too rich and powerful. King David himself was very generous to the Church. For example, in the *charter* granting land to the monks of Holyrood he also gave them money, the important fishing rights at Stirling, Berwick and Renfrew, freedom from paying *tolls* and the right to build their own burgh of Canongate outside the burgh wall of Edinburgh. No wonder a later King of Scotland, James VI, called David 'a sore saint for the crown' because he gave so much money to the Church. (Why do you think kings and nobles were so generous?)

So it is not surprising that Churchmen came to like wealth and comfort too much. They began to think more about their land and flocks and less about their promises to God.

When this happened two men, one an Italian and the other a Spaniard, had the same idea. They saw that monasteries did good work such as giving alms to the poor but, they asked, why should the poor have to come for help? Christ himself went among ordinary folk and taught his disciples to do the same. So these two men gathered round them followers who, though they might live in monasteries, went alone into towns and villages to tell people about God and help them in many ways. These preachers were called friars. They were forbidden to own any possessions and they even had to beg their food and shelter.

What were the names of these two men? One was Francis of Assisi in Italy, whom you may have heard about already, and the other was Dominic. Their followers were called Franciscans and Dominicans. The Franciscans wore a simple greyish-brown cloak and so were called Grey Friars; the Dominicans wore a black coat and hood over a white tunic and were named Black Friars. The Grey Friars and Black Friars reached practically every town and village in Scotland, preaching, teaching and caring for the sick.

We have not said anything about the bishops and priests that David and his brothers encouraged to come to Scotland.

From about the time of Margaret, Scotland was divided into ten districts, called dioceses, each under a bishop. The chief church in a diocese was called a cathedral because that was where the bishop's throne (in Latin 'cathedra') was placed. Each diocese was divided into parishes, each with its own church or kirk and parish priest.

The parish priest looked after the needs of the folk in his parish. He baptised them, married them and buried them, and tried to help the needy in any way he could. In return, the people were expected to give an offering as we do today for the work of the Church. But in addition they were expected to give a tithe or teind of everything that they produced. This meant that a tenth of a person's harvest went to the Church every year, and this was a heavy burden for many poor folk.

Some of the parish churches standing today go back to the time of David and his brothers, such as those at Dalmeny, near South Queensferry (shown here), and Birnie, near Elgin. When was the oldest church in your district built?

So David's work was important both for himself and for Scotland. The new bishops, monks and priests were loyal to their king. The beautiful new abbeys and churches reminded folk both of God's power and of the king's power. The Scottish Church was now firmly part of the Roman Catholic Church.

THINGS TO DO

1   Find out all you can about Saints Benedict, Bernard, Francis and Dominic. Write about each of them in your notebook.

2   Where is the nearest abbey or monastery to your home or school? Try to find out such things as what Order it belonged to, and when it was built. Write these down in your notebook.

3   Can you think of any place-names near you, or somewhere else in Scotland, with 'Blackfriars' or 'Greyfriars' in them? Make a note of any you know, and try to find out something about them.

4   A fifteenth-century Scottish poet, Andrew of Wyntoun, wrote this about King David:

> He illumynyd in his dayis
> His landys wyth Kyrkys and wyth Abbayis.

Write a paragraph to say why King David encouraged the Church and built so many 'kyrkys' and 'abbayis'.

20 Life at Melrose Abbey

Who looks after sick people nowadays? Who helps the poor and out-of-work? Who shows farmers how to make the best use of their land? Who gives travellers shelter? Who teaches the young and passes on knowledge to others? Who writes and makes books? Who keeps libraries?

'Don't be silly,' you may say. 'These things are all done by a great many people: doctors, nurses, hotel-keepers, the government, teachers, authors, printers, publishers, librarians. Anyway, what has all this to do with life in a monastery or an abbey?'

Well, let us see. Imagine you are a merchant travelling on horseback from Edinburgh to York in the year 1200. Yesterday you had a long and tiring journey along a dusty road (through woods that

Monk tasting brew

might be hiding wolves and robbers) and you stayed the night at Melrose Abbey. There are no hotels along this lonely stretch of road and the monks keep a special 'guest house' for weary travellers like yourself.

Here you had a refreshing sleep and a hearty breakfast. Just now one of the monks asked you if you would like to look round the abbey. You must not delay long, but you are very glad to see more of this beautiful place.

The guest house is a little distance away from the main buildings of the abbey. As you walk towards them, your guide tells you about life in the abbey.

'We produce nearly everything we need here, you know. You may have heard already about our famous flocks of sheep. Just now we have about four thousand! There is not time to show you all the grounds, but over there you can see our vegetable and herb gardens, and beyond them our hives. The buildings yonder are the bakehouse and the brewhouse. Farther away are the stables and the workshops. We do a lot of work ourselves, but we have about two hundred *lay brothers* to help us as well. But here we are. Go through this doorway.'

You go along a short passage and find that the buildings of the abbey which seemed to be all packed together are actually built round the four sides of a square courtyard. In the middle is a large lawn, about a hundred paces each way, and round this is a passageway which is open on the lawn side. You must look surprised, because your guide smiles. 'Yes, this is the centre of the abbey. There is the kirk on the south side of the lawn or garth. As you see, all the other buildings open on to these open passageways or cloisters. Let us go in the church first.'

You walk along two sides of the cloisters. Some monks are sitting on the stone benches reading and look up as you pass. One smiles, another is deep in thought and hardly seems to see you. A group of younger monks is gathered round an older man, listening carefully to what he is saying. Your guide tells you that these are novices, young men who are learning to become monks.

So you reach the church. It is a beautiful lofty building, all of stone. On your left as you enter is the high altar. In the centre is a great crucifix and on each side is a tall candle in an iron candlestick, which casts a dim, flickering light over the white cloth and colourful tapestry round the altar. The nave, or west part, of the church is cut off from the chancel, or east part, by a richly carved screen of stone pillars. Down each side stretches a line of tall pillars which support the roof. Some carry carvings, like this one of a musician.

In answer to your questions, your guide explains. 'We spend nearly six hours here every day, you know. We worship eight times a day and that includes a service at midnight and another at dawn. It was

113

pretty hard at first getting out of bed in the middle of the night. You soon get used to it though. After all it is only right that we give thanks to God for the gifts that He has given us.'

As you come out of the kirk the first building you come to is the chapter house. Here the monks meet every morning in a kind of 'parliament' to discuss the work of the abbey. Here, too, any monk who has disobeyed the rules is given his punishment.

Next door is a little room called the parlour (from the French word 'parler', meaning to speak). Here the monks can talk freely to visitors: elsewhere they generally have to be silent. On the other side of the parlour is the dormitory (where they sleep) and next to this a small warming-room where the shivering monks can warm themselves after an early-morning service in the cold kirk. Your guide also shows you the infirmary where monks who are old or sick are looked after.

Farther along the cloister is the refectory or dining hall. At the door you will see a large water-trough where the monks wash their hands. The dining hall is a long bare room with rushes on the floor. Wooden trestle tables stretch along it, and at the end is a little platform with a small reading desk beside it. On the platform sits the abbot, the head of the abbey, and at the desk a young monk reads from a religious book at mealtimes. Next to the dining room, as you would expect, is the kitchen.

'There is one more place I would like you to see,' says your friend, and he takes you to the library. Here you see shelves of large leather-bound books and in the centre of the room three desks rather like old-fashioned school desks, where monks are writing books by hand.

One of them shows you his work. There are designs in rich colours all round the page, but you find the writing difficult to follow, because it is in Latin. It takes the monk days to do one page, so you can imagine all the time and labour that are needed to make a single book. Naturally, such books are valuable and rare.

You walk back with your guide to the gatehouse. Outside there is a group of poor people who are waiting for 'alms': broth, or bread and ale, or perhaps money, which will be given them at mid-day.

But here is a servant with your horse. You bid farewell and ride away, thinking of all the good work which must be going on in hundreds of abbeys and monasteries all over Europe.

THINGS TO DO

1   In the Middle Ages Scotland would have been a more backward and less happy land without the monks. Make a list of all the things they did which helped other people.

2   We saw a herb garden and hives at Melrose. Why were herbs and honey more important then than they are today?

3   Do you know what monks wrote on and what they wrote with? Try to find out.

4   In your notebook, draw a careful plan of an abbey. Illustrate your note on the work of the monks.

5 This is what you might have read any day in a monk's diary (if he kept one):

2 a.m.	Got up for Vigils (the first service). Prayers and psalms until dawn.
Dawn	Matins (the second service, although some call it 'Lauds').
6 a.m.	Prime (the third service) followed by Mass, then Tierce (the fourth service).
8 a.m.	Returned to dormitory to change robes, then to lavatory to wash before going to chapter house meeting.
9.30 a.m.	Worked in fields (while others worked in the scriptorium, the brewhouse et cetera).
Noon	Back to church for Sext (the fifth service).
2 p.m.	Then Nones (the sixth service) and the first meal: bread, fruit, vegetables (as usual, no meat). Very hungry after working hard in fields all morning!
3 p.m.	Much to be done in fields so back to work there: no reading today.
Dusk	To church for Vespers (the seventh service).
Nightfall	Compline (the eighth service). Then supper—and bed!

Imagine you are a monk at Melrose and write an account of a day in your life.

(In summer or harvest time, Tierce, Sext and Nones were held in the fields to allow work to be done.)

21 Life in the burghs

You will remember from Chapter 18 that William the Lion was able to buy back Scotland's freedom from Richard Lionheart of England. The rest of William's reign was happy and peaceful. He was succeeded by Alexander II and Alexander III, and during the reigns of these strong rulers Scotland became so contented that men later looked back on this time as Scotland's 'Golden Age'. This is the seal of Alexander III.

The two Alexanders overcame dangers from within Scotland, from England, and from Norway. Where they had had foes before, they made not only friends but relations too, for they arranged marriages to keep friendly with other kings and lords.

In Scotland itself there was trouble from Galloway's Celtic lord, so his three daughters were married to Norman friends of the king. The beautiful Sweetheart Abbey at Dumfries was founded by one of these daughters, Devorgilla, in memory of her husband. As far as England was concerned, the two Alexanders kept friendly with Henry III by marrying his sister and his daughter!

Norway and Scotland had been quarrelling for a long time over the Western Isles and both the Alexanders and King Haakon of Norway tried to win them. After the Battle of Largs by the Clyde in 1263, when the Scots drove the Norsemen back to their ships, this quarrel was settled peacefully too. Alexander III bought the Hebrides and arranged for King Eric of Norway to marry his daughter Margaret, who became the mother of Margaret, 'the Maid of Norway', whom you will read about later.

Now let us see how folk lived during this 'Golden Age'. Most Scots people still lived in the countryside, in small villages. (We shall look at life in the countryside in the next chapter.) But meanwhile towns had been growing up.

They grew up where there was a good deal of trade and of course there was most trade where most people were living. As you would probably expect, most of these old towns were in the fertile land of the east and the south of Scotland. Often they were at river crossing-places or near important castles or abbeys.

Edinburgh grew up beside the king's castle. It was safe there and there were many more customers when the king and his court came to stay. Overseas trade helped other towns to grow. To the sea-ports and river-ports came Scottish ships, and also ships from Germany, Holland and France, bringing goods such as wine from France and Germany and tapestries, spices, and silks from Eastern lands. In return, Scottish merchants sold abroad cloth, wool, skins and hides. Some of the richer men would buy more goods than they themselves needed and sell them in, or outside, the town for a profit. These men, of course, were the merchants of the burgh.

These craftsmen and merchants wanted to spend all their time making things or buying or selling. But, you must remember, they all lived on the land of some lord: a baron or abbot, or perhaps the biggest landowner of all—the king. So they still had to do their share of work on the lord's land and were ruled by the lord's bailiff or manager. This was very annoying for them, and they wanted to be freed from this work and allowed to rule themselves.

If the town was on a royal estate, the only person who could give them this permission was the king. So the people of a town would ask him to grant them a 'charter' which freed them from having to work on the lord's land. It would also allow them to choose a council which would govern the new 'burgh'. For example, the king ordered that 'Berwick shall be governed by twenty-four good and trustworthy men'. At the head of this council were a provost and four bailies.

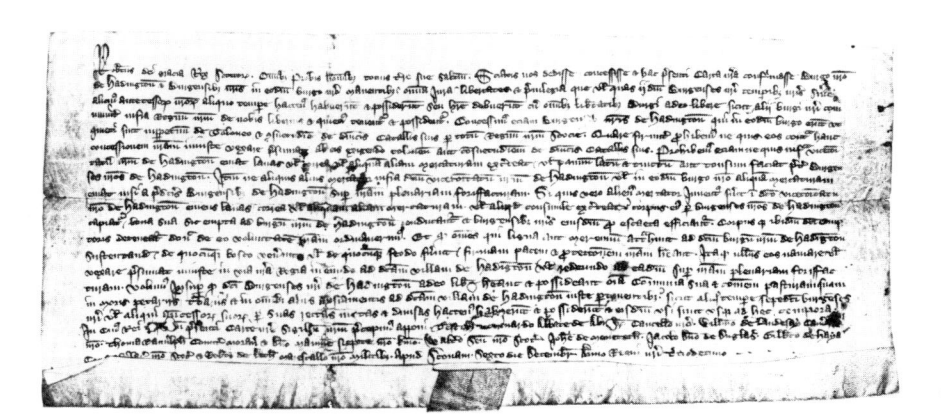

The charter of Haddington

For these valuable rights the burgh folk or 'burgesses' paid money. This took the form of rents of about 5p a year depending on the size of house or land as it was known. The king could also expect money from tolls paid by travellers entering a burgh and *customs* paid by merchants. So you can see that the growth of burghs increased the wealth and power of the king. Sometimes folk were encouraged to stay in a new burgh by being offered a 'land' free of rent for a year. In dangerous parts of the country this could be increased. In Dingwall, new burgesses could stay for ten years without paying rent.

By 1286 many burghs had been given charters by the king. Some barons and abbots copied the king's example and gave charters to burghs on their estates.

The wealthiest and most important group of people in the burghs were the merchants, who banded together in a Merchant Gild. There was a separate gild in each burgh and its members looked on merchants from other burghs as 'foreigners'. These 'foreigners' were sometimes allowed to come and sell their goods in the district round the burgh (if they handed over some of their takings). Usually, however, they were allowed to sell only to the merchants of the burgh they were visiting. The Merchant Gild drew up all kinds of rules for its members. These rules settled what prices merchants should charge, what wages they should pay, what hours their people should work, and so on. If any member fell ill or died leaving a widow and a young family, the Gild would look after them.

In 1286 you would find a great many craftsmen in a burgh like Edinburgh: hat-makers, masons and wrights, weavers, hammermen, goldsmiths, lorimers and saddlers, cutlers, armourers and fleshers, coopers, waukers, bonnetmakers, surgeons and barbers, candle-makers, bakers, tailors, skinners, furriers and cordiners. Here you can see a fishmonger hard at work. These men banded themselves together in separate Craft Gilds.

These gilds were very important. Only members of the gild were allowed to practise their craft. The gild set down standards of work,

119

hours of work and prices that could be charged. If a craft member produced poor work then he could be fined by the gild. The gild controlled the training for each craft. You could join as an apprentice when you were in your teens. After seven years of hard work for very little pay you passed a test of your craft skill to become a journeyman. After another seven years you could apply to become a master craftsman. To do this you had to produce an example of your best work—your masterpiece. Here we can see two journeymen being examined by the head of the gild.

A burgh, as you see, was a busy place, especially on its market-day each week. Even busier and gayer, however, were the fairs. Merchants from other burghs and travelling merchants called 'dusty-feet' were allowed to set up stalls in the street. Acrobats and jugglers, minstrels and men with performing bears came to add to the fun and the noise. A special court was set up to deal with troublemakers. Even today some of our older Scottish burghs have Fair Weeks which remind us of these fairs which our forefathers enjoyed so much.

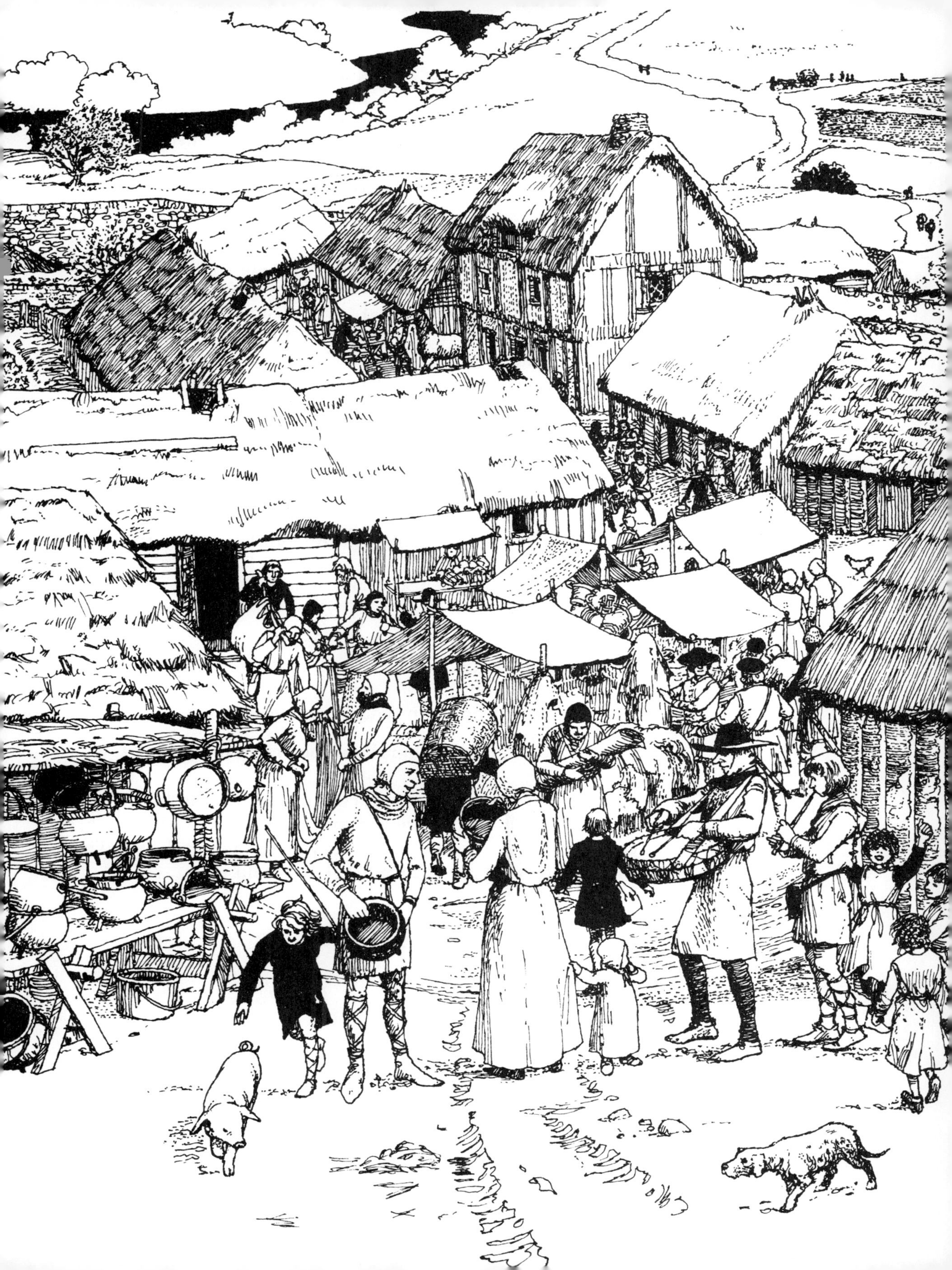

Try to imagine these Scots folk of 700 years ago living in these little burghs. The craftsmen's huts would seem very uncomfortable to us. The merchants' houses would be better, but all were made of timber with thatched roofs. We have thought of them as town-dwellers, but we must remember that they also cultivated fields outside the burgh on the burgh-muir and kept animals. (Burgesses were ordered to keep their pigs in sties and not allow them to wander through the streets!)

By the middle of the thirteenth century, then, towns were becoming more popular as places to live. They gave money to the king; they helped the merchant and the craftsman sell their goods and they gave some protection to people in times of trouble. We must remember though that these burghs were very small—only a few hundred folk at most. The majority of Scotland's population continued to live in the country.

THINGS TO DO

1 Do you live near one of the older Scottish burghs? Try to find out something about its history and who gave it its first charter.

2 We have mentioned several reasons for the growth of burghs. Try to find an example of:

(*a*) a burgh that grew up beside a castle
(*b*) a sea-port burgh
(*c*) a river-port burgh
(*d*) a burgh that grew up where roads meet

Why do you think your burgh, or the one nearest you, grew up?

3 You have come up from the country to visit your burgh relatives. Write a letter home, describing your impressions of the burgh, how you found your relatives and your visit to the burgh fair. The text and pictures on pages 120 and 121 will help you.

22 Life in the country

Although we have spoken about life in the towns first, we must remember that most Scots folk at this time (and for a long time to come) lived in the country. They were not merchants or craftsmen, but farmers.

Think what our countryside looks like today. Some of you Highlanders may think of crofts, Border folk may see hill sheepfarms, but most of you will think of neat fields of grass or crops, separated by fences or dykes with a neat stone-built farm here and there and a village every few miles along the road.

In the time of the Alexanders things were very different. To begin with, there were no roads, as we know them, to make travel quick and easy. There were just tracks, and while in winter your horse would have to wade through a sea of mud, in summer it would raise clouds of dust as you rode along. It was very difficult, you can imagine, for wagons and even pack-horses to carry goods along such roads. So the country people grew and made everything they could for themselves. Each village, we say, was 'self-sufficient'.

These villages or 'touns' were not big places, but simply clusters of a few cottages: eight, perhaps ten, not often more. The cottages were not very comfortable, but they were strong and easily built. Most of them were made by placing several branches or slender tree-trunks upright in the ground in two opposite rows, and each pair was tied together at the top. Along the top of all these was tied a long pole or 'roof tree'. This was the framework of the house. Next they built what was really a drystane dyke along the upright posts on each side and at the end. Where stone was not available, peat or turfs were used instead. The roof was made of divots or thatch on a framework of branches and kept in place by stones and ropes woven from heather. 'Windows', if there were any, were simply holes in the wall, with shutters of wood or hide. The door was of oxhide on a framework of wood, the chimney a little hole in the roof.

This is the inside of an old house which has been preserved at Torthorwald in Dumfriesshire.

The villagers might have been quite glad to have the reek from the peat fire, because the house was often divided by a low wall and the family's animals would be kept in the other part! The furniture was very simple: heather mattresses on wooden boards and a wooden bench were practically all they needed. The floor was the bare earth, trodden hard.

It was in these simple houses that children sat at the feet of their parents or grandparents listening to the old songs which were handed down by word of mouth: because, of course, they could not read or write. They would be told, too, the familiar tales of Scots warrior-heroes and of the 'wee folk' who, they believed, lived in the glens and the mountains. Do you know any of these songs or tales?

Winter must have been the great time for this storytelling, when the rain beat on the turf roof and the wind whined round the stone walls. Apart from the fire, the only light would be from an oil lamp like this known as a cruisie. In spring, summer and autumn there was too much work to be done in the fields.

Now, in a country such as ours, where much of the land is not very suitable for growing crops, men remained shepherds rather longer than in sunnier and more fertile lands. When they did begin to clear and till the ground they used a foot- or hand-plough. (A tool like this, called in Gaelic the 'cas-chrom', was used until quite recently in the north-west for ploughing.) But when they wanted to clear bigger patches with heavier ploughs drawn by oxen, a group of men worked together. They had to, because the rough wooden plough required up to twelve oxen to pull it—and most men owned only two. Folk reckoned a furlong—or furrowlong (200 metres)—to be the distance a team of oxen could pull the plough before needing a rest. An acre was the area that could be ploughed on a good day. A man's holding of some 8 to 14 acres was known as an 'oxgang'—for he was able to send one ox to the village plough team.

When they had ploughed one big patch each man wanted a fair share of the good land and not more than his fair share of the bad. So each man was given strips of land in various parts of the patch and each of these strips was made into a ridge or rig. Down the channels between these raised rigs ran the rainwater, and there was usually too much of that. As there was no other way of draining the fields, the flat valley land was too marshy for farming. Most rigs were to be found on higher ground.

As they needed more land, they cleared other patches. These all together were called the 'in-field' and were looked after carefully. All the other ground was called the 'out-field' and bits of it were ploughed over and cropped for two or three seasons and then allowed to rest for several years.

You may think that this was very awkward, having to go round all one's scattered rigs. But all the heavy work was still done together: ploughing, sowing and harvesting.

Even so, it was harder work than it is now. The big plough-team required several men to look after it. The oats (for oatcakes and porridge) and the bere or barley (for home-brewed ale) were sown broadcast (scattered) by hand. The crops were harvested with hand sickles, threshed with flails, winnowed by throwing handfuls into the air on a breezy day and sometimes ground by hand between stones. As well as the oats and barley they grew vegetables—kail, peas and beans—in their tofts, the little plots of ground round their cottages.

Peats had to be cut and wood collected. When they were not working in the fields, the womenfolk would be spinning and weaving. The whole family were kept busy.

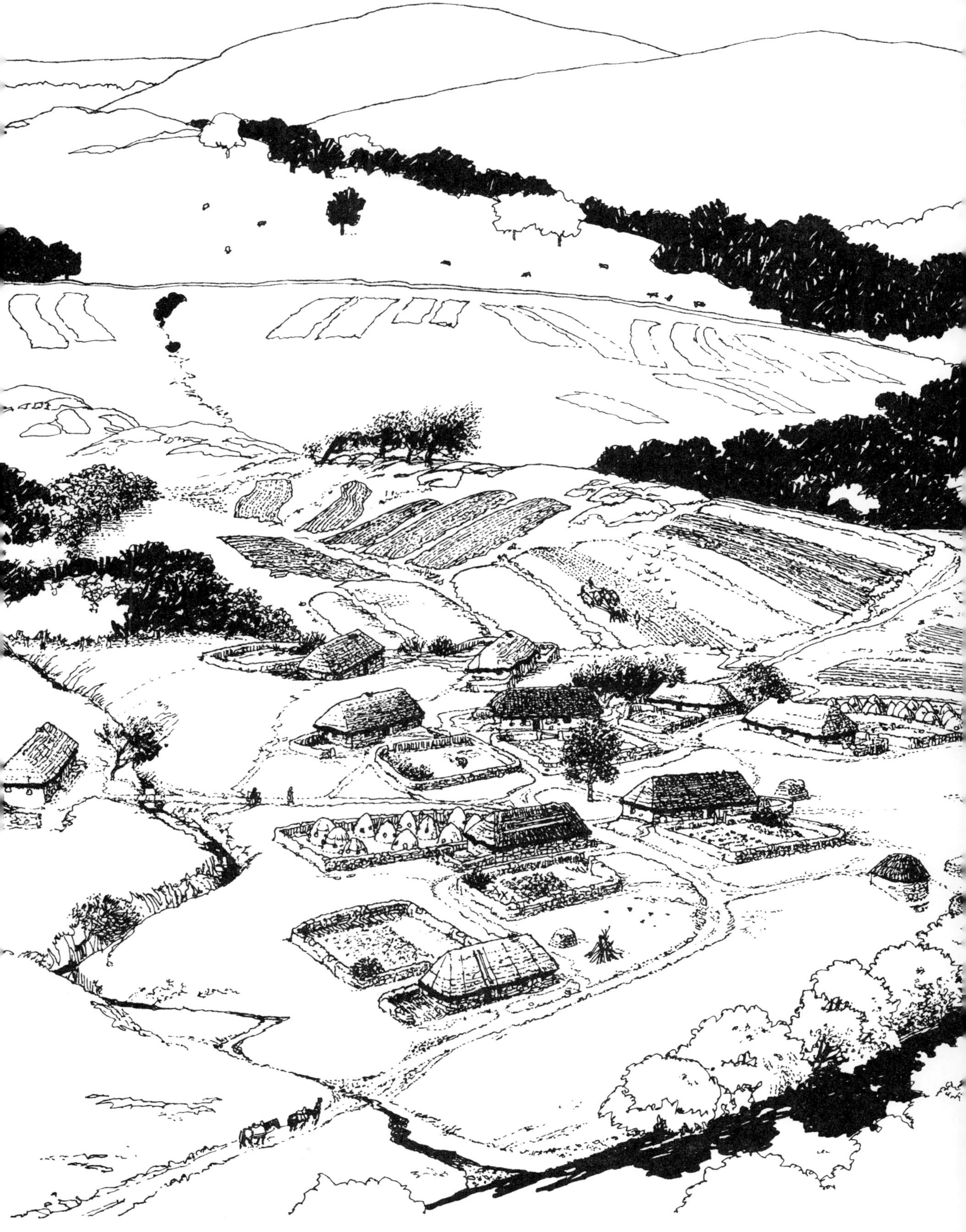

The children helped their parents at home or in the fields. Often they were given the job of watching the animals grazing in the outfield, keeping an eye open for wild animals or raiders. The cattle, sheep and goats were very small creatures: much smaller and thinner than our farm animals today. There was not enough winter fodder for them all: only a little hay, for turnips were unknown. So most of the beasts had to be killed at Martinmas (November 11th) and the meat salted, as there was no other way of keeping it fit to eat. This is why they were so anxious to have spices from the East for flavouring. You can become very tired of salt meat. (You will learn more about this spice trade in Chapter 27.)

So, you see, it was a tough life for these hardy ancestors of ours. Most of them were not free to go where they liked, as we are today. They rented their land from the laird and paid for it in food-rents and by giving so many days' work on the laird's land every year. At Kelso in 1290 each family had to pay 38p in rent or give farm produce equal to that amount; they had to do five days' reaping for their laird and one day's carting of peats. They had to help at other important times in the year such as sheep-shearing and Martinmas. All their grain had to be ground at the laird's mill. They could not leave their land. If a man did try to run away, the laird could bring him back—unless he was able to hide in a burgh for a year and a day!

Why did more people not try to run away? Because the laird gave a man the use of something he wanted—land. With his cottage and family, his cattle, sheep and goats, his oats and barley, his folktales and songs, and—last, but most important of all—his church, he was reasonably content.

THINGS TO DO

1 Write about 'A Year's Work for a Scots Farmer about 1250'. Divide your story neatly into paragraphs about spring work, then summer, autumn and winter. Illustrate what you have written.

2 Try to read some old folktales. Many of them are in 'Scottish Folk Tales and Legends' by Barbara Ker Wilson. You could borrow it from your public library.

3 Some place-names remind us of these farmers of long ago—even though they may not seem to be in likely places. In the mining district of West Lothian is the village of Fauldhouse, 'the house on land that was ploughed but is now fallow'. Not far away is Blackridge, which got its name from the rigs ploughed in the dark-coloured soil. Is there any place near you with a name like High Rigg, Easter (East) Rigg, or simply The Riggs? Again, another name for a strip of land was just 'land' or 'lands'. The meaning of Langland is obvious, and you should know what Souterland means, too. Milton is 'the town by the mill', Kirkton 'the town by the kirk', while the words 'Mains' means the land farmed by the laird himself. Can you find some more?

4 If you live in the north, see if any of your oldest friends or relations can tell you about old farming methods, especially digging with the cas-chrom.

5 We have said that in Scotland up to quite a late time men preferred to keep flocks instead of ploughing land which was stony and infertile. But kings wanted to encourage the growing of crops to increase the country's food supply. Here is a law made by Alexander II in 1214. Notice the fine that had to be paid if the law was not obeyed.

> 'At Scone in the year of grace 1214 Alexander, through the grace of God King of Scots, with the advice of his lords has made this law for the good of the country. He has decreed that all bondmen living in steads and touns during the past year must begin to plough and sow with all their study and might beginning the 15th day before the Purification of Saint Mary the Virgin. [That is, beginning on January 18th.]
>
> Also he and his lords ordain that a man who has more than 4 kye shall rent land from his lord and shall plough and sow to feed his family. All men who dwell in selde [rented] land, have less than 5 kye, and cannot plough with oxen, shall with their hands and feet delve the earth so that they may sow and grow food for their families. And those men that have oxen shall sel [hire] them to others that have land to plough.
>
> And if any lord will not thole this in his lands he shall pay a fine of 8 kye to the king.

23 The Hammer of the Scots

In 1286 Alexander III was killed at Kinghorn when, in the stormy darkness, his horse slipped and threw him down the cliffs. Men mourned him, and later were to look back on his death as a very great disaster for Scotland; for it was to lead to terrible wars with England which lasted for more than a hundred years.

Alexander had no son to succeed him as king. The nearest heiress was Margaret, Alexander's granddaughter, the 'Maid of Norway' we have already mentioned (see page 117). The little girl was three, too young to come to Scotland, when Alexander was killed. In England, King Edward I thought this was a wonderful chance to join together England and Scotland. He had already conquered Wales and hoped that his son would rule over a united Britain. Edward, therefore, arranged with Eric of Norway that Margaret should marry Edward's son.

The seal of Edward I

The Scots lords were quite willing to let the marriage take place, but they insisted that if Britain ever had one ruler all the rights and laws of Scotland should be kept. They were willing to be joined to England, but not swallowed up in England. In the marriage treaty signed at Birgham in 1290 Edward agreed to this. But it was all in vain. As Margaret sailed towards Scotland from Norway, she became ill and died in the Orkneys. Scotland had to find a new ruler.

Thirteen men claimed the throne because they were descended from kings. We need worry about two of them only—Robert Bruce, Lord of Annandale, and John Balliol, both of whom were descended from David I. There was a real risk of *civil war* breaking out, and most men were pleased when Edward of England offered to act as judge and to decide which of the claimants had most right to the throne of Scotland. They were staggered when Edward, taking advantage of Scottish weakness, insisted that first the men who wanted to be king should accept him as their overlord. They all accepted. After thinking things over Edward decided that John Balliol had the best right to the throne. In 1292, then, King John was crowned at Scone on St Andrew's Day.

His reign was short, from 1292 to 1296, and unhappy. Edward made it plain from the beginning that he, and not King John, was the real ruler of Scotland. He ordered King John about as if he were an English baron. To many of his disappointed Scottish subjects King John was known as 'Toom Tabard', which means 'empty coat'. He looked and dressed like a king but had no powers. But Edward went too far. So when England was at war with France, King John made a treaty with the King of France in 1295 agreeing to help the French in the war against the English. This alliance with France—the Auld Alliance—which lasted till 1560, was very useful to us both in our wars against England and in keeping us in touch with civilised Europe. But at first it brought a terrible revenge.

Soldiers looting a captured town

In 1296 Edward came north with his army, captured the great Scottish port of Berwick and had the people of the town butchered like beasts. From Berwick he marched north, destroying the countryside and capturing many castles, while the Scottish barons rushed to tell him how loyal they were to him. At Stracathro King John himself appeared before him, humbly dressed with a white wand in his hand, to surrender to him the kingdom of Scotland. John was for some years a prisoner of the English. He died in exile in France in 1314.

On his way home Edward took some of the treasures of Scotland. From Holyrood he removed the Black Rood, the piece of Christ's cross which St Margaret had brought with her. From Scone he took what he thought was the Stone of Destiny, the throne on which the kings of Scotland had been crowned for centuries. The stone Edward took away is still in Westminster, under the chair on which kings and queens have sat to be crowned.

One thing remained to be done—to appoint Englishmen to rule Scotland. De Warenne, Earl of Surrey, was made governor of Scotland with other Englishmen to help him. Scottish castles were garrisoned by Englishmen. Scotland in 1296 was just a province of England. Edward must have been very pleased: it had been so easy. He did not know that the war was not ended, but scarcely begun.

In the north and in the south leaders came forward to drive out the English and bring Balliol back as king. The first and greatest of these was William Wallace of Elderslie near Paisley, not a great noble but a laird. In 1297 he made his first attack on the English when, at the head of a little band of thirty men, he attacked Lanark, killed Hazelrig, Edward's sheriff, and drove out the English troops. From all parts of Scotland men joined him, especially the men of the north-east under Andrew of Moray. He was able to attack Scone and to besiege Dundee before he was called back to Stirling by the news that de Warenne was gathering a large army to attack the north. The attack failed. Wallace placed his men on the north side of the narrow wooden bridge that crossed the Forth in those days.

The Scots watched and waited as the first English soldiers crossed the bridge. When about 5000 were over, Wallace gave the signal for attack. The Scots army rushed forward and butchered them. The rest of the English army were then thrown into confusion and fled from the battle. Many Englishmen were killed that day—including Cressingham, the Treasurer. He was so hated by the Scots that they skinned his body and kept pieces for souvenirs! Now Wallace was free to drive south into England. There, during the winter, the Scots laid waste the land, burning farms, driving off cattle and sparing only Hexham Abbey.

For a few months Wallace and Moray had control of Scotland. Describing themselves as 'commanders of the army of the kingdom of Scotland', they wrote to the German towns of Lubeck and Hamburg. Their letter said that Scotland had been freed from the English and that trade with them could begin again.

But the triumph was short-lived. The next summer Edward was back in Scotland at the head of a great English and Welsh army. He met the Scots at Falkirk. Wallace drew up his spearmen in a formation known as a 'schiltron'. This was a huge spear-ring—perhaps 1000 men in each one with their spears, 4 metres long, bristling out like the spines of a hedgehog. Between the schiltrons he placed his archers from the Ettrick Forest. His small cavalry force was kept in reserve. As soon as the English attacked, the Scottish knights fled. The unprotected archers were mown down by the English cavalry. Then Edward's archers cut great gaps in the ranks of the Scottish spearmen and the English knights charged in to drive the Scots off the battlefield.

Edward's work was not yet done. He had another five years of fighting before he could say that Scotland was conquered. At last, in 1305, all seemed over: Wallace was betrayed and captured. There was no doubt about Wallace's fate. He was carried off to London, tried and executed, and his limbs were sent to be shown in Newcastle, Berwick, Perth and Stirling. The judges decided that he was a traitor to Edward. We know that he was not a traitor to Scotland.

THINGS TO DO

1 Here is the oldest piece of Scots verse we have, written about 1300. It describes the sadness of the people after the death of Alexander III:

	When Alexander our kynge was dede,	
	That Scotland led in law and le,	loyalty
plenty	Away was sons of ale and brede,	
	Of wyne and wax, of gamyn and gle.	
	Our golde was changed into lede.	
	Cryst, borne into virgynte,	
	Succoure Scotland and remede	
placed	That stad is in perplexyte.	

Can you make it out?

2 One of the first great poems in Scots was about Wallace and was written by Blind Harry. Here are some lines from his poem. They tell how Wallace hid himself after killing the son of the English ruler of Dundee.

	The house he knew his Eme had lodged in	uncle
	Thither he fled, for out he might not win.	escape
	The Goodwife there within the close saw he,	
	And 'Help', he cried, 'for Him that died on tree.	
	The young captain has fallen with me at strife.'	
	In at the door he went with this Goodwife.	
	A russet gown of her own she him gave	
clothes	Upon his weed, that covered all the lave.	rest
dirty	A suddled courch over neck and head let fall	head-cloth
	A woven white hat she braced on withal.	
distaff	Gave him a rock, syne set him down to spin.	

Now describe the adventure of Wallace in your own words: either in a paragraph of modern English or, if you like, in blank verse.

3 Try to imagine that you are defending Wallace at his trial. What would you say to prove that he was no traitor?

24 The saving of Scotland

This was the darkest hour of the war. Wallace was dead; all Scotland was in Edward's power; Edward was about to make Scotland part of England. All seemed lost. At this very moment Robert Bruce was making his plans to lead Scotland to freedom again. Before he died he had succeeded completely, being recognised even by the English as the king of an independent Scotland.

Who were these Bruces? We met a Robert Bruce first in the reign of David I. You will remember that he was one of the Normans brought in by David and given the lands of Annandale. When he died his family had continued to hold these lands in Annandale as well as the Bruce estates in England. His great-great-grandson was one of the men who claimed the throne, unsuccessfully, on the death of Alexander III. The Bruces, then, were large landowners in both England and south-west Scotland, and now were of royal descent. The Robert Bruce who became king was a grandson of the man who claimed the throne.

Until the death of Wallace, the Bruces did little for Scotland. Wallace was fighting to bring John Balliol back as king: the Bruces did not want him back.

Indeed, in 1302 Robert Bruce made his peace with the English. The agreement stated that 'Robert and his men and his tenants of Carrick will be guaranteed life and limb, lands and tenements, and will be free from imprisonment'.

When Wallace died all that changed, and Robert Bruce took over the leadership of Scotland. But first he tried to come to an agreement with Balliol's nephew, John Comyn, Lord of Badenoch. In 1306 the two men met in the Grey Friars' church at Dumfries. They quarrelled and Bruce knifed Comyn, wounding him badly. One of Bruce's men went into the church and finished the killing. That was a foolish as well as a wrong action. From now on Bruce had as his enemies all Comyn's followers and friends. This meant that large parts of Scotland—Buchan, Argyll and Galloway—were against him. There was also the anger of the Church, which rightly considered a murder committed in a church as a most dreadful crime.

The statue of Bruce at Bannockburn

The Church condemned Bruce, but in fact some of the principal Scottish clergymen supported him. When he was crowned king at Scone in March 1306 both the Bishop of St Andrews and the Bishop of Glasgow were present.

The two bishops were to suffer for this. Edward of England was furious when he heard of the fresh rising in Scotland. The two bishops were imprisoned; Bruce's wife and daughter were put in prison; three of Bruce's brothers were executed; all Bruce's lands were given to others. Edward himself hurried north at the head of an army, swearing he would have vengeance on Bruce.

At first the war went badly for Bruce. His little army was defeated at Methven. When he fell back to the west along Loch Tay they were attacked by Comyn's friends, the Macdougalls of Lorn. Finally Bruce had to flee from Scotland and spend the winter on Rathlin Isle off the coast of Ireland. Hope alone remained. It says much for his courage that he was ready to go on.

In the spring of 1307 he began to fight back, helped by his brother Edward and by Sir James Douglas, the Good Sir James who was to be with him till the end. Douglas had an old score to settle with the English. His own father had died in the Tower of London and, like Bruce, his lands had been stripped from him.

Bruce crossed again to Scotland to land near Turnberry in Ayrshire and for the next two years had very hard fighting against Comyn's friends. He was helped by the death of Edward I, whose son Edward II was weak and unwarlike, so there was no longer the same drive from England. The old king ordered that his son should continue the advance into Scotland, bearing his father's bones in a leather bag at the head of the English army. But Edward II preferred his pleasures in England to the fighting in Scotland.

Bruce carried out a brilliant campaign of *guerrilla warfare*. Using speed and surprise he carried the fight to the English. By the summer of 1308 Bruce had been joined by many supporters, including men from the Highlands and Western Isles. He was even able to call his first Parliament at St Andrews. By 1311 his army was strong enough for him to begin to capture the great stone castles where the English soldiers held out. After he had taken them Bruce was too wise a soldier to try to hold them. He preferred to destroy part of their walls, to make them useless to the English, and abandon them, keeping his army together for fighting battles. This also meant that his small army could be kept together, instead of being used to defend castles up and down the country.

But capturing these castles was a difficult task. The Scots did not have the great catapults or towers needed for a long siege. Instead they had to rely on surprise. Perth was taken in a night attack, Linlithgow was taken by a trick. The assault party was hidden in the haycart of a local farmer, who drove it into the castle and stopped right under the great *portcullis*. The assault party leaped out. The alarm was given and the English tried to drop the portcullis. It was held up by the haycart long enough to let the main body rush in and seize the castle.

Sir James Douglas's men took Roxburgh on Shrove Tuesday, scaling the walls and surprising the garrison at a party. Bruce's nephew, Thomas Randolph, led the attack on Edinburgh Castle, up the steep cliffs and over the castle walls. They left only St Margaret's chapel standing. At last only two big castles were left in English hands—Bothwell and Stirling.

A 17th-century drawing of Stirling Castle

Bruce's brother Sir Edward Bruce was given the job of capturing Stirling. Rather than risk a direct assault he made an agreement with the governor of the castle, Sir Philip Mowbray. If the English did not relieve the castle by the midsummer of the following year, 1314, then Stirling would be surrendered to the Scots.

Robert Bruce was furious with his brother. He had avoided fighting a pitched battle with the English, but now King Edward had a whole year to gather an army together. King Robert ordered his brother to fight. We are told that Sir Edward Bruce was ready for this: 'Let the King of England marshal his whole people down to the very schoolboys against us yet, as God is my witness, we will give them a lesson they will never forget.' Both sides made their preparations for battle.

In 1314 the great English army began to move north. There were more than 20 000 men, including over 2000 knights and many of the archers, with their dreaded longbows, who had broken the Scots at Falkirk. Eye-witnesses reported that 'all who were present agreed that never in our times has such an army gone forth from England.... If they had been lined up end to end they would have stretched for twenty miles.'

Bruce prepared to meet them behind the Bannock Burn. Part of his front line was defended with holes, from the bottom of which spikes stuck up. This is a spike, called a calthrop, which was actually used at Bannockburn. The holes were covered with branches and turf to make traps for the enemy cavalry.

Bruce's army of 10 000 men blocked the road to Stirling. On June 23rd a party of English knights led by Lord Clifford tried to break through to Stirling. They were driven back by a schiltron of spearmen led by Randolph. Meanwhile Bruce had killed Sir Henry Bohun, with one blow from his battleaxe, in single combat. This was a good start for the Scots.

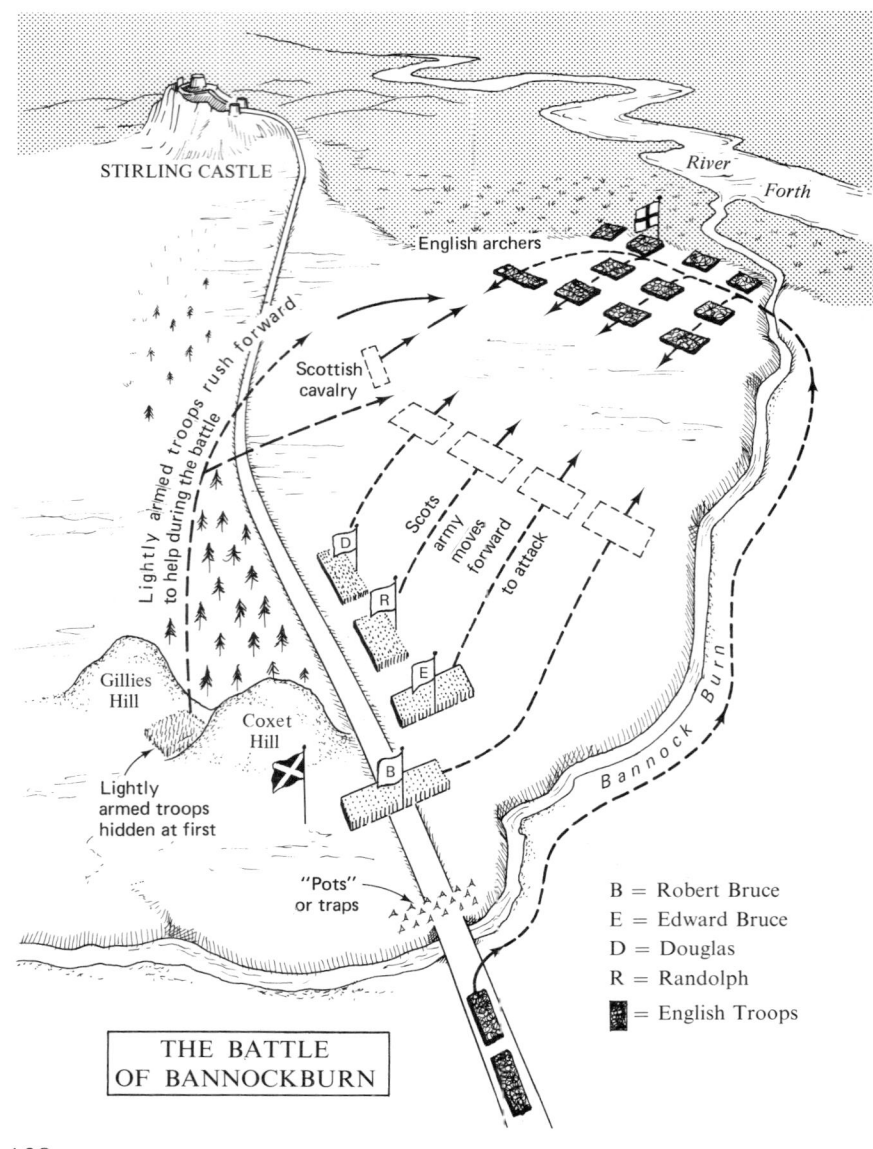

THE BATTLE OF BANNOCKBURN

B = Robert Bruce
E = Edward Bruce
D = Douglas
R = Randolph
▓ = English Troops

King Edward tried to reach Stirling by a roundabout way and spent a miserable night on the marshy ground along the Forth. There the Scots attacked him on the morning of the 24th, Midsummer Day, going forward in good order with their spears ready. The English archers were scattered by the Scottish cavalry. Then, when the battle was at its height, the lightly armed Scottish camp followers —many of them Highlanders—came streaming forward to turn the battle into a great victory. The heavily armoured English knights were trapped in the marshy ground, few of the English escaped and the Scots gathered a great plunder from the dead. Edward himself fled to Berwick, hotly pursued by Douglas, and only just managed to escape. This fourteenth-century print of the battle, the earliest that we have, show Bruce killing Bohun with his axe. Stirling Castle is in the background.

Bannockburn was the decisive battle of the war. Scotland was finally free.

The Declaration of Arbroath with the nobles' seals attached

But the fighting dragged on for another fourteen years, during which Edward's lands suffered from Scottish raids. A Scottish expedition went to Ireland to fight the English there. Indeed, the Scots were so successful in Ireland that for a short time Edward Bruce was King of Ireland. He was killed in battle in 1318, however, and the Scots withdrew from Ireland.

During this later fighting the Scots nobles, meeting at Arbroath, wrote a long letter to the Pope, justifying the war against England. Today we call it the Declaration of Arbroath, and it is one of the greatest documents in our history; for in it the nobles explain how the war was started by Edward I and go on to argue that freedom is the best thing a nation can have. If need be, they said, they would drive out Bruce himself if he failed to keep Scotland free.

Bruce set about governing the country. He made many laws to restore the peace. In 1328 he invited the people of Edinburgh to send six representatives to his Parliament—a sure sign of the growing importance of the burghs. In the same year the long war ended in the Treaty of Edinburgh-Northampton. The new King of England, Edward III, finally recognised Scotland as a completely independent country and King Robert Bruce as its sovereign.

So at last Bruce had peace to enjoy his kingdom. But not for long. Leprosy, an illness common at the time, killed him at Cardross in 1329. He was fifty-five. He had always wanted to make a pilgrimage to the Holy Land to make up for the crime of Comyn's murder. As death approached, he asked that his heart should be taken there. So his body was buried in Dunfermline Abbey after his heart was cut out. It was encased in a lead casket and taken by faithful Sir James Douglas on this *crusade*. Sadly, Douglas was killed fighting in Spain and Bruce's heart was brought home to be buried in Melrose Abbey.

Read the stirring words of part of the 'Declaration of Arbroath' of 1320:

> But if he [King Robert Bruce] were to give up the work he has begun, or wish to bring us or our kingdom under the rule of the king of the English or the English people, we would at once try to drive him out as our enemy ... and we would choose another king to rule over us who would be equal to the work of our defence. For so long as one hundred men remain alive, we shall never under any conditions submit to the rule of the English. It is not for glory, or riches, or honours that we fight, but for freedom alone, which no good man gives up but with his life.

THINGS TO DO

1 In Sir Walter Scott's 'Tales of a Grandfather' you will find many stories about Bruce and his men. Try to read some of these stories and learn one well enough to tell it again.

2 If you live near any of the places connected with the wars or with Bruce, find out all you can about what happened in your neighbourhood at this time.

3 Write an obituary for King Robert Bruce.

4 Up to the time of Robert Bruce there are few books or documents describing Scottish events. Not much was written down and what was has often not survived through the centuries. King Edward I took many Scottish documents away with him in 1296. From the start of the fourteenth century onwards, historians have much more in the way of written evidence. Here is part of a description of a Scottish raid into England made in 1327. The raid was led by Douglas. This account was written by a Frenchman, Jean Froissart, as part of his 'Chronicles'—a kind of history book. He did not witness the raid but took this description from another Frenchman, Jean Le Bel, who had fought against the Scots in 1327.

> The Scots are a bold hardy people, very experienced in war. At that time [1327] they had little love or respect for the English. When they cross the border they advance 60 to 70 miles in a day and night, which would seem astonishing to anyone ignorant of their customs. The explanation is that, on their expeditions into England, they all come back on horseback, except the irregulars who follow on foot. Because they have to pass over the wild hills of Northumberland, they bring no baggage carts and so carry no supplies of bread or wine. They cook their meat in the hides of the cattle it is taken from, after skinning. This does away with the need for pots and pans. Since they are sure to find plenty of cattle in the country they pass through, the only things they take with them are a large flat stone placed between the saddle and the saddle-cloth and a bag of oatmeal strapped behind. They lay these stones on a fire and mixing a little of their oatmeal with water, they sprinkle the thin paste on the hot stone and make a small cake rather like a wafer. Hence it is not surprising that they can travel faster than other armies.

(*a*) From what you have learned from Chapters 23 and 24, why did the Scots have 'little love or respect for the English'?

(*b*) How far were the Scots able to travel 'in a day and a night'?

(*c*) How were they able to move so quickly?

(*d*) What did they have to eat?

(*e*) Where did they get this meat from?

(*f*) How did they cook this meat?

(*g*) The last part of the extract describes a favourite Scottish food—what is it?

25 The story of the Auld Alliance

In the chapter about the Vikings we said that many of our Scots words were brought to us by Norsemen. Kirk, gait, rowan, shieling and many others entered our language this way. Other words have come to us from France, brought either by Frenchmen who visited Scotland or by Scots returning from France. Our word ashet comes from the French word 'assiette', tassie from 'tasse', fash from 'fâcher'. Some words, such as douce, have not changed in spelling or sound.

All this reminds us that for nearly three centuries Frenchmen and Scotsmen were very friendly indeed. Scots students went to the University of Paris, for there was no university in Scotland till St Andrews was founded in 1412. France was Scotland's 'auld ally', her trusted friend. Whenever the English threatened Scotland, the Scots turned to France for help. When France was in danger, Scottish soldiers went to fight with the French against the English invaders.

The story of friendship can really be said to begin in 1295 when, as we have already read in Chapter 23, Edward I tried to order King John Balliol about as if John were an English baron. Balliol allied with France, and Edward took his terrible revenge on Berwick which led to the War of Independence.

Scotland's independence was in danger again just after the death of Bruce, when his eleven-year-old son David II was king. Edward I's grandson, Edward III, was anxious to teach the Scots a lesson and force Bruce's son off the throne. So King Edward helped Edward Balliol, son of King John, to invade Scotland. Balliol landed in Fife and beat the Scots army at Dupplin Moor, near Perth. Although the Scots were beaten again at Halidon Hill, near Berwick, Balliol was forced to leave Scotland. Now young David II, who had been sent to France out of harm's way, was able to come back to a country which was still free.

By this time Edward III had begun a war with France which lasted, off and on, for over a hundred years and is known as the Hundred Years' War. Kings of England had once owned a large part of France. Edward still owned Gascony, and now he claimed the whole kingdom. He took an army of 12 000 men to France, all anxious to follow him for the booty that was to be won.

The years 1346 and 1356 were important for England, France and Scotland. In 1346 at the Battle of Crécy the French army tried to stop a plundering raid by the English, but the English archers won the day. Their arrows, we are told, flew so thick they looked like snow falling, and the French knights were mown down. David II tried to help the French in the same year by invading England, the common enemy, but he was beaten at the Battle of Neville's Cross, near Durham. David himself was taken prisoner, and was released only when the Scots agreed to pay a very heavy *ransom*.

The years after Neville's Cross were hard indeed. The Black Death, a fearful *plague* from Eastern lands, swept across Europe and into Scotland. The ransom had to be paid, and when David did come back he actually suggested that the crown of Scotland should pass to the son of Edward III. This roused the anger of the Scots clergy, nobles and burgesses and nothing came of it.

The Black Prince (from the figure on his tomb in Canterbury Cathedral)

By 1356 the English attacks on France had begun again, led by Edward's son, the Black Prince—so called because he always wore black armour. Once more the French tried to stop the English march through the north of France, but at the Battle of Poitiers in the south they were again beaten by the English bowmen. Now Edward determined to punish the Scots for carrying on the Auld Alliance. He came north but, after burning villages, crops and even churches, from the Border almost to Edinburgh, he had to return home. This 'Burnt Candlemas' was his last attempt to conquer Scotland.

In 1385, a force of 1000 French knights was sent to Scotland to lead an invasion of England. This operation was not a success. The French did not think much of the guerrilla tactics of the Scots that we read about on page 136. They thought this method of warfare beneath them. As knights they wanted to fight pitched battles. While the Scots and French argued, the new English king, Richard II, the son of the Black Prince, invaded Scotland. The abbeys of Melrose, Dryburgh, Newburgh and Holyrood were destroyed. Edinburgh itself was captured and burnt. The Scots as usual concentrated on making life as difficult as possible for the English. This was not proper fighting, the French thought, and they went home in disgust.

In 1415 Henry V of England took up the claim to the French throne and led an army through the north of France as Edward III had done. The French army tried to stop them at Agincourt, quite near Crécy.

The story of Crécy and Poitiers was repeated, although the English were outnumbered four to one. After this the French king agreed that Henry V should be the next ruler of France, and it looked as if France might be swallowed up for a time by England. And then what would happen to little Scotland, the auld ally of France?

In 1420, the French king, Charles VII, pleaded with the Scots for help. A force of 10 000 men, led by the Earl of Buchan and Sir Archibald Douglas, sailed for France. At first the Scots were not popular with the French, who thought that they spent too much time eating and drinking!

The Scots, though, won a great victory at the Battle of Baugé. Many leading Englishmen were killed or captured. King Henry V's own brother, the Duke of Clarence, was among the dead. In a book written shortly after the battle we are told that the King of France turned on those who had been complaining about the Scots:

> O you who were wont to say that my Scots were useless to the King and the kingdom, worth naught save as eaters of mutton and guzzlers of wine, see now who have earned the honour, victory and glory of this battle.

From then on things started to improve for the French. They were helped still further by the bravery of Joan of Arc. A simple peasant girl from the village of Domrémy, she put new hope into the faint hearts of the French leaders and rode at the head of the French troops. The English were then besieging Orleans and you can imagine how thunderstruck the rough English soldiers were to see a young girl in armour riding at the head of the French reinforcements. Orleans, and France—and possibly Scotland—were saved. Joan of Arc later fell into the hands of the English. Later she was tried as a witch and burnt at the stake. So died this brave and wonderful girl: and the king whose kingdom she had saved did not lift a finger to save her.

Thanks to Joan, the French kings now ruled a strong, united people, proud of being French. England, on the other hand, fell on bad times in the Wars of the Roses, when two noble families fought each other for the throne.

We left Scotland in 1385. Before we finish the story of the Auld Alliance, which was by no means ended, we must look at Scotland once more to see what was happening there.

THINGS TO DO

1 Write in your own words what you mean by the **Auld Alliance** and why it was so important for Scotland.

2 You are one of the French knights who has come to Scotland in 1385. Write a letter home saying what you think of the Scots and their ways of fighting.

3 Here is part of an account of the Battle of Agincourt written shortly after the English victory. Read it carefully and use the information to write about the battle as though you were an English archer telling it to your family as you return home.

> The place [Agincourt] was narrow and very advantageous for the English, and, on the contrary, very ruinous for the French, for the said French had been all night on horseback and it rained and the *pages*, grooms and others leading about the horses, had broken up the ground which was so soft that the horses could with difficulty step out of the soil. And also the said French were so loaded with armour that they could not support themselves or move forward and with all these mischiefs there was this, that most of them were troubled with hunger and want of sleep. Then the English archers began to send their arrows on the French with great vigour. The said archers were for the most part in their *doublets*, without armour, their stockings rolled up to their knees and having hatchets and battle-axes or greatswords hanging at their girdles. The English archers did much damage, breaking the line in several places; so many of the horses were wounded by the English arrows that their riders could not control them and they caused many more knights to fall. As soon as the English saw this disorder they all entered the fray and throwing down bows and arrows, they took their swords, axes, mallets, bill-hooks and staves and struck out at the French, many of whom they killed.

26 Stewart kings and unruly nobles

The reign of David II was an unhappy time for Scotland. When David died in 1371 he left no son to succeed him. His sister, Marjorie Bruce, had married Walter Fitzalan, the *High Steward*. Their son became Robert II, the founder of the Stewart line of kings.

During his reign, and that of his son, Robert III, there was more trouble, especially in the Borders and the Highlands. In the Borders the Scottish Douglas and the English Percy, Earl of Northumberland, were old rivals and they met at the Battle of Otterburn in 1388. Have you read in the ballad how a 'dead man won a fight'?

There were rivalries in the Highlands too. On the North Inch at Perth two 'teams' of thirty men on each side fought the 'Clan Fight' to end the long quarrel between Clan Chattan and Clan Kay. The king himself, we are told, watched this fight to the death. His own brother, the Earl of Buchan, was better known as the Wolf of Badenoch: a wild character who obeyed no law but his own. His worst crime was the burning of Elgin Cathedral because he had quarrelled with the Bishop of Moray.

Robert III seemed powerless to stop this sort of violence. A writer of the time said:

> In those days there was no law in Scotland, but he who was stronger oppressed him who was weaker, and the whole kingdom was a den of thieves; murders, herschips [ravagings] and fireraising, and all other misdeeds remained unpunished; and justice, as if outlawed, lay in exile outwith the bounds of the kingdom.

Worse was to follow. The king's own son, the Duke of Rothesay, was murdered in Falkland Palace—starved to death, it was said, by his uncle, the Duke of Albany.

No wonder Robert III decided to send his other son James over to France to be educated and kept safe. But after the prince had set sail from North Berwick, he was captured by the English and kept a prisoner by Henry IV of England. Poor King Robert died that same year, 1406, claiming to be 'the worst of kings and the most miserable of men'.

So for several years Scotland was without a king. Scotland was very unlucky with her Stewart line of kings. Some were weak, some were too young to rule, and the strong ones were killed in the wars with their nobles or with England.

James I

When James was a prisoner in England, he fell in love with an English lady and, it is believed, wrote a long poem, 'The Kingis Quair' (The King's Book), which you might read some day.

But meanwhile the Lord of the Isles was trying to conquer a large part of James's kingdom—from Inverness to Dundee. He was stopped by an army, which contained many townsmen of Aberdeen, at the battle of Harlaw in 1411. However, other things were going on in James's absence: the next year the first Scottish university was founded at St Andrews by the bishop there.

At last in 1424 James was released from captivity and came back to Scotland determined to make his kingdom peaceful. In his own words, he wanted to 'make the key keep the castle, and the bracken bush the cow'. One of the first things he did was to call a Parliament at Perth and ask it to pass laws to stop the private wars between Scottish barons.

But he realised that it was not enough just to pass laws. He had to show these Lowland barons that he really meant what he said. He had his own cousin arrested, put on trial and executed at Stirling Castle. A little later he gave the Highland chiefs a lesson too. He ordered a Parliament to be held, at Inverness this time, which the chieftains were to attend. As each one entered the room where the Parliament was to meet, and approached the king, he was pounced upon and hustled away to a dungeon. The poet-king, we are told, sat on his throne amusing his courtiers with this:

> To a castle strong let us lure the throng,
> For by Christ's wrong they deserve not to live long.

Three of the chiefs were executed. The rest were released after a short spell in prison. James had made his mark on the Highlands, however.

Naturally, all this made James many enemies, including his *Chamberlain*, Sir Robert Stewart, and Sir Robert Graham who had been put in prison by the king. In 1437 he was staying at Black Friars' Monastery at Perth. One night, when he was chatting to the queen and her ladies-in-waiting, the shouts of his enemies were heard outside. James was killed—although Lady Catherine Douglas did her best to save him. (Do you know the story of 'Kate Barlass'?)

The murderers were tracked down and cruelly tortured to death. James was sadly missed. A popular rhyme of the day was

> Sir Robert Graham
> That slew our king
> God give him shame.

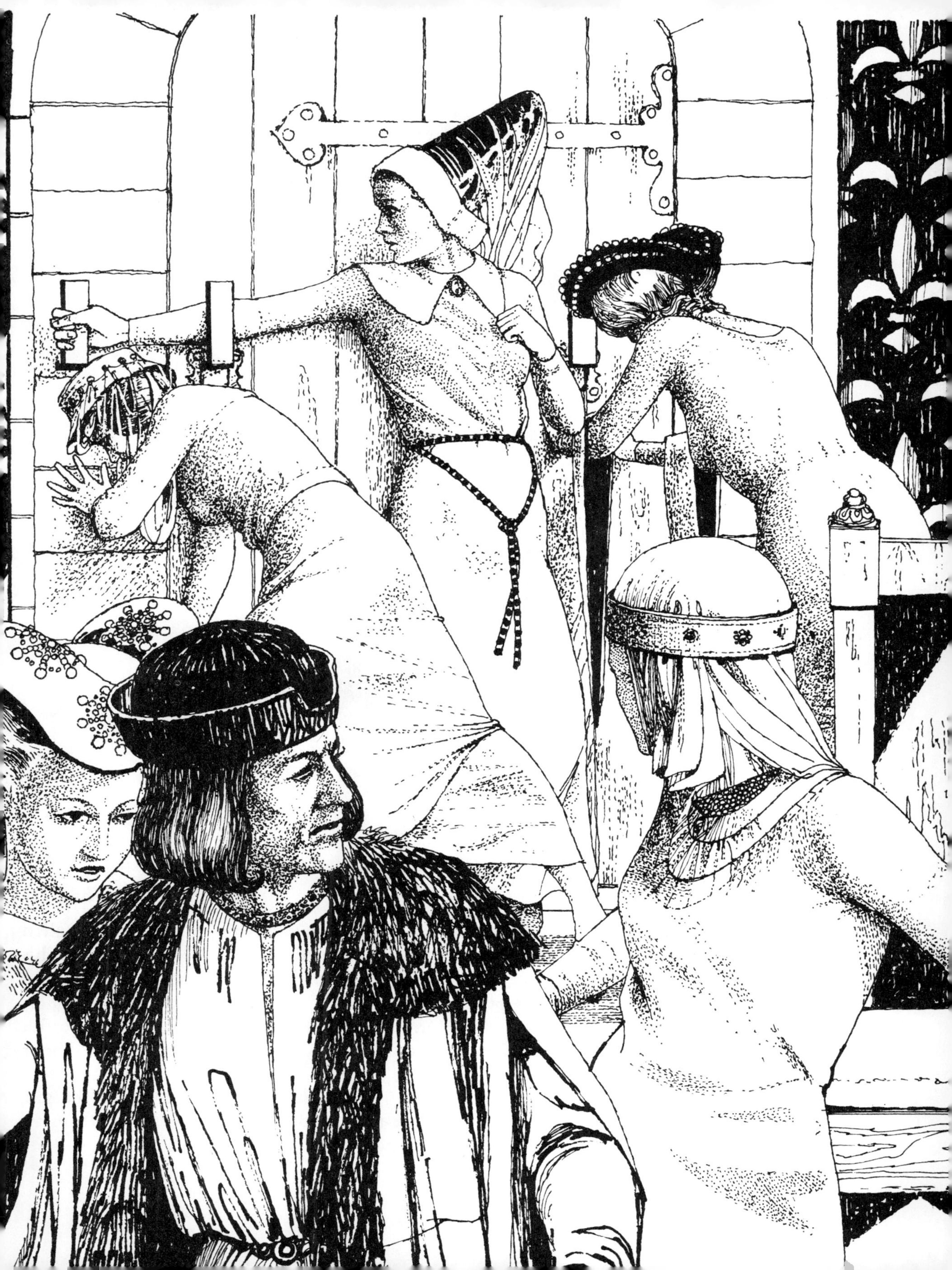

James II

So his son became king of a country that needed someone to rule it firmly. But James was only seven and was in the power of two nobles named Crichton and Livingston. These two invited their enemy, the Earl of Douglas, to a dinner at Edinburgh Castle. We are told that at the end of the dinner the servants brought in a bull's head on a platter and placed it in front of Douglas as a sign that he was about to die. Whether this actually happened or not, just after the so-called 'Black Dinner' Douglas and his brother were beheaded on the crest of the castle rock near St Margaret's Chapel.

Here is a rhyme written soon after the event:

> Edinburgh castle, Toune and Towre
> God grant them sinke for sinne
> And that even for the Black dinoir
> Earl Douglas gat therin.

(Do you think the writer supported the king or the Douglases?)

James grew up to be a ruthless man like his father. He was called Fiery-faced James because a scarlet scar covered one cheek: and his subjects soon found that his temper was just as fiery. As a boy he may have wept at the death of a Douglas after the Black Dinner, but as a man he realised that the Douglases were far too powerful. He asked the new Earl of Douglas to Stirling Castle. After dinner he told him that he must end his friendship with men who were the king's enemies—such as the Lord of the Isles. Douglas refused, and immediately the quick-tempered king drew the dagger from his belt and stabbed Douglas to death.

Cannon being used at the siege of the castle

Scotland had peace for a few years after this and James, in 1460, decided to try to recapture the Border castle of Roxburgh which was in the hands of the English. James took a great interest in artillery and was very proud of the new weapons of war that he had bought. His cannon had already pounded the walls of the Douglas castles Threave (Kirkcudbrightshire) and Abercorn. We read of 'a gret gun, the quhilk a Frenchman schot richt wele'. Perhaps this 'gret gun' was Mons Meg, which you can still see at Edinburgh Castle. These cannon were very dangerous, however. At Roxburgh, one of his guns burst and James was killed by a flying piece of metal.

James III

For the second time in thirty years Scotland had a boy-king, for James was only eight when his father was killed. To begin with, the wise Bishop Kennedy of St Andrews was there to advise him, but even after the bishop's death James seemed to be ruling wisely.

He married the daughter of Christian, King of Denmark, Norway and Sweden. Christian promised to pay a large *dowry* and allowed James to keep the Orkneys and Shetlands until the dowry was paid. However, after four years James became tired of waiting and added the islands to his kingdom! So it was in this strange way that they became part of Scotland. James made himself stronger still. He attacked the Lord of the Isles and took away some of his possessions; and he made peace with the English king, Edward IV.

Despite this, James was not really a warlike man. We are told that 'he delyttit mair in singing and playing upoun instrumentis nor [than] he did in defense of the bordouris or the ministration of justice'. He surrounded himself with favourites. These were not nobles but quite ordinary men like Robert Cochrane, an architect, and James Hommyle, a tailor. These men worked with the king in a Secret Council. All this angered the nobles.

When war broke out with England in 1482, James marched towards the Borders, not knowing that his nobles were plotting with the English king against him. At Lauder they were afraid to face the king until their leader, the Earl of Angus, went to 'bell the cat', and James was arrested. Many of his favourites were hung at Lauder Bridge.

James's brother, the Duke of Albany, was the first leader of rebel nobles. After he fled and James regained his power, the nobles found a new leader—the king's own son—and the king was defeated at the Battle of Sauchieburn. Prince James gave very strict orders that his father should not be harmed, but the king was murdered in a mill nearby by a man who pretended to be a priest.

You may think that this story of Scotland from 1371 to 1488 is nothing for us to be proud of. Well, of course, it is not. But you should know that all over Europe nobles were rebelling against their rulers. In England there were the Wars of the Roses. In France and Germany the nobles were building castles, keeping private armies and making trouble. What Scotland (and other countries of Europe) needed at that time was the strong rule of a wise king. Only then could the country be peaceful and the people happy.

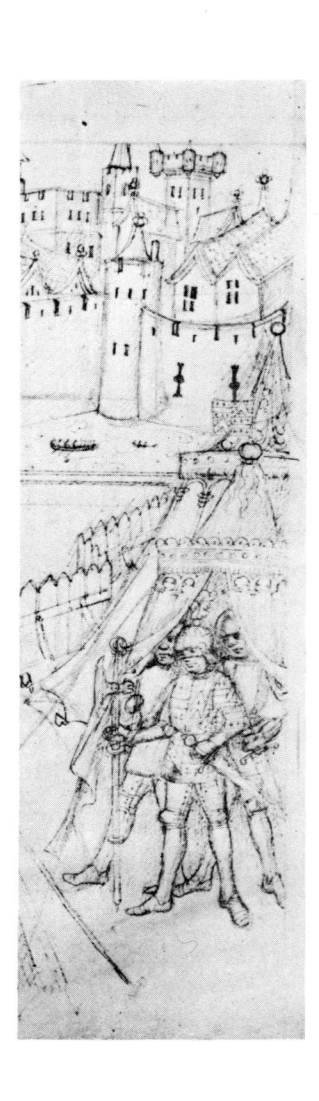

THINGS TO DO

1 You can read some of these stories in old ballads or other poems. Read 'The Ballad of Otterburn':

> It fell about the Lammas tide,
> When the muir-men win their hay,
> The doughty Douglas boun'd him to ride
> Into England to drive a prey.

Douglas dreamed the night before the battle:

> 'But I hae dream'd a dreary dream,
> Beyond the Isle of Skye;
> I saw a dead man win a fight,
> And I think that man was I.'

> He belted on his guid braid sword,
> And to the field he ran;
> But he forgot the helmet good,
> That should have kept his brain.

There is another good one called 'The Battle of Harlaw' which ends:

> And gin Hielan' lasses speer at you
> For them that gaed awa',
> Ye may tell them plain and plain enough,
> They're sleeping at Harlaw.

Another poem was written long after the events it describes, but it tells a thrilling story:

> And now the rush was heard on the stair,
> And, 'God, what help?' was our cry.
> And was I frenzied or was I bold?
> I looked at each empty stanchion-hold,
> And no bar but my arm had I!

> Like iron felt my arm, as through
> The staple I made it pass:—
> Alack! it was flesh and bone—no more!
> 'Twas Catherine Douglas sprang to the door,
> But I fell back Kate Barlass.

It is called 'The King's Tragedy' and is by Dante Gabriel Rossetti.

2 As you read, James II was killed by one of his own cannon. Although artillery was becoming more important, the three Jameses ordered ordinary men to practise archery so that they could fight for the king when needed. They had to begin at twelve years of age. Here is a law of James I. Can you make it out? Read it carefully and answer the questions below:

> It is decretyt and ordanyt that wapinschawingis be haldin four tymis in the yere. And at the fut ball ande the golf be utterly cryit doune and nocht usyt. And at the bowe merkis be maide at ilk parroch kirk and a pair of buttis and schuting be usyt ilk sunday and that ilk man schut sex schottes at the lest under the payne to be raisit upone thame that cumis nocht at the lest ii d. [2 pence] to be giffin to thame that cumis to the bowe merkis to drink.

(Do you know of any place near you called The Butts or Bow Butts? Is it near the kirk?)

(a) What do you think a wapinschawing was?
(b) How often were they to be held?
(c) What sports were forbidden during a wapinschawing?
(d) Where was the archery practice to take place?
(e) How often were the men to practise?
(f) How many arrows were they to fire?
(g) What happened to those who did not turn up?

3 There were no newspapers in those days, but imagine that there were. Use the information on page 151 about James II and the early cannon and write the story that goes with this headline: KING JAMES KILLED BY EXPLODING CANNON.

PART THREE
Explorers and reformers

A coin of James the Fourth

27 Travel in the Middle Ages

Travelling is something that we accept as part and parcel of our lives. Whether it is travelling to school or work, travelling to a new home in a different part of the country or travelling for a holiday, we all spend a good deal of time travelling. Indeed in the course of our lives we will travel perhaps thousands of miles by bike, bus, car, train, boat or plane.

In the last two chapters we tried to imagine living in a society where very little change was taking place. It was also a time when very few people travelled. Most folk living in these times would spend all their lives in the village of their birth. Why did so few people travel? Well, there were very few reasons for travelling. People worked close to their homes. There were no package holidays as we know them. If you did decide to travel then your journey would be hard, long and dangerous. There were few proper roads. What roads there were had been built by the Romans nearly a thousand years earlier! The rest were just like farm tracks, dusty in summer and muddy in winter. There was little choice as to how you travelled. You went on foot, by horseback (if you could afford it) or by boat. Without any form of police force as we know it, travellers had to face the dangers of robbers and outlaws who lurked in the many forests. Travellers by sea risked their lives in small boats and were often at the mercy of pirates.

These were real dangers. There were others, though, that kept people at home. We have already seen just how ignorant people were. There were no schools as we know them. They knew so little about the world that they imagined there were strange, unknown lands, peopled by amazing creatures, and that the seas were teeming with terrible monsters. 'Travellers' tales' made up by men like Sir John Mandeville just added to people's fears.

This lack of knowledge can be seen in these maps. On the next page you can see how confused they were. How much help could this be to a traveller? Many maps put Jerusalem at the centre of the world (can you guess why?) and surrounded the earth with water. Some even included a Garden of Eden. It is little wonder, then, why so few people were prepared to travel.

This 13th-century map can still be seen in Hereford Cathedral.

The diagram below shows more clearly the most important places marked on the map.

What continents are missing?

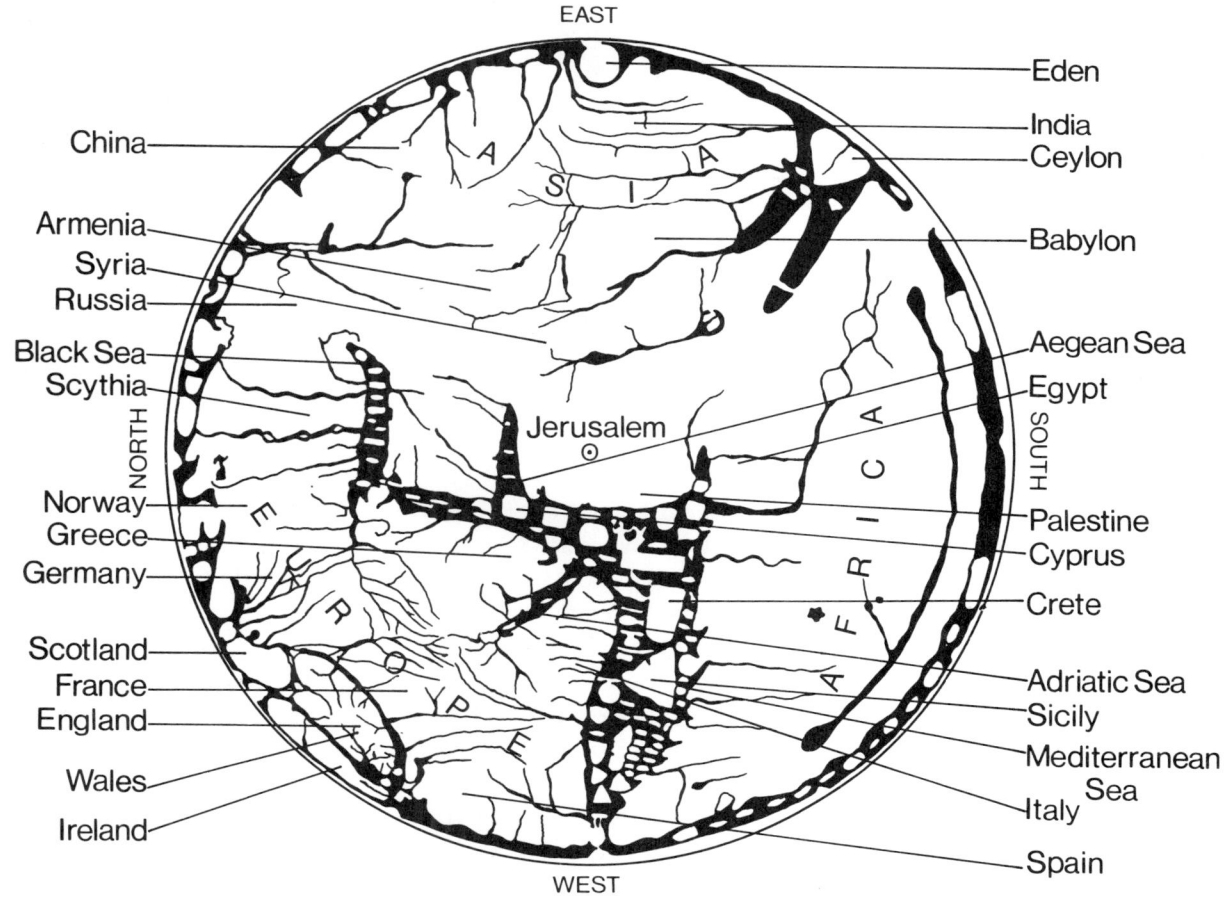

157

There were some travellers, however. What sort of folk would you have met on the roads? You would certainly see companies of soldiers on the move. Many of these men travelled about Europe fighting for pay. Today we would call them 'mercenaries'. They were often dangerous men who would seize what they could from the local folk. There would be pilgrims on the road, too. They travelled to holy places such as St Andrews or Canterbury to seek a cure for illness or forgiveness from God. Perhaps you would meet a group of travelling entertainers, known as troubadours, on their way to a fair or a market. The last sort of traveller that you might meet could be a merchant carrying his goods for sale. In his packs he would perhaps have silks, precious jewels or spices.

These spices were very important. Remember there were no fridges or freezers; no tinned or preserved foods as we know them. Meat and fish could be kept eatable only by smoking it or salting it. Spices such as cloves or pepper helped to hide the taste of the meat, so were in great demand. Most of them came from the East and, because they had to be carried such distances, these spices were very expensive. Here is a collection of some of the most important spices—peppers, cloves, ginger, nutmeg and cinnamon. In the centre is rosemary, a popular herb used in cooking by poorer folk who could not afford spices.

By the beginning of the fifteenth century, the spice trade was threatened by the Turks, who occupied much of the land that was used by traders bringing the spices to Europe. When Constantinople was captured in 1453, there was a real danger of this trade being cut off altogether.

Europeans had to find a new route to the East. This route would have to be by sea. Think of the dangers, however. Poor boats, poor maps and a fear of the unknown discouraged would-be sailors.

How were these difficulties to be overcome?

28 The New Age

We hear a lot nowadays about progress, about the speed of change. Just think of some of the discoveries of this century—radio, 'talking pictures', television, the computer, nuclear power. In 1903 Orville Wright's tiny aircraft flew for twelve seconds. In 1969 another American, Neil Armstrong, walked on the surface of the moon—after a journey of four days.

Think also of changes in such things as fashion, art and pop music. It is difficult for us to imagine living in a society where there was very little change. Can you imagine yourself wearing the same kind of clothes, eating the same kind of food, doing the same kind of work with the same kind of tools, as your parents and grandparents before you?

This was what life was like for almost everybody in Western Europe at the beginning of the fifteenth century. Look again at the picture of *peasants* working in Anglo-Saxon England in the eleventh century (page 86) and compare it with this fifteenth-century picture. How much change can you see? Why was this?

For perhaps a thousand years there had been very little progress in learning. Apart from things to do with fighting—armour, castles, gunpowder—science had stood still. Ideas in mathematics, chemistry, physics, biology, *astronomy* and medicine had been understood better by the men of Ancient Greece and Rome. Much of their learning had been destroyed by the barbarians who broke up the Roman Empire—but some of their books and ideas were still kept in Constantinople, the capital of the old Eastern Roman Empire. Most folk in Western Europe, however, were completely ignorant of such ideas. In fact, very few could read or even write their own names.

There were no schools as we know them. What schools there were trained a few young men for careers in the Church. Most people still lived and worked on the land. Most youngsters learned only from their parents, who taught them the skills of farming, cooking, weaving—or perhaps the skills of a trade. The sons of better-off folk were trained to fight; although some were sent to the Church.

Most education, then (at least, as we know it), was controlled by the Church. Men were not encouraged to find things out for themselves. The Church felt that the Bible gave the answers to questions about science as well as religion. Look at this picture. This is how people in those days saw our solar system. They placed the Earth at the centre with the sun and the other planets circling round it. (Can you guess why they did this?) Some people even believed that the stars were holes in the night sky through which the light of heaven shone.

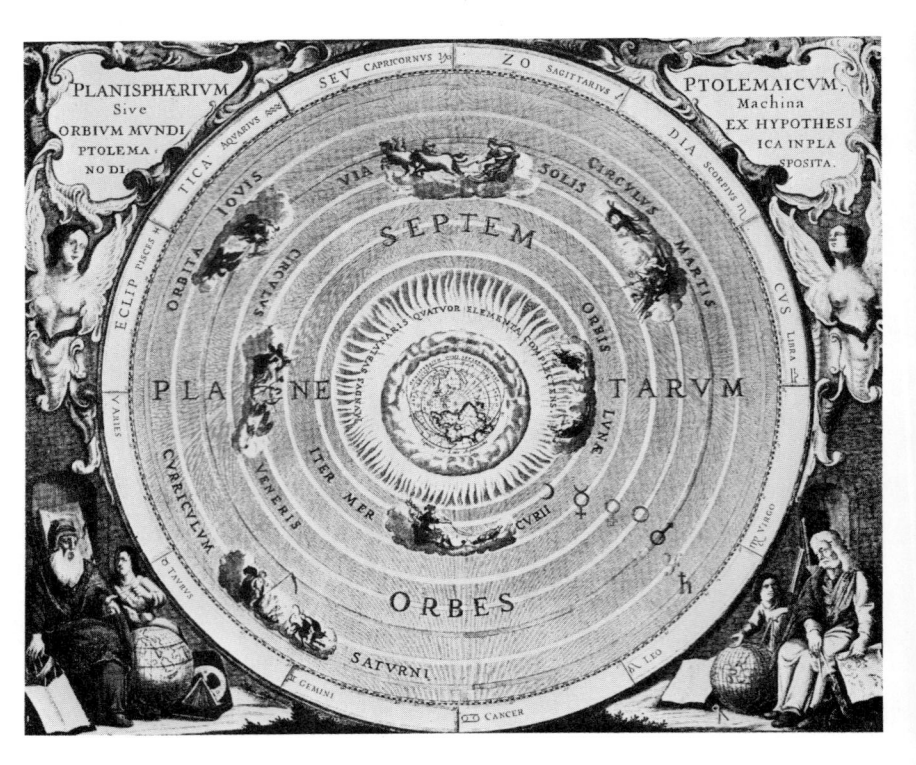

There were other reasons why people knew so little. Not only were there no television, films, radio or newspapers: there were scarcely any books. In 1450 there were only about 100 000 books in the whole of Europe. (There are more in a single university library today.) Each book had to be slowly copied out by hand: even a good scribe would take four to five months to copy a 250-page book.

With so few schools, so few books and so little interest in learning, it is little wonder that progress was so slow. And yet people talk of the century from about 1450 to 1550 as the time of a Renaissance—a rebirth of learning. Why was this?

In 1453 Constantinople was captured by the Turks after a long siege. Many refugees fled by sea to Italian ports such as Venice and Florence. They brought with them many of the books and ideas of the Greeks and Romans. Some people read these with great interest and began to question much of what they had been taught.

In Florence and Venice merchants had made fortunes out of trading. They used this money to build beautiful palaces, to collect books and to encourage the brilliant artists who copied the rediscovered ideas of Greece and Rome.

One of the greatest of these artists was Leonardo da Vinci. He is best known as the painter of the pictures 'The Last Supper' and 'Mona Lisa'—but he was also an architect, sculptor, poet and musician. He studied astronomy and anatomy too! Then, as a hobby, he made drawings of things he thought were possible: steam engines, submarines, aeroplanes and 'tanks'. Here is a sketch of what he thought a 'tank' would look like. And, remember, this amazing man died in 1519.

Other great Italian artists were Raphael, Titian and Michelangelo (who painted the wonderful ceiling in the Sistine Chapel in Rome and the famous picture 'The Holy Family'). Their work was very different from the stiff, flat, unlifelike paintings in the religious books of the previous centuries like the one you see here. These new paintings were natural-looking and full of life.

Madonna and child
by Lorenzo Monaco

163

From Italy these new ideas in art spread north to Germany and the Netherlands and west to Spain. You may have heard of the Germans Holbein and Durer, of the Dutchmen Rubens and Rembrandt, and of the Spaniard Velasquez.

Painting and sculpture were not the only kinds of art that owed much to the Greeks. Buildings were now being built differently. Instead of plain, even ugly, castles wealthy men now built beautiful palaces and houses. They were planned carefully from the beginning, with columns and domes copied from the buildings of Ancient Greece and Rome.

When the new ideas in architecture reached Scotland they were 'grafted' on to the old style of building. George Heriot's School in Edinburgh shows this mixture of Renaissance ideas and the old idea of building for strength. The school was carefully planned from the beginning. The central dome is there; everything is nicely 'balanced', according to Greek 'rules'. But the towers and the little turrets, which remind us of the old Scottish castles and keeps, are there too.

But the Renaissance was not just a rebirth of interest in art and architecture; it was a rebirth of interest in reading and writing too. The study of the old writings in Greek and Latin helped men to write better in the language they used every day. In Italy, Boccaccio wrote short stories in Italian for the ladies of Florence. In Scotland Dunbar and Henryson wrote great poetry in Scots (as we shall see in Chapter 30).

All these books could be bought more cheaply because about 1450 a German named Gutenberg had invented a printing-press with type which could be used over and over again. By 1476 William Caxton was printing books in London; by 1507 Chapman and Myllar had set up their press in Edinburgh. All over Europe these new presses were printing books far more quickly than a scribe could copy. Indeed, by 1500 there were nine million printed copies of books for people to buy and study.

The printing-press was not the only important invention of the Renaissance. A Dutchman named Lippershey invented the first telescope and an Italian, Galileo, improved it. These scientists were continually asking questions and trying to answer them. Galileo discovered the law of gravity; a Polish astronomer, Copernicus, discovered that the earth moved round the sun and not the sun round the earth—as men had believed before.

The Renaissance, as you can see, was a time of great change. Men were curious to find out more about the world they lived in. In the next chapter we shall see how this curiosity led to a series of exciting voyages of discovery.

THINGS TO DO

1 From the information in this chapter, list as many reasons as you can to explain why there was so little progress in learning before 1450.

2 GUTENBERG INVENTS THE PRINTING-PRESS

Imagine this is a headline from a German newspaper of 1450. Write the article to go with this headline. Your story should be in three parts:

(a) How books have been 'printed' until now.

(b) How the printing-press works (the picture on page 165 will help).

(c) Why you think this is an important invention.

29 The great discoverers

So far we have been concerned with what men did in Europe and the Mediterranean lands. Now a great change was to come. The men from the coasts of western Europe—from Portugal, Spain, France and England—were to sail beyond Europe and to conquer vast new lands in America, Africa and the East Indies. In 1500 North America contained about one million Red Indians of various tribes and languages. Today it holds about 220 million people, most of them descended from Europeans.

Before 1500 men did not know much about the world. (We looked at the reasons for this in the last two chapters.) But they had heard about India and Cathay (the old name for China) where their spices came from. They heard the tales of the Arab traders who brought these goods to such ports as Constantinople and Alexandria; and of other Arabs who traded over the Sahara from the Niger to Algiers. They knew the tales of Marco Polo, the Venetian who had travelled to Cathay, written down two centuries before.

Most of the voyages of discovery, however, were made by Portuguese sea-captains. A prince of Portugal, Prince Henry, did all he could to encourage them. He came to be called Prince Henry the Navigator—although, in fact, he made no great voyages himself.

Prince Henry knew the problems facing sailors. He started a school for Portuguese sea-captains at Sagres on the south-west tip of Portugal. Here, the sailors were taught the most up-to-date methods of navigation using the compass and the *astrolabe*. They were shown the most up-to-date maps that were available and they helped to develop a new type of ship—the caravel. This ship, with its sturdy build and strong sails, was a great improvement, but we must remember how tiny these ships were. The caravels which sailed round Africa to India, which reached America, and which later sailed round the world were little bigger than modern trawlers or ocean-going tugs.

At first, Prince Henry's captains were afraid to sail farther south than Cape Bojador. They were frightened of tales that farther south the sea was boiling hot. In 1434, however, one of his captains, Gil Eannes, went beyond Cape Bojador and returned safely. Others soon followed. What were they looking for? They were trying to make

SOME GREAT JOURNEYS OF DISCOVERY

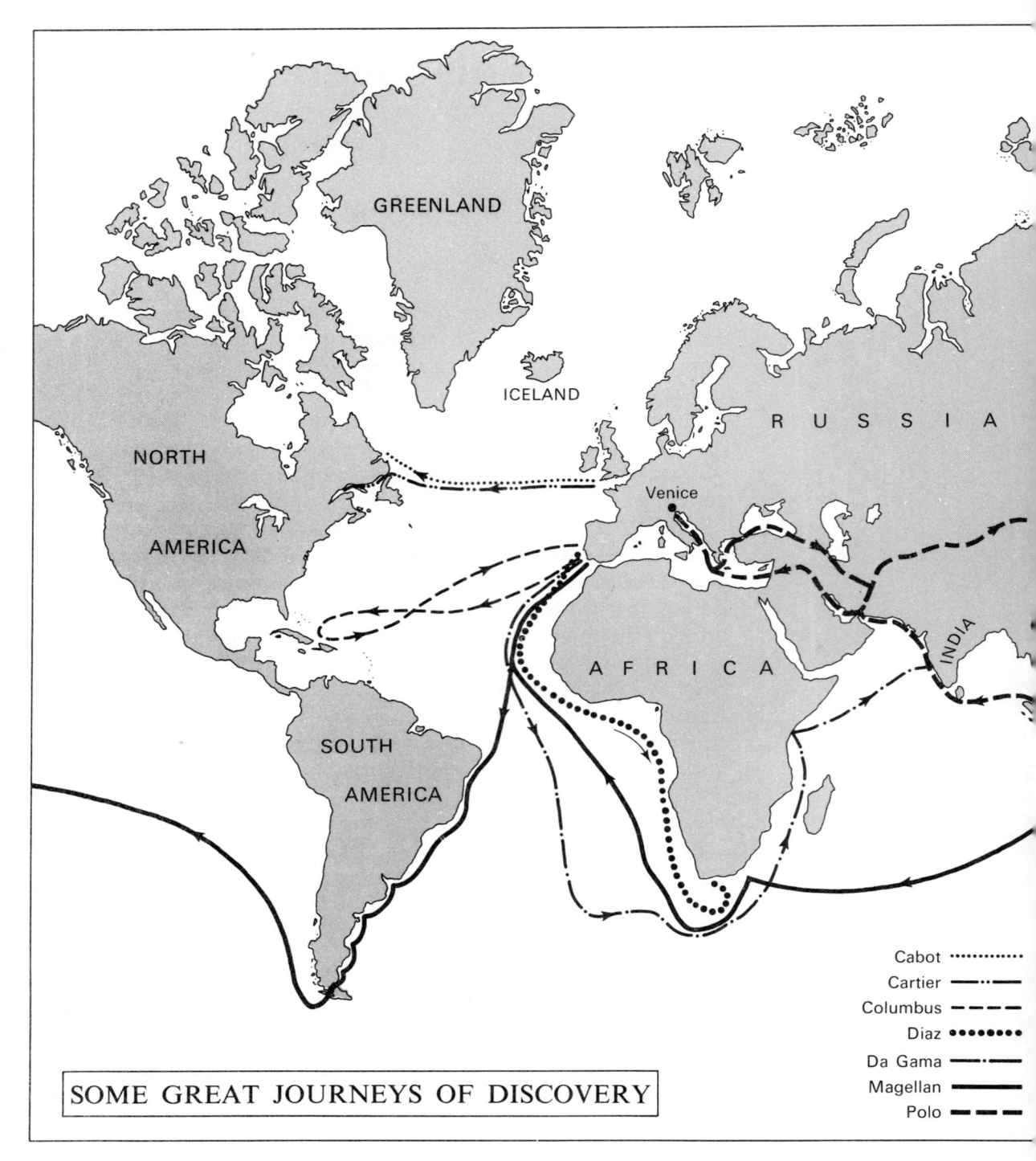

Cabot ·············
Cartier —··—··—
Columbus ———
Diaz ●●●●●●●
Da Gama —·—·—
Magellan ————
Polo ▬ ▬ ▬

the Africans Christians and to reach India. They were also trying to get gold, ivory and slaves, and they began a profitable trade in these. Prince Henry died in 1460 but his work was carried on.

In 1488 Bartholomew Diaz sailed farther south than anyone had

168

done before. While sailing down the coast of Africa he ran into a terrible storm, out of sight of land, and was blown far to the south. When the storm died down he thought he just had to sail east back to land—but there was no land there! So he turned northwards and discovered that the coast ran from west to east. He had found that there probably was a way round Africa to the east. But his men had had enough and he had to sail back home round the cape he first called the Cape of Storms. However, as this name was a frightening one for other sailors, it was changed to the Cape of Good Hope.

A few years later, in 1497, another Portuguese sea-captain, Vasco da Gama, sailed round the Cape of Good Hope and made his way northwards, At Christmas-time he named the land he was sailing past 'Natal', and in a few weeks he reached a port where he managed to get a pilot who promised to take him to India. He set sail north-east and, blown by the steady *monsoon*, reached the great port of Calicut. At last da Gama had found a seaway to India from Europe.

One big question puzzled men and they wanted to know the answer to it. They knew the earth was round, so why should they not sail west across the sea to get to India and Cathay? Not knowing of America (although Vikings had visited there) they thought it could be done. One man who believed this was an Italian, Christopher Columbus, who said the ocean dividing Europe and the East must be quite narrow. But most men thought it must be too wide to be crossed—even with their stronger ships and better compasses.

For a long time Columbus was not able to do what he wanted because he had no money, men, or ships—only ideas. The King of Portugal was not interested, so Columbus went to the King and Queen of Spain. They were not interested at first, either, but in the end they gave Columbus the help he needed. On August 3rd, 1492, he set sail from the port of Palos—with three little ships, the 'Santa Maria', the 'Nina' and the 'Pinta', and eighty-eight men.

After nearly six weeks' sailing out of sight of land and safety, they found they were in a sea covered with weed. This was sargassum weed, and they had reached what we still call the Sargasso Sea. After four more weeks of weary sailing, Columbus's men were restive. Why should they continue to obey a madman who sailed west, on and on, to unknown dangers? Why not mutiny and turn the ships eastwards for home? But one evening the look-out sighted land. The next day, October 12th, Columbus landed on what he called San Salvador in the Bahamas. From there he sailed on round the islands. Columbus believed that he had sailed right round the world and that these islands he had found were the Indies, the Spice Islands, he was looking for. In fact, they were far away from the Spice Islands, but we call them the 'West Indies' still.

Columbus made three more voyages to these islands and explored the neighbouring coasts. Back to Spain he and his men took plants,

Christopher Columbus

birds and animals they had never seen before. More important for the Spanish, he brought back some gold ornaments. Were these the riches of the East?

The Spanish soon realised that this was not the East but a huge new continent waiting to be explored. Other sailors followed Columbus. Amerigo Vespucci—after whom America was named—sailed along the coast of Brazil. He explored the mouth of the Amazon and in January 1502 discovered a river he called the River of January—Rio de Janeiro. These rivers, he knew, must come from a huge country, because at their mouths the water was fresh for miles. But another explorer, Balboa, heard natives' tales of a great ocean not far to the west of the land known as Darien. After a long march of more than three weeks, through forests and marshes and the lands of hostile tribes, he saw, away in the distance, a great sea. It was the Pacific Ocean.

The last great voyage of discovery we can talk about is that of Ferdinand Magellan, a Portuguese who sailed for the King of Spain. He thought that he might be able to reach the Spice Islands if only he could sail round the south of South America. In August 1519 he sailed from Spain with five ships and about 280 men. From Rio de Janeiro he made his way down the coast and finally found a way through the narrow strait that is named after him. As you can see from an atlas, if he had sailed farther south he would have found he could sail round Cape Horn. But Magellan believed that there must be another continent to the south and for a long time it was known as the 'Southern Continent' or 'Terra Australis'.

Once through the strait he found himself in the ocean that Balboa had seen. He named it the Pacific. By this time his fleet had been at sea for over a year. There had been a mutiny and one ship had deserted. He sailed north-west towards where he thought the Spice Islands must be. For many days, they sailed on into the unknown. They began to run out of food and water. Men were dying of disease and starvation. At last they sighted land. He had found the East by sailing west, and the dream of Columbus had come true. Magellan was tragically killed by natives on one of the islands later called the Philippines. The survivors headed for home under the command of Captain Juan de Elcano. At last on September 8th, 1522, one battered ship—the 'Vittoria'—reached Spain. Only eighteen men were left, but they had succeeded in being the first to sail round the world.

Soon these explorers of America were followed by more and more Spaniards, but they came for other reasons. Perhaps you have heard of the Spanish 'conquistadores' or conquerors. The empire of the Aztec Indians in Mexico was conquered by Cortes: the Inca Empire in Peru by Pizarro.

These adventurers were looking for gold and they found it in vast amounts. The people that they conquered were not simple savages.

They were highly civilised. They produced beautiful works of art and lived in large stone-built cities. This is the Inca city of Macchu Pichu.

Tenochtitlan, the capital of the Aztecs, was built on a lake. It was bigger than any city in Europe: perhaps as many as 300 000 people lived there. The Spaniards were amazed at what they saw. Bemal Diaz, one of Cortes's soldiers, wrote: 'We were astounded. These great towns and cities and buildings rising from the water, all made of stone, seemed like an enchanted vision. It was all so wonderful, this first glimpse of things never heard of, seen or dreamed before.'

One thing about the Aztecs shocked the Spaniards, however. Their religion demanded human sacrifices. Each year thousands of people had their hearts cut out to please their gods. Perhaps this is one reason why the Spaniards in turn treated them so cruelly.

These great empires were conquered by only a few hundred conquistadores. How was this possible? Both the Aztecs and the Incas thought the Spaniards were gods. Later, when they realised their mistake, they fought the invaders. But their warclubs were no match for the armour, steel swords, guns and horses of the Spaniards.

So the Aztecs and the Incas were defeated. Spain now had a huge empire to control.

What were the results of all these discoveries? Well, from now on the old trade routes were less important, and so were the old ports of Venice, Genoa and Marseilles. Spain and Portugal built up powerful empires and became very rich from all the trade in gold, silver and spices which their ships brought to Europe. Other countries followed their example. France and England sent ships and colonists to North America. We have not space here to look at their adventures, but perhaps you could find out for yourself about Jacques Cartier, John Cabot, Walter Raleigh and Francis Drake.

One thing was certain. In little more than the space of a lifetime man's knowledge of the world had increased tremendously. Look at this map published in 1570. Compare it with the map on page 156. There is much still to be discovered, but see how much has been found out by these great explorers. Notice, too, that the map still shows sea-monsters!

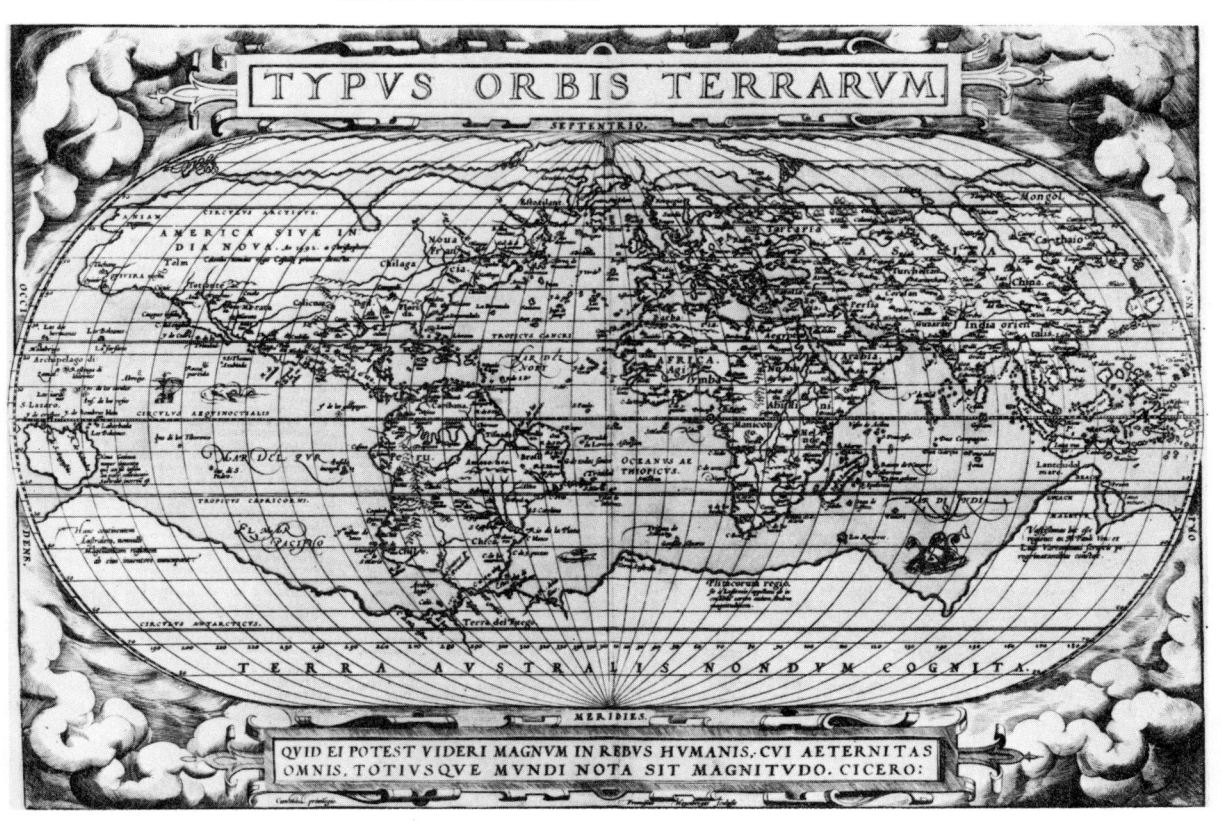

THINGS TO DO

1 On a blank map of the world mark in with different coloured crayons the routes taken by the discoverers. Shade Portugal red and mark all Portuguese voyages with a red line. Shade Spain blue and mark all Spanish voyages with a blue line.

2 Mark in, using the same colours, the lands these countries conquered.

3 Try to find out as much as you can about the ships, compasses, guns, etc. used by these early discoverers.

4 What new goods did Europeans gain from these discoveries?

5 Write an obituary for Prince Henry the Navigator. You should mention the problems he faced and what he did to overcome them.

6 It is March 15th, 1493. Christopher Columbus has just arrived back in Spain. Imagine that you are a reporter from the local radio station. You are sent on board the 'Nina' (the 'Santa Maria' was wrecked in the West Indies) to interview Captain Christopher Columbus. Write down the interview that you had with him.

30 James the Fourth

James IV was King of Scotland at the time when Columbus discovered America: in other words, he was one of the kings of Scotland during the Renaissance. As we would expect, there was much more interest in books and learning during his reign. But first James had to make his kingdom more peaceful and happy than it had ever been under his father. You will remember that James III had been murdered after the Battle of Sauchieburn. James IV was only fifteen when he came to the throne, but he quickly showed that he meant to be a strong king.

First of all, he had to 'make the key keep the castle and the bracken bush the cow', as his great-grandfather James I had said. For the old troubles went on. The Lord of the Isles was trying to get back the land of Ross that James III had taken from him. In the Border country, cattle thieves still carried on their business, and the king's laws were not being properly obeyed even in the Lowlands.

Six times James IV had to invade the Hebrides before he was sure they would stay peaceful. The Lord of the Isles surrendered and was forced to spend the rest of his life in a monastery. In the Borders, James set up courts at Jedburgh and other places. Most important of all, he made each judge, or justiciar as he was called, go round his district twice a year. These justiciars stopped in country towns to try and punish lawbreakers. So in these ways Scotland became more peaceful and law-abiding.

James wanted all justiciars and sheriffs to be well educated for their important work. So his Parliament passed the Act of 1496 which ordered all barons and other landowners to send their eldest sons to school to learn Latin, and then send them to the university to learn law. The king wanted to encourage men to learn other subjects as well. He founded the College of Surgeons in Edinburgh, and King's College at Aberdeen. In all this work he was helped by Bishop Elphinstone of Aberdeen. James also encouraged architects. The building of Holyrood Palace had begun and improvements were made to his castles at Stirling, Inverness, Linlithgow and Falkland.

Writers and poets were encouraged too. The most famous poet or makar was William Dunbar, who wrote 'The Thistle and the Rose' for the marriage of James to Margaret, the daughter of King

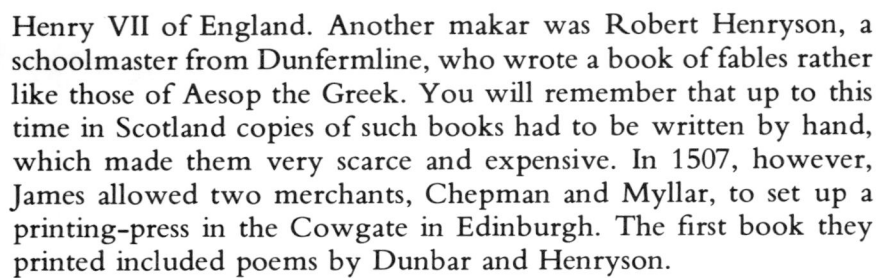

Henry VII of England. Another makar was Robert Henryson, a schoolmaster from Dunfermline, who wrote a book of fables rather like those of Aesop the Greek. You will remember that up to this time in Scotland copies of such books had to be written by hand, which made them very scarce and expensive. In 1507, however, James allowed two merchants, Chepman and Myllar, to set up a printing-press in the Cowgate in Edinburgh. The first book they printed included poems by Dunbar and Henryson.

In fact, as you can see, James wanted to help learning in any way he could. He set a good example to his people, for James himself was a clever man. The Spanish ambassador to Scotland said that the king could speak Latin, French, Flemish, Italian and Spanish, besides 'the language of the savages who live in some parts of Scotland and in the islands'—which was, of course, Gaelic. James was also a curious man. He paid a man 14 shillings so that he could pull his teeth out and often used to dissect bodies at his new College of Surgeons! Sometimes his eagerness to learn brought strange people to him like the Italian, John Damien, who said he could fly, and others who said that they could change lead into gold. Despite this, James continued to encourage new ideas. He has indeed been called the Renaissance King of Scotland. In fact, he sent one of his sons, Alexander, to Italy to study at Padua, the home of the Renaissance.

James was wise and clever enough to see that a small country like Scotland had to be properly defended. In particular, she needed a strong navy. Fortunately, she had sea-captains—Sir Andrew Wood, Andrew Barton and others—as brave and skilful as any in the world. Scotland needed them too: for seafaring was very dangerous then. English sea-captains attacked Spanish ships, Dutch attacked Scottish—and Barton attacked Portuguese, even though Scotland and Portugal were at peace.

James saw that armed trading ships were not enough, and he began to build ships like the 'Great Michael'. The ship was one of the biggest afloat. She was nearly 80 metres long and was sailed by a crew of 300. There was also room for 120 gunners and 1000 soldiers. She was so huge that 'she emptied all the woods in Fife except Falkland Wood, beside all the timber that was brought out of Norway'. This coin of James IV, showing a Scottish warship, lets us see how important the navy was to him.

Although Henry VIII of England and James were brothers-in-law they quarrelled—partly over the pirate raids of their seamen, but over other matters too. France, the auld ally of Scotland, was being threatened by a *league* of other nations, including England. The careful Bishop Elphinstone advised James to keep out of war, but the king renewed the Auld Alliance.

Next, the Queen of France sent to James a letter, appealing to him to lead an army against her enemy Henry, and with it she sent a ring

Andrew Myllar's 'trademark'
What does it show?

The 'Great Michael'

which James carried with him to the end. So in 1513 he decided to throw in his lot with France and attack his brother-in-law's kingdom.

He crossed the Tweed with an army of some 20 000 men and took up a strong position on Flodden Hill. The English general, the Earl of Surrey, saw this and sent a *herald* to suggest that they should not fight for three days. Unwisely, James agreed. The English army, also about 20 000 strong, marched round the Scottish army and placed themselves between the Scots and Scotland—so that there was no way of retreat for them.

But the battle was decided before it was fought. The English were now armed with the bill-hook, a long powerful weapon, with which they hacked down the long spears of the Scots soldiers who fought closely side by side. There was a dreadful slaughter. With their king there perished two bishops, three abbots, nine earls, fourteen lords and three Highland chiefs. James's son Alexander was killed beside his father. Together with them died hundreds of ordinary Scotsmen, some of whom came from Ettrick Forest. We do not know their names, but you can think of them when you hear the pipes playing the lament for Flodden, 'The Flowers of the Forest'.

THINGS TO DO

1 Make a heading in your notebook: 'James IV (1488–1513), a Renaissance King'.

From what you have learnt in this chapter and in Chapter 30, make a list of the things that James IV did that you think were to do with this 'rebirth'.

2 Here is a description of Damien's attempt to fly in 1507. It is written in the Scots tongue of the time and there are some rather odd spellings. Read it carefully and you will find it easy to understand. It is taken from a history of Scotland written by John Leslie, Bishop of Ross, in 1570.

> Ther wes ane Italiane with the King, quha wes maid Abbott of Tungland. ... This Abbott tuik in hand to flie with wingis ... and to that effect he causit maik ane pair of wingis of fedderis, quhilk beand fassinit upon him, he flew off the castel wall of Striveling [Stirling] bot schortlie he fell to the grund and braik his thie-bane, bot the wyte thairof he ascryvit to that thair wes sum hen fedderis in the wingis, quilk yemit and covet the midden and not the skyis.

(a) Who is 'the King' in the text?
(b) What title did he give to Damien, the Italian?
(c) What were the wings made of?
(d) Where did he try to fly?
(e) What happened to him?
(f) The text finishes with Damien's excuse for his crash. Try to put it in your own words in modern English.
(g) Why do you think he crashed?

3 Do you know any of the poems written by William Dunbar? Don't be put off because they are written in old Scots. It is quite easy to read.

We shall see later how humorously (but not very politely) he described the Edinburgh of his day. But he also wrote serious poems, such as 'Lament for the Makars' and 'The Dance of the Sevin Deidly Synnis'. You would like some of this, especially the last verse which tells what happened to the Seven Deadly Sins:

> Thae termagants, with tag and tatter
> Full loud in Erse begouth to clatter
> And roup like raven and rook;
> The Devil sa deavit was with their yell
> That in the deepest pot of hell
> He smoorit them with smoke.

Do you notice how Dunbar repeats the same sounds? This trick was used by many Scots poets in his time.

4 DISASTER AT FLODDEN
   KING JAMES AMONGST THOSE KILLED

It is September 12th, 1513. Write the newspaper story that goes with this headline. In your story explain why the Scots invaded England, describe the battle (perhaps from the account of an eye-witness) and say why the death of James is such a loss to Scotland.

31 The Protestant and Catholic Reformations

In the last three chapters we have read much about changes in the world. Changes took place in the Church too. In the second part of this book we spoke about the great work it did. Think again of all the good done by priests, monks and friars, not only in Scotland but in every country of Europe. You will remember that David I made very large grants of land to abbeys such as Melrose and Holyrood so that their work would go on after his death.

Long afterwards another Scots king, James VI, called David 'a sore saint for the Crown'. By this he meant that David had actually given too much land to the Church and had made it too rich and powerful.

What happened when the Church became too rich and powerful? It attracted the wrong kind of men. No longer was it just the religious, learned man who became a monk or a priest. Now many men who loved an easy and comfortable life saw that they could have it in the many rich abbeys all over Scotland and other countries. Kings were often to blame, too, for they gave positions in the Church to men who should never have had them. Even children were given important offices so that their families could have the money. James IV made his own son, Alexander, Archbishop of St Andrews when he was only thirteen.

There were other criticisms made of the Church. You will remember from Chapter 28 just how ignorant people were. Many poor folk were taken in by a group of churchmen called 'pardoners'. These men went round the country selling pardons. People were persuaded that they could buy forgiveness for their sins from these pardoners. Pardoners made fat profits from this. Some of these pardoners also made money by selling fake holy relics. It was the wish of every church to own something that once belonged to Jesus or to one of the saints. Most of the relics sold by pardoners were worthless, however. Geoffrey Chaucer, an English poet writing in 1390, described one of these pardoners. This man sold a pillow-case which he claimed was the veil of the Virgin Mary. He also carried a bottle of pigs' bones which he sold to people as the bones of dead saints:

> On one short day, in money down he drew
> More than the parson [priest] in a month or two.

But not all churchmen were dishonest or loved the good life too much. Many still tried to do their best for the people in their care. Chaucer also described a priest who did all he could to help his parishioners:

> Wide was his parish, with houses far asunder
> Yet he neglected not in rain or thunder.
> In sickness or in grief to pay a call
> On the remotest, whether great or small.

Sadly, however, too many churchmen ignored their duties.

So it is not surprising that such churchmen were criticised. The poor people were very bitter, because often they had to make heavy payments to their priest or monks. Every year a peasant farmer had to pay to the Church 'teinds' or 'tenths': that is, a tenth of all the produce from his lands and flocks. Even when he died his widow had to pay very heavily. His second-best beast and his best outer garment —the 'kirk coo' and the 'umaist claith'—went to the priest as the 'corpse present'. This would have been bad enough if all the churchmen had been good men, but when so many of them were not, it was more than the poor folk could bear.

In the burghs, too, men were becoming more and more discontented with the Church. From ports such as Leith, Berwick and Aberdeen, Scots merchants traded with Germany, and in 1520 they began to hear stories about a certain Martin Luther.

Luther, the son of a German miner, had become a monk and then a professor at the University of Wittenberg. He did not like the greed and slackness of many of the men of the Church, for many of the German bishops had more than one position and, of course, could not do their work properly. What made it worse for Germans was that many of their rich priests were Italians.

One day, in 1517, Luther could control himself no longer. A friar from Rome, named Tetzel, appeared near Wittenberg, and Luther disagreed very strongly with what he taught. In addition, Tetzel was selling a special kind of pardon called an indulgence. The money raised from selling these indulgences was to be used to build the new St Peter's Church in Rome. So Luther made out a list of ninety-five things he wanted to discuss and he nailed this list to the church door. A very learned scholar did have a debate with him, but Luther refused to stop criticising some of the churchmen and their ideas.

So the Pope decided to excommunicate Luther, that is, expel him from the Church—a terrible punishment in those days. To the astonishment and horror of almost everyone, Luther actually burnt the Pope's letter in the middle of the market-place for all to see. After that the emperor, Charles V, tried Luther and declared that he was an outlaw. From now on he remained in hiding, studying and translating the Bible into German.

Martin Luther

Luther's teachings spread over Germany and into France. In France his followers were tried and many were put to death. A young Frenchman named John Calvin watched some of these Lutherans being burnt in Paris and, as he too followed Luther's teachings, he fled to Basel in Switzerland and then to Geneva. He taught that church services should be as simple as they were in the early days of the Christian Church.

Below you can see some of the first of Calvin's followers at worship. Secondly, he said that there should be no bishops, but each church should choose its own rulers. This sort of church is called *presbyterian*. The Church of Scotland is a presbyterian church. We shall be taking a closer look at the organisation of this church in Chapter 32.

John Calvin

Luther and Calvin were protesting against the churchmen of their own day and they hoped to reform or change the Church. They are called Protestant reformers. In the end, though, they broke away from the Roman Catholic Church altogether. But many Catholics inside the Church saw that reform and change really were necessary. One of these was a man called Ignatius Loyola, a Spanish army officer who had been so badly wounded that he could no longer fight for the King of Spain. So he decided to fight for the Church instead. He gathered together six friends and they decided to try to travel to Palestine to fight for the Holy Land. When they found that they were unable to do that, they banded themselves into a new company of monks who obeyed orders as strict as those for soldiers. The head of this 'Company of Jesus' was even called 'general'; his 'monks' were called Jesuits. Here some of the first recruits are taking the oath of loyalty to the Company of Jesus.

The Jesuits did wonderful work for the Catholic Church. First, they set up schools, and many of them taught in these schools and in the universities of many countries of Europe. Secondly, many Jesuits became missionaries to countries that were not Christian—to India, Japan, China, Canada and South America. Perhaps you have heard of that great missionary Francis Xavier, who was one of the six friends of Loyola. He taught and worked in unknown lands, among lepers and other poor folk, in all kinds of danger. And Xavier was just the first of many Jesuit missionaries. Thirdly, many Jesuits acted as Catholic missionaries in the countries of Europe where people had followed the teachings of Luther and Calvin. If the Jesuits were discovered, there was often only one punishment to expect—death. One Jesuit missionary, John Ogilvie, was put on trial and executed in Glasgow.

We have read about two Protestant reformers, Luther and Calvin, and two Roman Catholic reformers, Loyola and Xavier. All these men, and others, worked in their own way for what they believed to be right.

Today in Europe you find Lutheran churches in Germany and Scandinavia. There are strong Calvinist churches in Scotland and in Holland. In Italy and Spain nearly everyone is Roman Catholic. These differences were carried by Europeans to the new lands overseas. Today, for example, North America is mainly Protestant and South America mainly Roman Catholic.

In Europe these differences led to bitter wars which we cannot describe here, for we must now turn to Scotland again.

THINGS TO DO

1 Imagine that you are Martin Luther. Prepare a short speech listing what you think is wrong with the Catholic Church.

2 Write an obituary for Ignatius Loyola.

3 A lad called David Lindsay was a page at the court of James IV and performed in masques or plays before the king. Later he became Sir David Lindsay, poet and play-writer. He wrote 'The Three Estates', which showed how the churchmen, nobles and merchants were selfish and greedy, and did not care for the poor folk of the land. The churchmen, for example, were blamed for taking corpse-presents and teinds from the poor: the customs we have read about in this chapter.

In this play a poor man tells his sad tale:

>My father was an auld man with grey hair
>And was of age fourscore of years and mair,   eighty
>And Maud my mother was fourscore and fifteen;
>And with my labour I did them baith sustain.
>We had a mare that carryt salt and coal,
>And every year she brocht us hame a foal.
>We had three kye that was baith fat and fair,
>Nane tidier hence to the toun of Ayr.
>My faither was sae weak of blude and bane,
>That he deit, wherefore my mother made great mane
>Then she deit within ane day or two,
>And there began my poverty and woe.
>Our guid gray mare was grazan' on the field
>And our land's laird took her for his hire-yield.   rent
>Our vicar took the best cow by the heid   priest
>Within an hour, when my father was deid.
>And when the vicar heard tell how that my mother
>Was deid, frae hand he took frae me another.
>Then Meg my wife did mourn baith even and morrow
>Till at the last she deit for very sorrow.
>And when the vicar heard tell my wife was deid,
>The third cow he cleikit by the heid.
>Their hindmost claes that was of rapploch grey,
>The vicar gart his clerk bear them away.
>When all was gane I micht mak nae debate,
>But with my bairns passed for to beg my meat.
>Now I have told you the black verity   truth
>How I am brocht into this misery.

Read the poem carefully. Imagine that you are an interviewer for a local radio station. You are interviewing the poor man of the poem, whom we will call Andrew Ross. Write down the questions that you, the interviewer, want to ask and the answers the poor man gives, using the information in the poem. For example, your first question could be:

Interviewer: Good afternoon, Mr Ross. How old were your parents when your troubles began?

4 You have read how the English poet Chaucer described a 'pardoner'. Sir David Lindsay, too, described how pardoners sold worthless relics, pretending they were bones of saints or cords which saints had worn round their waists. Lindsay tells what a pardoner might have said with a little more truth!

<pre>
Though ye have nae contrition   repentance
Ye shall have full remission   forgiveness
   With help of books and bells.
Here is ane relic, lang and braid
Of Finn MacColl the richt chaft blade
   With teeth and all together.
Of Colin's cow here is a horn
For of eating of MacConnel's corn
   Was slain into Balquhidder.
Here is ane cord both great and lang
Which hangit Johnnie the Armstrong
   Of gude hemp soft and sound.
Gude haly people, I stand for'd,
Wha ever beis hangit with this cord
   Needs never to be droun'd!
</pre>

32 Scottish rulers and the Scottish Church

When James IV died at Flodden his heir, James V, was only a year old. So Scots barons began fighting all over again. At one time, in 1520, the Douglases and the Hamiltons fought a pitched battle in the High Street of Edinburgh. The blood of seventy men flowed in the streets of the town during this fight known as 'Cleanse the Causeway'.

But the country was ruled by a firm hand when James was old enough. As the 'Gudeman of Ballengeich' he often went about in disguise to see how the common folk were faring. He saw that his laws were kept in the Highlands and the Borders, where the well-known thief Johnnie Armstrong was hanged. Here you can see one of his coins. James is wearing a bonnet rather than his crown. We are told that James used to 'sit on horseback night and day in the coldest winter so that he might catch the thieves unawares'. Most important of all, he founded the Court of Session in Edinburgh in which his subjects could be sure of getting a fair trial.

It was in the reign of James V that news of Martin Luther began to reach Scotland. By 1525 Scots ships trading with German ports were bringing back not only stories of Luther's doings, but also copies of the New Testament in English. Then Patrick Hamilton returned from Germany and began to spread the new ideas. In 1528 he was arrested, tried and burnt at the stake at St Andrews: the first Scotsman to die for the Protestant faith.

At this time Henry VIII, James's uncle, was on the English throne. Henry quarrelled with the Pope, made himself head of the Church in England, and hoped that James would follow his example in Scotland. He was angry when James remained loyal to the Pope and furious when James married Mary of Guise, a member of the most powerful Roman Catholic family in France.

The last years of his reign were unhappy for James. His two infant sons died. Many of his nobles were angered by the way he tried to enforce his laws. In 1542 Henry was at war with France. James raised an army to invade England, but his soldiers refused to cross the Border, fearing another Flodden. James never recovered from this blow to his pride.

Henry now sent an English army north, and the Scots troops

James V

were beaten at Solway Moss. A month later, as James lay dying at Falkland Palace, the news reached him that a daughter had been born at Linlithgow Palace. The unhappy James did not think that a Stewart queen would be able to keep the crown of troubled Scotland. 'It came with ane lass [meaning Marjory Bruce] and it will pass with ane lass', he murmured, and 'turned his face unto the wall'.

There was bound to be trouble. With a girl-child as ruler of Scotland, Henry VIII tried what Edward I had tried to do—to join Scotland to England. He failed as Edward I had failed, but Scotland again had to pay dearly. Henry made a treaty with the Scots which would put the young Princess Mary in his care until she was old enough to marry his son Edward. But there was a strong group of Scots, led by Cardinal Beaton, who wanted the Auld Alliance to continue, and they refused to agree to the marriage treaty.

Again Henry did what the Hammer of the Scots had done. His armies invaded Scotland and burned the beautiful Border abbeys of Melrose, Kelso, Dryburgh and Jedburgh. Altogether the damage done was tremendous. Farms, crops and animals were destroyed. Some 240 villages and towns were burnt, including Edinburgh—all to force the Scots to agree to the marriage treaty. This 'Rough Wooing' of Scotland continued after the death of Henry in 1547. The Duke of Somerset was Protector, or Regent, for Henry's young son Edward VI, and he sent another English army which defeated the Scots at the Battle of Pinkie.

'Rough Wooing' like this did not win Scotland over, and the young queen was kept out of harm's way. Finally she was sent to France, where she later married the Dauphin, the heir of the king. While she was away from Scotland the country was ruled by her mother, Mary of Guise.

In Scotland the struggle went on between the Roman Catholics and the rebels against the Church. One of the rebels, or 'heretics', was George Wishart, who was burnt by Cardinal Beaton in front of St Andrews Castle. Later Beaton, who had watched Wishart's death from a castle window, was himself killed and his body left hanging outside the same window.

Henry VIII

For nearly a year Beaton's enemies took refuge in the castle, and gave in only when the French fleet arrived and landed guns and soldiers. Many were punished by being sent to serve in the French *galleys*. One of these galley slaves was John Knox of Haddington, who had been Wishart's bodyguard. In 1549 he was freed after eighteen months' captivity. He made his way to Geneva in Switzerland, where he met John Calvin.

But the Protestant ideas continued to spread. Some nobles, who came to be called the Lords of the Congregation, banded together to try to set up a Protestant Church in Scotland. (Many of them were not really very interested in the religious ideas. They saw in the Reformation the chance to get their hands on Church land.) They had the new English Prayer Book used in the churches they controlled, and they cleared these churches of everything that reminded them of the Roman Catholic faith. In 1558 Queen Mary Tudor of England died and was succeeded by her half-sister Elizabeth, a Protestant. Now England finally got the Protestant Church most people wanted. In Scotland things began to move quickly too.

On New Year's Day 1559 a notice was posted on the doors of all abbeys and monasteries in Scotland. In the name of 'the blind, crooked, bedridden, widows, orphans, and all other poor' it ordered the monks and friars to get out of their buildings—or they would be turned out. A few months after this 'Beggars' Summons' John Knox, who had returned to Scotland bringing Calvin's ideas from Geneva, preached a strong sermon at Perth against the Catholic Church. Some people who had been listening to him went away to destroy all the statues and stained-glass windows in the churches of Perth. The same thing happened in other towns. To Mary of Guise, the Queen Regent, all this looked like a declaration of war. So French troops came to Scotland to defend the Roman Catholic religion and keep up the Auld Alliance.

But Elizabeth, Queen of England, did not want to have French troops or a strong Roman Catholic Church north of the Border. In 1560 she sent troops to help the Lords of the Congregation. Soon the French troops were shut up in Leith and surrendered. By the Treaty of Edinburgh which followed, the French had to leave Scotland. The Treaty marked the end of the Auld Alliance. From now on Protestant England, not Catholic France, was to be the ally of Scotland.

In 1560 the 'Reformation Parliament' met. It passed various Acts, ending the Pope's rule of the Church in Scotland, and stopped Roman Catholic services. It agreed to the 'Confession of Faith', which said what members of the new Church were to be taught. John Knox, the leader of the reforming ministers, wrote the First Book of Discipline, a plan for the running of the new Church. It contained many good ideas, such as a plan for a school in every parish in Scotland, but not all these ideas could be made to work at once.

The Protestant Church in Scotland soon had *elders*, *kirk sessions*, *presbyteries*, a *General Assembly* and—above all—a strong belief in reading and obeying the Bible. But the quarrels in religion were not ended, because men had not yet learned to allow each other to worship freely as we do today.

THINGS TO DO

1 From the information on page 186 write a paragraph to explain why James was nicknamed 'the Gudeman of Ballengeich'.

2 It is 1549. Prepare an interview with John Knox in Geneva after his release from captivity. You could ask him about his criticism of the Church, the siege of St Andrews Castle and his time as a galley slave.

3 Find out what happened in Reformation times in your own town or district.

4 Read the ballad 'Johnnie Armstrong'.

5 Here is an eye-witness description of the destruction of Edinburgh during the 'Rough Wooing'. It was written by an English soldier.

> It was determined utterly to ruinate and destroy the said town with fire, which, for the night drew fast on, we omitted thoroughly to execute on that day, but setting fire in three or four parts of the town, we repaired for the night into our camp. And the next morning very early we began where we left, and continued burning all that day and the two days next ensuing, continually, so that neither within the walls nor in the suburbs was left any one house unburnt besides the innumerable booties, spoils, and pillages that our soldiers brought from thence, notwithstanding abundance which was consumed with fire. Also we burnt the abbey called Holyroodhouse, and the Palace adjoining the same.

Imagine that you are one of the Scottish soldiers watching this from the safety of Edinburgh Castle. You later watch the English march away to the border in the south. You are asked by a friend from outside Edinburgh to describe what happened. Use this description to tell the story. You should begin by saying why the English came in the first place. (See page 187.)

33 Mary, Queen of Scots

The birth of a daughter did not bring happiness to James V as he lay dying. He thought that a girl would never be able to keep the crown of Scotland in the Stewart family. He was not quite right: the crown passed to her son, though she could not keep it herself. James saw unhappiness and difficulties for his daughter: in fact, most of the unhappiness and difficulties came through Mary's own fault.

The 'Rough Wooing' of Scotland by Henry VIII made the Scots take very good care of their young queen. For a while she was kept at Inchmahome Priory, on an island in the Lake of Menteith in Perthshire. When she was six she was sent to France for a stay that was to last thirteen years. She was brought up at the French court by Queen Catherine and in 1558 was married to the Dauphin François, the heir to the French throne. The next year her sickly husband became king; the year after that he died suddenly. Mary was left a young widow.

She had already made enemies. In 1558, the year of Mary's marriage, Elizabeth Tudor became Queen of England. Elizabeth was not recognised by Roman Catholics as the rightful queen, because she was the daughter of Anne Boleyn, whom Henry VIII had married after he divorced his first wife. The Roman Catholic Church said that there was no such thing as 'divorce': a marriage was ended only by death. Who did Roman Catholics, including the kings of Spain and France, say should be the ruler of England? Mary Stuart—the granddaughter of the Margaret Tudor who had married James IV. (Mary changed her name from Stewart to Stuart after her marriage to the Dauphin.) Mary and her husband François had, in fact, been declared rulers of France, Scotland and England.

Would Mary be welcome in Scotland? Remember what had happened there in the year 1560. A civil war had broken out between the Reformers—the Protestant ministers led by Knox and the Lords of the Congregation—and the Regent Mary of Guise, helped by French troops. In June, Mary of Guise died and the French troops surrendered at Leith. In August the 'Reformation Parliament' met and began the Protestant Church in Scotland. The south-east of the country, at least, was now firmly Protestant. Then in December Mary's husband died and she, a Roman Catholic, decided to return home.

Mary and François

A real dour Scots haar hung over the port when the queen landed at Leith, where her mother's soldiers had been defeated less than a year before. 'The very face of heaven', said Knox, 'did speak what comfort was brought into this country with her—sorrow, misery, and darkness.' How poor Mary must have felt as she splashed along the muddy roads to the grey palace of Holyrood, we can only imagine.

But it took more than the Scots weather to dampen Mary's spirits. She was only nineteen, and loved the gay life she had known in France. Many folk in Edinburgh did not like the dancing, music and merrymaking they heard at Holyrood. Still less did they like the *Mass* that was said in her chapel there, for Mary showed that she was not going to change her religion for anybody—not even for John Knox, who preached sermons at her and did his best to make her change. They had several heated arguments and Mary was sometimes left in tears.

Mary did not, as you might expect, try to make all her subjects Roman Catholic: she left the arrangements of the Reformation Parliament alone. Her chief advisers at this time were her half-brother, Lord James Stewart, who was a Protestant, and Maitland of Lethington. Quite early in her reign the powerful Earl of Huntly rebelled against her, and was crushed by Lord James at the Battle of Corrichie. Mary herself rode north with him and her army. She seems to have enjoyed it, for she said she wished she were a man, so that she could ride with her soldiers in 'jack and knapscha' (jacket and head-piece). It seemed that Mary could be a popular queen.

Darnley

Not long afterwards, however, Mary took the first step along the road which was to lead to her death. She fell in love with her cousin Lord Henry Darnley, who was, like her, a Roman Catholic. She married him secretly at Stirling Castle and later publicly at Holyrood. Neither Elizabeth nor the Scottish Protestant lords liked this marriage. Lord James Stewart, now the Earl of Moray, and other Scots lords rose up in rebellion, but the queen's army forced the rebels over the border into England.

This success did not make Mary happy, because she now learned how worthless and unreliable her husband was. She had given Darnley the title of king, but he was not content and wanted the full powers of a king. Mary, advised by her Italian secretary, David Rizzio, refused. The jealous Darnley joined a plot to kill Rizzio. As you probably know, this led to the murder of Rizzio outside the queen's little supper-room in Holyrood Palace.

After this, Mary won Darnley over from his fellow-plotters and even allowed the Protestant lords to return to the country. In 1566 her son James was born in the little room you can see today in Edinburgh Castle. Everything seemed right, but Mary was only acting. She hated and despised Darnley—and had now fallen in love with the Earl of Bothwell. The lords hated Darnley too....

You know the story? One night the peace of Edinburgh was shattered by an explosion in buildings attached to the old Kirk o' Field. The body of Darnley was found in the garden. He had been strangled. Opposite is a contemporary sketch of the murder scene. Who was responsible? Bothwell? The citizens of Edinburgh believed he was. Mary? Surely not, and yet—what followed?

Three months later she visited her young son at Stirling Castle. On her way back to Edinburgh Bothwell met her and because, he said, she was 'in great danger' he carried her off to Dunbar Castle. Less than a month after this Mary married Bothwell, whom many believed to be the murderer of her former husband.

Bothwell

Now almost everyone was against her. She and Bothwell fled to Dunbar, raised an army and marched back towards Edinburgh. At Carberry Hill, south of Musselburgh, Mary and Bothwell found that their way was barred. Bothwell fled back to Dunbar and escaped to Norway. He never saw Mary or Scotland again and died in a Danish prison in 1578. Mary was taken to Lochleven Castle and kept a closely guarded prisoner. There she was made to give up the throne and young James became king.

But Mary was not closely enough guarded. Young Willie Douglas stole the keys of the castle and helped her to escape to the west. Her new army was defeated at Langside, where Hampden Park football ground is now. She escaped to England by crossing the Solway and landed at Workington in Cumberland. Later she was the 'guest' of the Queen of England in various castles in the Midlands. Meantime fighting went on in Scotland. The Earl of Moray, now Regent for the young James VI, was murdered in the street in Linlithgow. Edinburgh Castle, the last stronghold of Mary's supporters, held out under Kirkcaldy of Grange for nine years until 1573.

Mary was a constant worry for Elizabeth. The Protestant Queen of England would have felt much safer with her rival out of the way, but she shrank from doing her 'guest' harm. But then Mary was accused in Scotland and in England. In Scotland the Protestant lords said that the Casket Letters (found in a silver casket belonging to Bothwell, and said to be in Mary's handwriting) proved that Mary knew about the plan to murder Darnley. In England, attempts were made to put Mary on the throne in place of Elizabeth. As plot after plot was uncovered, Elizabeth could delay no longer. In 1587, after nineteen years in captivity, Mary was put on trial and, although she defended herself bravely and skilfully, she was found guilty and condemned to death.

The life of Mary Stuart was closed early one February morning at Fotheringay Castle in Northamptonshire. Although deserted even by her own son, Mary showed great coolness and courage at this terrifying time, and walked quietly to her execution.

THINGS TO DO

1 This is a description of the murder of Rizzio in 1566—written by Mary herself:

> Upon the 9th day of March we were having our supper in our cabinet with the Countess of Argyll, the Laird of Creich, Arthur Erskine, and certain other domestic servants, when our husband, the King, came in and sat down beside us at supper. Then the Earl of Morton, and Lord Lindsay, and their assistants clothed in warlike manner, to the number of eight score persons, kept and occupied the whole entry to our Palace of Holyrood House. In the meantime, Lord Ruthven entered demanding to speak to Rizzio, and we asked if the King, our husband, knew anything of this, but he denied it. We also said that Rizzio would go before the Lords in Parliament, if anyone wished to punish him. But Lord Ruthven and his accomplices advanced on Rizzio who had gone behind my back, and they laid violent hands on him—some struck him over the shoulders and others stood in front of me with pistols, and at the door of my room they stabbed him fifty-six times with swords and daggers, at which I was in great fear of my life. After this deed was done Lord Ruthven came into our presence and declared he and his accomplices were very much offended by my *tyranny*, and they thought I was much abused by David Rizzio, whom they had put to death. Then all that night we were kept in captivity.

Read this passage carefully then answer the following questions in sentences:

(*a*) When did the murder take place?
(*b*) Where did the murder take place?
(*c*) What were the queen and her friends doing when the murderers came in?
(*d*) Who was 'our husband, the King'?
(*e*) Who was Rizzio?
(*f*) Why do you think the king might have been jealous of Rizzio?
(*g*) How was Rizzio murdered?
(*h*) What happened that night to Mary, Queen of Scots?

2 Imagine that you are one of the servants of Mary, Queen of Scots. Describe the murder of David Rizzio.

3 Write in your own words the story of the life of Mary, Queen of Scots. Pay particular attention to any connections she had with your own district.

4 What in your opinion were Mary's mistakes? Make a list of as many as you can.

34 The Lowlands in Queen Mary's time

In many ways Scotland in Queen Mary's time was little different from the Scotland that Alexander III knew—especially in the countryside.

We spoke about villages in 'The Golden Age of Scotland'. You will remember that the cottages then were very simply built with stone or turf walls and thatched or turf roofs. In Mary's time they were built in much the same way. Several travellers in Scotland who have left us descriptions did not think much of them—inside or out. One Englishman said the cobwebs above his bed were so thick they might have been blankets; another said he saw 'sheep grazing on the tops of the houses, where there was hardly grass enough to graze a goose on'.

There had been little change in farming, either. Oxen, cattle and sheep were kept—and shut up in the houses at night for safety. The same crops were grown in the in-field and in the tofts. Do you remember what these crops were?

The country folk had other jobs besides farming. Spinning and weaving wool for the coarse plaiding they all wore was carried on everywhere. In some districts men earned their living by doing work that we do not connect with the countryside today. In Fife and Midlothian many men were colliers. They led a miserable life in the coal *heughs* (there were no deep pits) and were treated like slaves. In the Lothians, especially East Lothian, 'salters' worked at the salt-pans where salt was produced from seawater. Can you think of any place-name ending in -pans?

Most people still lived in the countryside, but the burghs were growing fast. Yet they were still small compared with modern towns. Edinburgh, with about 30 000 people, was by far the largest; Glasgow and Aberdeen each had about 4000. The other leading burghs were Dundee and Perth, then St Andrews, Haddington and Stirling. Then came the smaller burghs of Ayr, Kirkcaldy, Inverness, Dumfries, Cupar, Montrose, Elgin, Linlithgow and Dunfermline.

Let us have a look at a Scottish burgh in Mary's time.

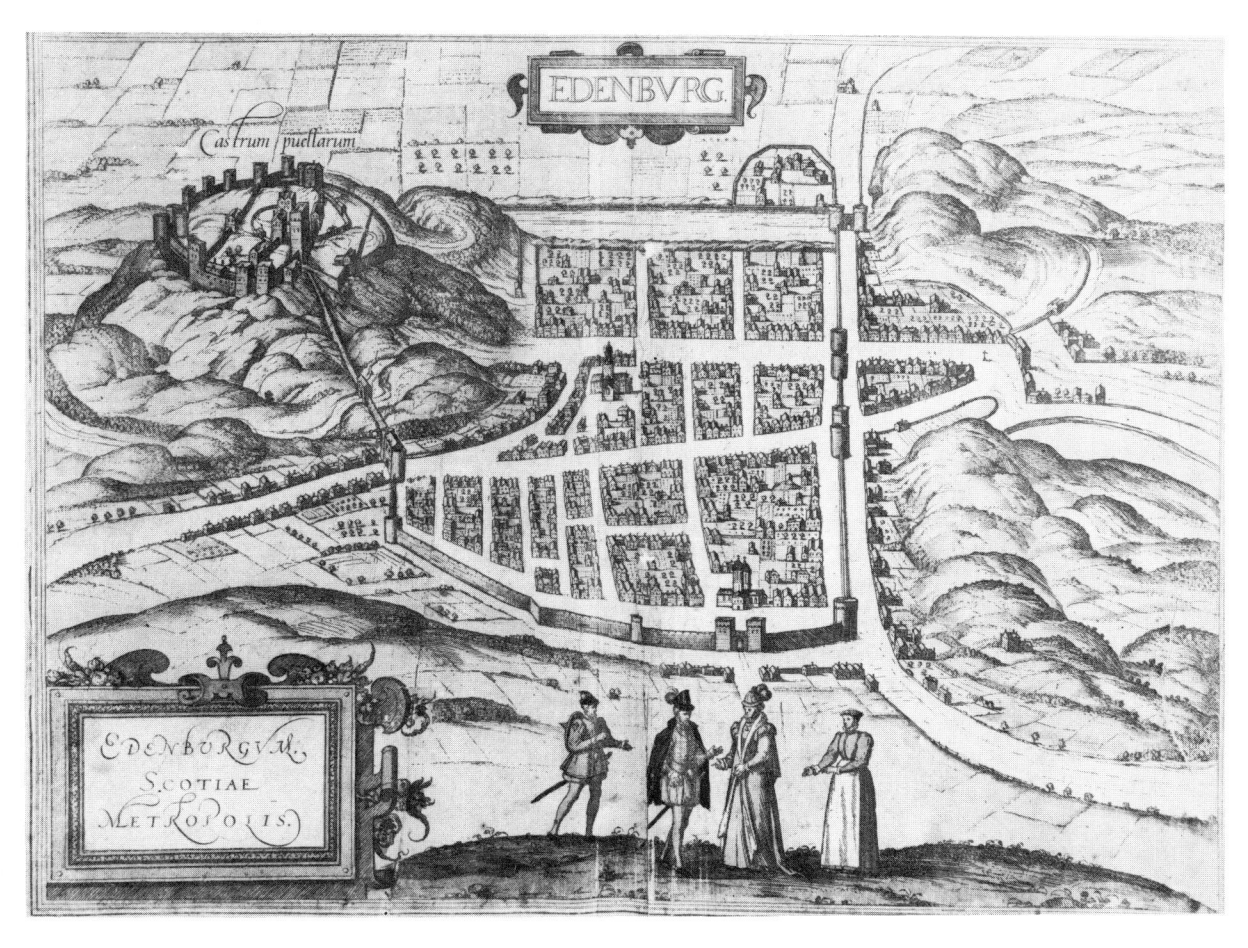

Before we reach the town we pass through the 'burgh rigs' where the townsfolk still produce much of their food, and the 'burgh muir' where their animals graze under the care of the burgh shepherd and cowherd. Not many Scots towns had walls that were any use for defence, though in Mary's reign Edinburgh still had the 'Flodden Wall' which had been hurriedly built after 1513. But they all had 'ports' or gates through which you had to leave and enter the town. This is the West Port of St Andrews in Fife.

The townsfolk have been busy since early morning. In 1574, the Town Council of Aberdeen gave orders to 'John Coupar to pas everie day in the morning at four houris and everie nicht at aucht houris throw all the rewis, playand upoun the Almany gulussil, with ane servand with him playand upoun the tabourine, quhairby the craftsmen, their servandis, and all uthiris laborious folkis being warnit and excitat, may pas to their labouris and fra their labouris, in dew and convenient tyme'. (We have already read on page 142 about the French influence on our Scottish language. In this passage there are several words borrowed from France. The 'rewis' were the streets, from the French word 'rue'. The 'Almany gulussil' was a German flute and the name came from the French word for Germany—'Allemagne'. 'Tabourine' was the French word for a small drum.)

Having passed through the burgh port, the first thing you notice is the smell. You may think that the poet William Dunbar was really being quite polite when he called it the 'stink of haddocks and of skates'. For in front of the houses are middens, where all the rubbish is thrown. They are supposed to be cleared away every Saturday, but it is very doubtful if they are. Anyway, the many pigsties in front of the houses prevent the air from being very sweet. The magistrates of Edinburgh have complained that the streets are 'overlaid and coverit with middinges and with the filthe and excrementis of man and beast'.

Once you are used to the air, you start walking up the Hie Gait or High Street. Only in Edinburgh is the High Street well paved and sloping to the sides. In most burghs it is roughly done, with flat stones (with many potholes in between), and an open gutter or sewer along one side. On each side of the Hie Gait are the houses, mainly of stone (for timber is scarce in Mary's Scotland), but in some the upper storeys are made of wood. Many houses are built in their own 'closes' or gardens. The look of many of these houses is spoiled by the wooden 'fore-stairs', or by sties or wooden stalls. Many of these stalls are booths (or shops) where the householder makes and sells his wares.

But you notice that some of the newer houses are built on a grander scale. One or two may be the town houses of a noble or local laird, but most of them are the houses of merchants who are becoming richer as trade prospers. Some have carved doorways.

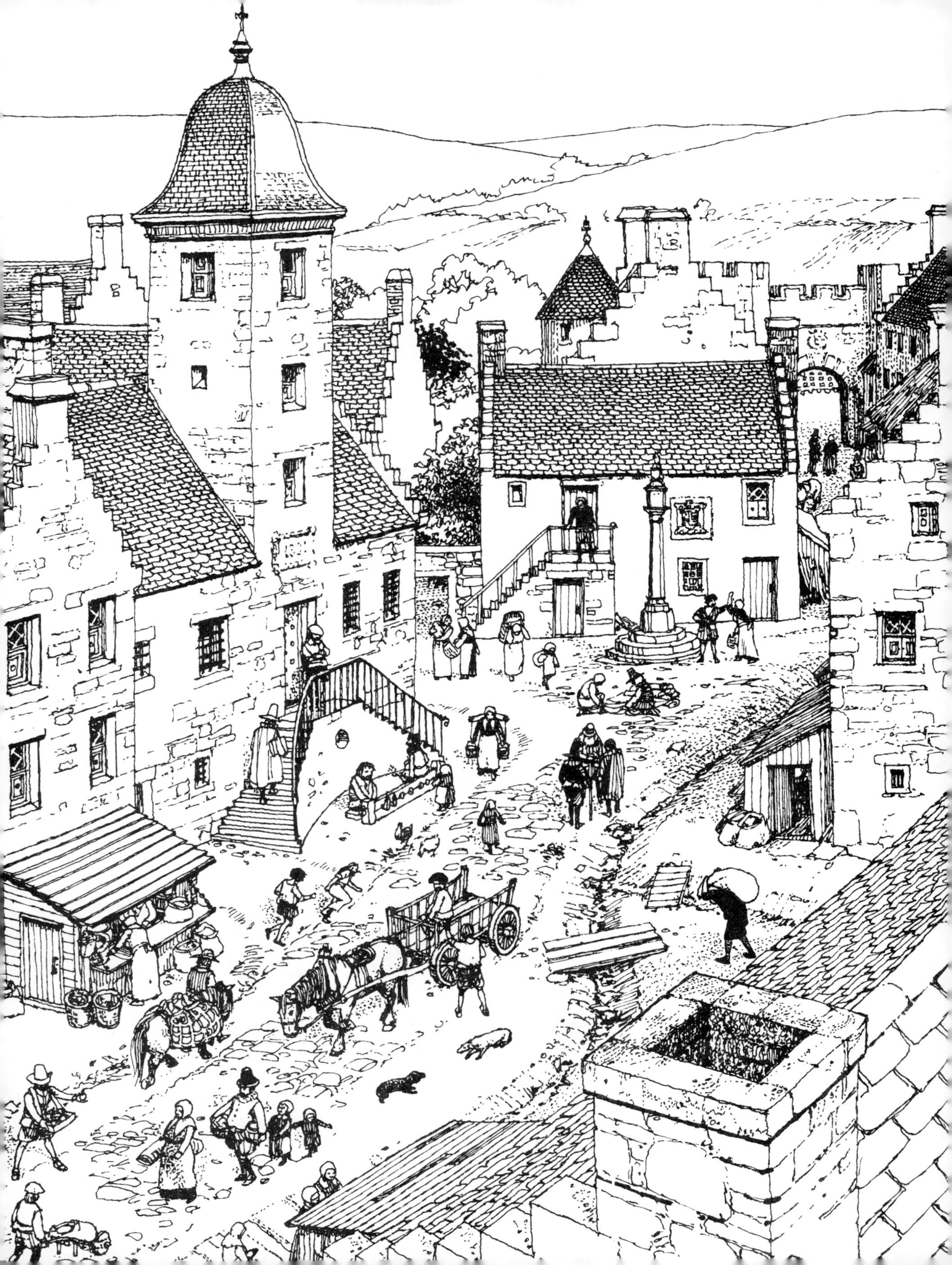

John Knox's house, Edinburgh

These houses have corbie-step gables, dormer windows and big chimneys. Inside these houses the wooden furniture is often beautifully carved. The family sleep in wooden box-beds, often with two or three people in each bed. The most important room is the solar, the living room. Those who are rich enough hang their walls with tapestries; others content themselves with looking up at their painted ceilings or perhaps sitting at their windows watching the hustle and bustle of the street.

As you walk along the Hie Gait you notice other streets running off on each side. Along one of these the animals are driven to the burgh muir. Past the well in the middle of the street you come to the Tron Gait, leading to the Tron or weighing beam where all goods bought or sold are publicly weighed. Next you come to the centre of the burgh—the Mercat Cross, where all important news is announced. (Here is the Mercat Cross at Culross in Fife.) Beside the Mercat Cross is the kirk in its kirkyard.

The kirk used to be the place where all the town's business was done and was a general meeting-place, but now (by Mary's time) most towns have Tolbooths where taxes are paid, where the Town Council sits and where prisoners are kept. Outside the Tolbooth you can see its 'trademarks', stocks and branks and jougs, as if to warn would-be wrongdoers to think again!

Down at the harbour there is as much activity as at the Tron. This is the old harbour of Crail, again in Fife. There are fishing boats and ships which trade with the countries of northern Europe. They carry salt, saltfish and hides abroad and bring back iron ore from Sweden, timber from Norway and wines from France. All this coming and going, to and from Europe, is bringing changes in the habits, houses and speech of the folk in the Lowland burghs.

These old burghs are interesting places. If you live in one, or there is an old burgh near you, try to find out all you can about its history.

201

THINGS TO DO

1 Draw a plan of a Scots burgh in Mary's reign. If you can, make a plan of your own burgh, or of one near you, as it was then.

2 If there are any sixteenth-century buildings near you, make sketches or drawings of interesting parts of them. If you live in or near an old Scots burgh, find out as much as you can about one of its older buildings or places. Write a short report about it. If other people in the class do the same about other places, you could make an illustrated classbook.

3 Imagine that you are a visitor from the country who has come to stay in a burgh with your cousin. Write a letter home to your family describing your first impressions of the burgh. The picture on page 199 will help you.

4 We have said that the poet William Dunbar wrote 'The Thistle and the Rose' for the marriage of James IV to Margaret. When he went to London to make arrangements for the wedding, he wrote a poem which began 'London, thou art the floure of cities all'.

But he didn't think so much of Edinburgh—and probably it had not changed much in the time of Queen Mary!

>May nane pass through your principal gaits
>For stink of haddocks and of skates...
>
>Your stinking schule that standis dirk
>Halds the light frae your parish kirk;
>Your fore-stairs mak your houses mirk
>Like nae country but here at hame...
>
>At your Hie Cross, where gold and silk
>Should be, there is but curds and milk;
>And at your Tron but cockle and wilk,
>Pansches, puddings of Jock and Jame:
>   Think ye not shame,
>Sen as the world sayis that ilk
>In hurt and slander of your name?

35 The Highlands in Queen Mary's time

It has been said that Scotland is really two separate countries—the Highlands and the Lowlands. What do we mean by this? If you look at a map you will see quite clearly the geographical differences which give the two parts of Scotland their names. From Dumbarton in the south-west through Stirlingshire and Perthshire and then northwards through Angus to the Moray Firth runs the Highland Line. Here, the farmlands of the Lowlands give way to rough moorland and high mountains. You will remember from Chapter 5 how important it was for early settlers to have decent weather and soil for their crops to grow and their villages to thrive. The Highlands of Scotland, even today, are difficult to live in. There is little good farmland, the climate is harsh and the mountains, lochs and moors still make it difficult to move freely about the area. The ruined castle of Kilchurn in Argyllshire still guards a typical Highland scene.

The Scots from Ireland who settled in the Highlands in the sixth century lived in small groups cut off from much contact with the outside world. Their leaders fought to win and hold areas of land for their followers. (Here you can see the gravestone of one of these leaders, or chiefs, who was buried in Iona.) It was from these small groups that the clan system grew.

203

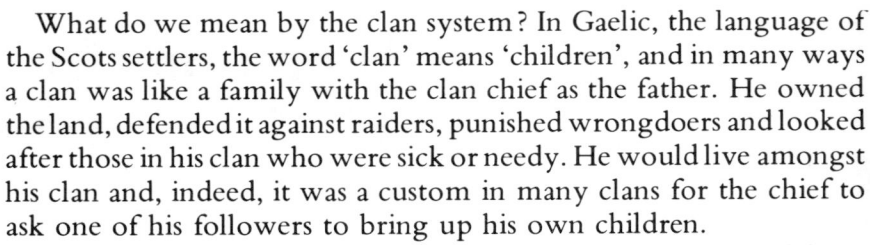

What do we mean by the clan system? In Gaelic, the language of the Scots settlers, the word 'clan' means 'children', and in many ways a clan was like a family with the clan chief as the father. He owned the land, defended it against raiders, punished wrongdoers and looked after those in his clan who were sick or needy. He would live amongst his clan and, indeed, it was a custom in many clans for the chief to ask one of his followers to bring up his own children.

Many chiefs built castles for their defence like the one at Kilchurn put up by a chief of the Campbells. Here in times of peace the chief entertained visitors. In the great hall, guests feasted and listened to the chief's piper, harpist, or bard telling stories of old heroes. From his castle, the chief controlled his clan. While the chief may have been a Campbell, Macdonald, or Cameron, not everyone in the clan would have the same name. This came much later, although clansmen often wore the same badge, perhaps a sprig of leaves or a feather, in their bonnets. The chief gave out his land rather like the feudal lord we read about on page 105. His chief tenants were known as tacksmen (a tack being a piece of land). Often they were related to the chief. In return for their land, they fought for their chief, collected his rent and kept the peace for him. They, in turn, let out their land to the ordinary clansmen. The clansmen paid rent in kind (that is with things that they made or grew) or by working for the chief. They had to obey the wishes of their chief even if it meant fighting for him. Those who refused could find their homes burnt down.

A chief reckoned his strength in the number of fighting men he could call out to follow him. Chiefs of the Campbells, the Donalds (the Lord of the Isles) and the Mackenzies could count on 3000 to 4000 men each. Some clans were linked under one chief. The Clan Chattan was made up of seventeen different clans, including the Macphersons, the Davidsons and the Macphails. Smaller clans like the Chisholms could count on only 100 to 200 men.

The clansmen had a reputation for being great warriors. They certainly had to know how to take care of themselves. Raids into the territory of a neighbouring clan or into the Lowlands themselves were common. So too were pitched battles between clans. In 1598, 280 Macleans were killed in Islay, while in 1603 the MacGregors massacred 200 Colquhouns in Glenfruin. John Taylor, an Englishman, visited the Highlands in 1618 and gave this description of the Highlanders' weapons: 'Now their weapons are long bows and forked arrows, swords and targets [shields], harquebuses [a type of musket fired from a tripod stand], muskets, durks and Loquhabor [Lochaber] axes.'

We have several descriptions of what the ordinary clansmen wore. They certainly did not wear a short tartan kilt of many colours. Many of our present-day clan tartans were invented in the nineteenth century! Instead they wore long linen shirts sometimes dyed yellow with saffron. The only other garment was either a plaid or 'great wrap', a long piece of woollen cloth wrapped round and over the body, or woollen trousers or trews. These were 'tartan' but not coloured as we know them today. A sixteenth-century Lowlander, George Buchanan, gives us this description:

> The Highlanders take pleasure in clothing of various colours, especially striped, and their favourite colours are purple and blue. Their forebears [ancestors] wore plaids of many colours and numbers still keep to this custom, but most now prefer to wear a dark brown, matching the leaves of the heather, so that, while lying among it in the day-time, they may not be revealed by a sight of their clothing. In these, wrapped rather than covered, they face the worst storms of the open, and at times will lie down and sleep, even in snow.

Women and girls wore long gowns and cloaks, again of tartan material.

Here you can see one of the earliest illustrations of Highland dress. This shows both the plaid and the trews. Notice that one of the men is barefooted. It was common for Highlanders—men, women and children—to go without shoes or stockings. This earned them the nickname 'redshanks' from Lowlanders.

As you read above, George Buchanan said that Highlanders were able to sleep out in the worst of weather. They certainly had to be tough to survive because their lives were very hard indeed.

What was life like for these ordinary clansfolk? Unfortunately none of them has left us a description of their conditions. We have to rely on the reports of visitors to try to re-create the scene.

They lived in scattered townships made up of six to twelve huts. These huts were very simple—often no better than the thirteenth-century cottages we read about on page 124.

Indeed this photograph of a nineteenth-century 'black house' (as it was called) shows that there has been little change over all these years. Inside the shelter of the rough stone walls, the family lived, ate and slept in one room with a bare earth floor. Apart from a wooden table, some stools and box-beds, there was no other furniture. Cooking was done on the open hearth in the centre of the floor. Visitors to these huts described how filthy they were, how the cold draughts swept in and how the thick peat smoke made their eyes water.

The folk had to be self-sufficient. Apart from the occasional visit of a wandering pedlar they had to grow, make and mend everything they needed. They grew what poor crops they could on the thin soil—oats, barley and some vegetables. They raised cattle—small, tough creatures, the ancestors of our present-day Highland cattle. They also kept some sheep. These thin wee creatures were no bigger than collie dogs. Nothing was wasted, so they were milked like the cattle. In the summer the animals were driven up to the shielings—high mountain pastures. There, they were tended by the women and young children. They spent these summer months living in bothies made of turfs, milking the cattle and sheep and making butter and cheese. The sheep were plucked by hand and the wool spun ready for weaving in the cottages during the long winter months. Meanwhile the menfolk would hunt and fish or perhaps go raiding for cattle from a neighbouring clan.

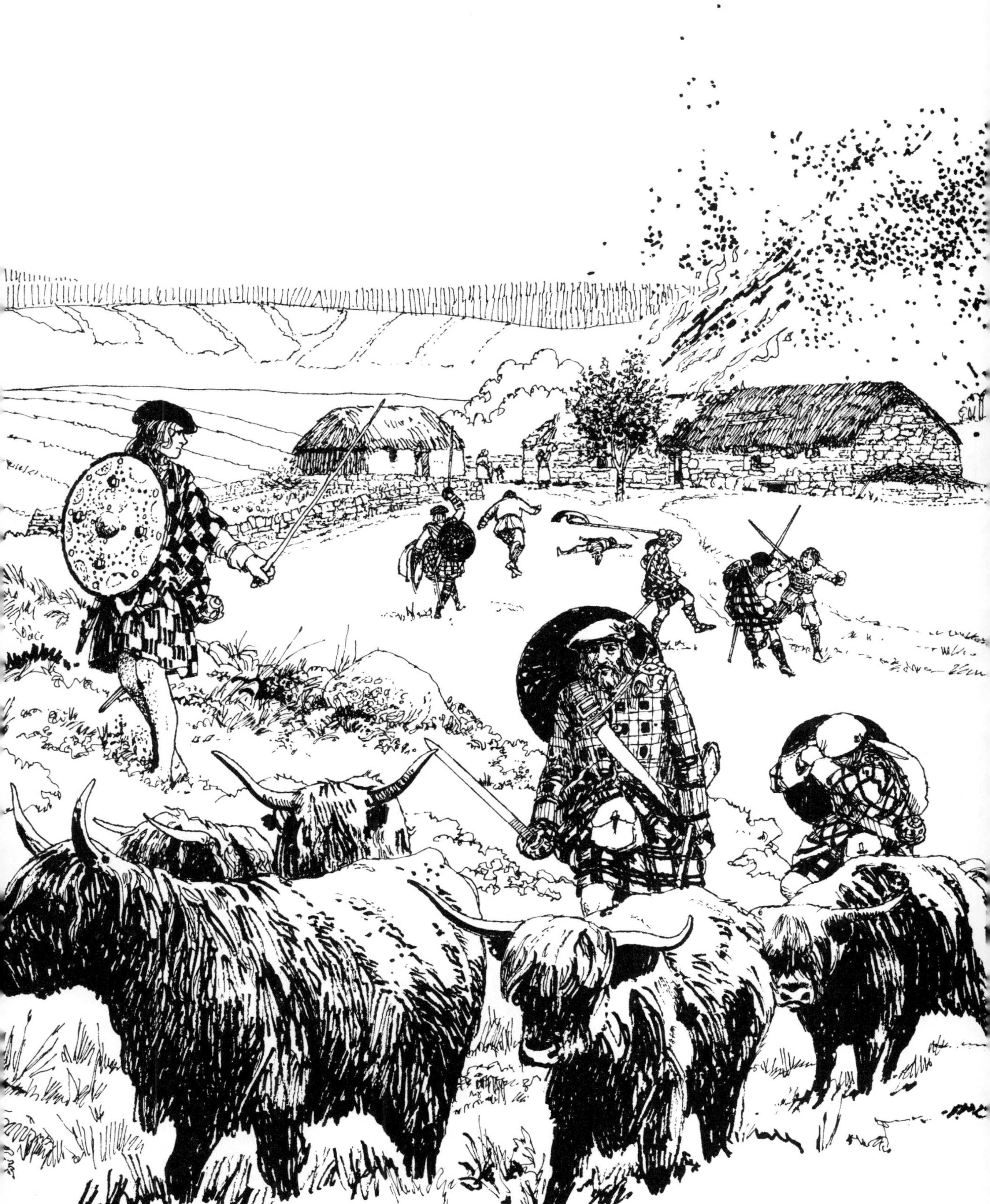

A powder horn

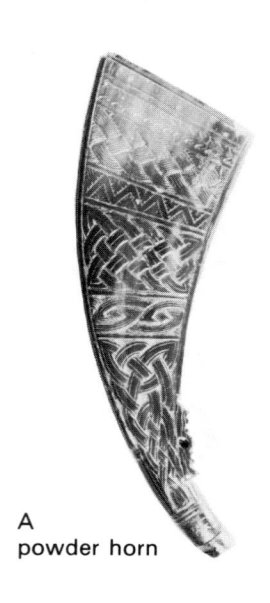

In the autumn, most of the cattle had to be killed. The Highlanders had little hay to feed them during the winter. Traditionally, the cattle were killed at Martinmas (November 11th). This was a time for great celebration—and for hard work! The meat was salted; the skins were used to make leather articles; the blood was mixed with oatmeal and onions to make a form of black pudding. Even the horns were not wasted. Only the important bull or milk-cow was kept. These beasts spent the winter in the cottage with the family.

Times were not all hard, however. There was much singing, storytelling and dancing—particularly during the short, warm summer nights in the shielings. Sometimes the chief would organise a hunt. Then the clansmen could compete in throwing competitions or races—the origin of our Highland Games.

To Lowlanders, however, the Highlanders were a savage race. They dressed differently, followed different customs and spoke a strange language. The new ideas of the Renaissance and the Reformation had not reached the Highland glens. We have read already about the trouble the Stewart kings had with some of the Highland chiefs. James VI, the son of Mary, Queen of Scots, compared Highlanders to wild beasts who had to be crushed. For Lowland folk living close to the Highland Line there was indeed the danger that the 'wyld, wykhed helandmen' would sweep down on their farms and villages burning, killing and stealing cattle. Some even paid the Highlanders protection money to keep them away. But only some clansmen bothered with this sort of life. Most were worried only about keeping themselves and their families alive.

THINGS TO DO

1 There were no tourists, as we know them, in the Highlands in those days. Imagine, though, that you had been invited to a hunt organised by a Highland chief. (In fact John Taylor whom we read about on page 204 had been asked to a hunt by the Earl of Mar.) Write a letter home describing your first impressions of the Highlands and the clansfolk. You could mention the scenery, the homes of the clansfolk, their dress, etc.

2 Use the picture on page 207 to describe a raid by clansmen on a Lowland farm. You can write either as a clansman or as a runaway Lowlander.

Glossary

(A list of words printed in *italics* in this book, with their meanings)

abbot	the head of an abbey or *monastery*
amphitheatre	an open-air theatre with rows of seats, one above the other, surrounding a large open space
ancestor	anyone from whom a person is descended by birth; a forefather
archaeologist	a person who studies the buildings, tools, etc., left by people of earlier times
archaeology	the study of such things in order to find out more about the way of life of the these people
archbishop	a chief bishop; the high ranking churchman in the Roman Catholic Church, the Scottish Episcopal Church, or the Church of England
architect	a person who plans and designs buildings
astrolabe	an old instrument, used like the modern sextant, to measure the altitude or height of stars to help sailors to find their position at sea
astronomy	the study of the stars and their movements
barbarian	any uncivilised person (The Romans used the word to describe anyone who was not a Roman.)
bishop	a churchman of a high rank (next to an *archbishop*) in the Roman Catholic Church, the Scottish Episcopal Church, or the Church of England (A bishop looks after all the churches in an area called a *see*.)
Chamberlain	an officer chosen by a king to organise the royal household and carry out other special duties
charter	a written paper or *document* showing the granting of land or other rights by a king to a noble, or by a king or noble to a town, monastery or abbey
civilian	anyone who is not a member of the armed forces
civil servant	any member of the civil service, the group of people who advise the rulers of a country and carry out their orders
civil war	a war between groups of people belonging to the same country
colony	a group of people who have left one country to settle

	in another, when the settlement they make is still governed by the parent country (The plural is *colonies*.)
consecrate	to set something apart for a holy use
crusade	a war-journey made in the Middle Ages by Christians to try to win back the Holy Land from the Turks, who were Muslims, followers of Mohammed (Nowadays any movement in a good cause may be called a 'crusade'.)
customs	taxes paid on goods coming into a country
depose	to remove a person (usually a king or queen) from a high position
document	a written statement which gives information, proof, or evidence about something
doublet	a close-fitting garment, something like a waistcoat, with or without sleeves, once worn by men
dowry	money and/or property brought by a woman to her husband when they marry
elder	a person in a *presbyterian* church who is chosen to help the minister in the work of the church (An elder is a member of the *kirk session*.)
exile	a person who lives outside his own country, either from choice or because he is not allowed by *law* to live in his own country; to drive a person away from his own country
extract	a part chosen from a book or *document*, usually to give details about a particular matter
galley	a long, low-built ship driven by oars
General Assembly	the chief meeting of ministers and *elders* in the Church of Scotland, held once a year
glaciation	the results of movements of large sheets of ice on the land they covered during the Ice Age
gladiator	in Roman times, a man trained to fight with other men or with animals for the amusement of spectators
guerrilla	a member of a small band which makes sudden attacks on a larger army but which does not fight on open ground
guerrilla warfare	a way of fighting in which many small bands acting separately make sudden raids on an enemy
heathen	a person who does not believe in the Christian God, especially one who worships idols
heir	a person who by *law* receives a title, land, or other property on the death of its owner
herald	a person who carries and reads aloud important messages or notices
heugh	a coal-pit, the shaft of a coal-mine
kirk session	in the Church of Scotland, a committee of the minister

	and *elders* of a particular church which looks after its affairs
lay brother	a working member of a *monastery* or abbey who is not a monk and does not take part in all the studies and services of the monks
law	the collection of rules according to which a country is governed; any particular one of such rules
league	a union of nations formed to help each other, either in peace (especially for trade) or in war
Mass	in the Roman Catholic Church, the communion service which reminds people of Christ's last supper with his disciples
midden	a rubbish (or dung) heap
monastery	a building or group of buildings where a group of monks and *lay brothers* live and worship
monsoon	a wind that blows in the Indian Ocean; the rainy season caused by the south-west monsoon in summer
mosaic	a picture or design made up of many small pieces of coloured glass, stone, etc.
noble	a person of high rank or birth, usually bearing a title such as earl, lord, etc.
page	a boy servant; a youth training to be a knight, being educated and having duties in the household of a knight or nobleman
Parliament	the chief law-making group of a nation; in Britain, the House of Commons and the House of Lords (The word comes from the French 'parler', to speak.)
peasant	a person, usually a poor one who does not own land, who lives and works on the land
plague	an infectious disease which can cause death, especially a disease carried by rat fleas
portcullis	a grating of crossed woodwork or ironwork which can be let down quickly to close a gateway in a castle or fort
presbyter	(in a *presbyterian* church, like the Church of Scotland, where affairs are managed by presbyters) a minister or elder A *presbytery* is a committee of ministers and *elders* from the churches in a district, and the same word is used for the district. (in the Roman Catholic Church) a priest below the rank of bishop, whose residence is called a presbytery
preservation	the act of preserving
preserve	to keep safe from harm, to keep in existence without risk of damage
ransom	the price paid for the freeing of someone who has been captured; to pay money to free a captive

republic	a form of government in which power is in the hands of the elected representatives of the people, with a president instead of a king; a country which is governed in this way
restoration	the act of restoring
restore	to repair (a building, painting, piece of pottery, etc.) so that it looks as it used to
scribe	a person who wrote letters, copied out *documents*, books, etc.
seal	a piece of wax, lead, or other material, with a design pressed into it and fixed on, or attached to, a *document* It showed that the document was genuine: that it was sent by a king, *noble*, or other person, and that it was approved by him
see	the district over which a *bishop* or *archbishop* has authority
site	a place where a town, village, settlement, or building stood; where an event (such as a battle) took place
steward	an attendant or someone who manages the affairs of someone else
	The *Lord High Steward* was one of the high officers of a king's household.
toll	a tax charged for using a bridge or road, or for selling goods in a market (The same word also means a road junction.)
tollbooth	the building where burgh *tolls* were paid
tomb	a grave, vault or chamber in which a dead body is placed
treaty	an agreement made between two or more kings or other rulers, usually after a war or other trouble between their countries
tyranny	the rule of a tyrant, a person who governs cruelly and unjustly
villa	in Roman times, a large country house, sometimes with other buildings, occupied by the owner, family and servants

The definitions in this glossary are based on entries in dictionaries published by W. & R. Chambers Ltd of Edinburgh. To them the authors express their thanks: in particular to Mrs E. M. Kirkpatrick, their Dictionaries Editor, for her help.

Index

Aberdeen 148, 175, 181, 196, 198
Adamnan 68, 71
Aerial photography 13, 14
Agincourt, Battle of 144, 146
Agricola 50–2, 54
Alaric 60, 66
Alexander II 117, 129
Alexander III 117, 130, 134, 135
Alexander the Great 36, 37
Alfred the Great 84–7, 89, 99
America 76, 79, 167, 173, 175, 183
Anglo-Saxons 60, 61, 66, 81, 82, 84
Anglo-Saxon Chronicle 72, 84, 86, 89, 92, 93, 98, 99
Antonine's Wall 54, 55
Aquilifer 38, 45, 52
Arbroath, Declaration of 140
Archaeology 12–17, 19–21, 24, 25, 28, 63
Architecture 7, 12, 13, 19, 20, 25, 26, 28, 32, 35, 40, 42, 43, 47, 68, 78, 98, 99, 106, 113, 122, 124, 125, 164, 196, 198, 200, 206
Ardoch 52
Armstrong, Johnnie 185, 186
Art 8, 31, 34, 163, 164, 200
Athens 33, 35
Attila 59
Augustinians 108
Augustus Caesar 39
Auld Alliance 131, 142–4, 176, 187, 188
Aztecs 170–3

Balboa 170
Balliol, King John 130–2, 135, 142
Bannockburn, Battle of 6, 138, 139
Barton, Andrew 176
Barlass Kate 148, 153
Baugé, Battle of 145
Bayeux Tapestry 92–4, 98
Beaton, Cardinal 187, 188
Benedictines 108
Berwick 109, 118, 131, 133, 139, 142, 181
Birgham, Treaty of 130
Black Death 143
Black Dinner 150
Black Prince 143
Boadicea 47
Bothwell, Earl of 192–4
Britons 45, 46, 48, 60, 61, 63, 81, 82
Broch 51
Bruce, Sir Edward 137, 140
Bruce, Marjorie 147, 187
Bruce, King Robert 135–40

Caesar, Julius 5, 39, 45
Caledonia 48, 50–5, 67
Calgacus 53
Callanish 2

Calvin, John 182, 183, 188
Caractacus 46
Carham, Battle of 82
Carriden 55
Carter, Howard 12
Carthage 37, 38
Casket Letters 194
Catacombs 39, 65
Caxton, William 165
Centurion 38, 39
Chapman and Myller 165, 176
Chaucer, Geoffrey 180, 181
Christianity 39, 44, 60, 65, 66, 68, 71, 74, 85, 103, 108, 110, 111
Cistercians 108
Clan system 203, 204
Claudius 46
Cleopatra 30, 39
Clothing 9, 10, 23, 25, 28, 29, 32, 41, 46, 48, 73, 74, 78, 97, 204, 205
Cnut 89, 97
Coloniae 47, 52
Columbus, Christopher 76, 169, 170, 175
Colosseum 43, 44
Comyn, John 135, 136, 140
Conquistadores 170–3
Constantine 39, 60, 65
Constantinople 60, 74, 76, 159, 161, 162, 167
Copernicus 165
Corrichie, Battle of 191
Cortes 170, 171
Craft gild 119, 120
Cramond 16, 52
Crécy, Battle of 143, 144
Crop marks 14
Cruisie 125

Dalriata 67, 68, 82
Damien, John 176, 178
Danegeld 85, 89
Danelaw 85
Darnley, Henry 192, 194
David I 104–11, 131, 180
David II 142, 143, 147
Denmark 60, 72, 80, 193
Diaz, Bartholomew 168
Domesday Book 99
Dominicans 110
Douglas, Sir James 136, 137, 139, 140
Dun 51
Dunbar, William 165, 175, 178, 202
Duncan 82
Duncan II 104
Dundee 132, 134, 148, 196
Duneiden 51, 82
Dunfermline 102, 140, 176, 196
Dunkeld 82
Dupplin Moor, Battle of 142

Edinburgh 10, 11, 16, 35, 43, 51, 52, 103, 109, 112, 117, 137, 143, 150, 186, 187, 189, 191–3, 196–8, 202
Edinburgh, Treaty of (1560) 188
Edinburgh–Northampton, Treaty of 140
Edington, Battle of 85
Education 23, 29, 30, 36, 40, 84, 86, 113, 142, 148, 161, 162, 175, 183, 189
Edward the Confessor 89, 92–4
Edward I 130–3, 135, 136, 142
Edward II 136, 137, 139, 140
Edward III 142, 143
Edward IV 152
Edward VI 187
Egyptians 12, 25–9, 31, 32, 36, 63
Elcanco, Jaun De 170
Elizabeth I 188, 190, 193, 194
Elphinstone, Bishop 175, 176
Entertainment 42–4, 78, 79, 125, 158, 208
Ericsson, Lief 79
Ethelred 89

Falkirk, Battle of 133, 137
Falkland Palace 147, 175, 187
Farming 12, 18, 23–7, 31, 33, 46, 63, 77, 78, 85–9, 92, 93, 113, 123–9, 161, 196, 197, 206, 207
Fergus Mór 67
Fertile Crescent 24, 25
Feudal system 105, 106, 204
First Book of Discipline 188, 189
Flodden, Battle of 177, 186
Food 9, 18, 23, 28, 42, 126, 141, 159, 206, 208
France 57, 60, 118, 131, 132, 142, 143, 152, 167, 176, 177, 182, 186–8, 190, 191, 198
Franciscans 110
Franks 57, 60, 63
Furniture 21, 28, 32, 78, 124, 200, 206
Futhark 80
Fyrd 85–7, 95–7

Galileo 165
Gama, Vasco da 169
Gaul 39, 45, 57, 59, 60
Germany 60, 63, 80, 118, 132, 152, 164, 181–3, 186, 198
Gladiators 42, 44
Glasgow 43, 136, 196
Glenlochar 14
Gododdin 82
Goths 57, 59, 60
Government and Laws 8, 26, 33, 38, 39, 48, 60, 87, 99, 106, 107, 109, 118, 119, 132, 136, 140, 148, 154, 175, 186, 204
Great Wall of China 58
Greece 32, 34–6, 161, 163, 164
Gregory, Pope 59, 66
Gutenberg 165
Guthrum 85

213

Hadrian's Wall   15, 48–50, 54, 55, 57
Halidon Hill, Battle of   142
Hamilton, Patrick   186
Hannibal   38
Harlaw, Battle of   148, 153
Harold Godwinson   93–8
Harold Hardraada   80, 95
Hastings, Battle of   96–8, 101
Hebrides   79, 117, 175
Hejira   5
Henry III   117
Henry IV   147
Henry V   144, 145
Henry VII   176
Henry VIII   176, 186, 187, 190
Henry the Navigator   167, 168
Henryson, Robert   165, 176
Hieroglyphics   29, 30
Holyrood Abbey   108, 109, 143, 180
Holyrood Palace   175, 191, 192
Housecarls   97
Hundred Years War   142
Huns   57–9
Hunting   18, 23, 24, 45, 77, 78, 92, 93, 105, 206

Ice Age   18, 24
Incas   170, 171, 173
Inchtuthil   52, 54
Inverness   66, 68, 81, 148, 175
Iona   66–72, 74, 82, 108, 203
Ireland   4, 66, 67, 71, 82, 140, 203
Italy   37, 60, 80, 162–5, 176, 183

James I   147, 148, 154
James II   150, 151, 154
James III   79, 152, 175
James IV   175–80, 186, 190, 202
James V   186, 187, 190
James VI   109, 180, 192, 194, 208
Jarlshof   78, 79
Jericho   25, 26
Jerusalem   39, 103, 156
Jesuits   183
Jesus Christ   5, 39, 65, 67, 110, 180
Joan of Arc   145, 146
Jutes   60, 84

Kirkcaldy of Grange   193
Knox, John   188, 190, 191

Langside, Battle of   193
Largs, Battle of   117
Legion   38, 39, 45–7, 50, 52, 54, 55, 57, 64
Lindisfarne   68, 72
Lindsay, Sir David   184, 185
Linlithgow   175, 187, 193, 196
London   6, 8, 47, 74, 96, 98, 133, 136, 202
Longships   73
Lords of the Congregation   188, 190
Loyola, Ignatius   183
Luther, Martin   181–3, 186

McAlpin, Kenneth   71, 82
Magellen, Ferdinand   170
Malcolm II   82
Malcolm III   102–4
Margaret, Maid of Norway   117, 130
Mary of Guise   186–8, 190
Mary Queen of Scots   8, 187, 190–6, 198, 201, 202, 208

Mary Tudor   188
Medicine   26, 30, 89, 112, 176
Mediterranean Sea   26, 37, 76, 167
Melrose Abbey   108, 112–16, 143, 180, 187
Mercat cross   201
Merchant gild   119
Methven, Battle of   136
Mohammed   5
Mons Graupius, Battle of   53, 55
Moray, Andrew of   132

Nectansmere, Battle of   82
Neville's Cross, Battle of   143
Nile, River   25, 26
Normans   77, 89, 92–7, 101, 104–8, 135
Northallerton, Battle of   107
Northumbria   66, 68, 82
Norway   71, 72, 89, 117, 130, 193

Odin   66, 74, 79
Ogham letters   81
Ogilvie, John   183
Oppida   51
Orkney Isles   19, 20, 77–9, 130, 152
Otterburn, Battle of   147, 153

Parliament   8, 39, 136, 140, 148, 175
Pepys, Samuel   8
Perth   133, 136, 142, 147, 148, 188, 196
Pharoah   12, 26–8, 30, 31
Picts   51, 57, 66–8, 81, 82
Pinkie, Battle of   187
Pizzaro   170
Poitiers, Battle of   143, 144
Polo, Marco   167
Pompeii   13, 17, 19
Pontius Pilate   39
Portugal   167, 169, 170
Preston Mill   17
Pyramids   26–8

Randolph, Thomas   137, 139
Reformation   180–6, 188, 208
Reformation Parliament   188, 190, 191
Register House   8
Renaissance   162–5, 175, 176, 208
Richard II   77
Richard Lionheart   107, 117
Rizzio, David   192, 195
Robert II   143
Robert III   143
Romans   9, 14, 15, 36–67, 84, 156, 161, 163, 164
Rome   37, 43, 54, 60, 65–7, 84, 163
'Rough Wooing'   187, 189, 190
Russia   58, 76, 80

Sagas   78–80, 95
Sauchieburn, Battle of   152, 175
Schiltron   133, 138
Scribe   26, 29–32
Second World War   8, 9, 11
Self-sufficiency   23, 123, 206
Senate   39
Septimus Severus   55, 64
Shetland Isles   74, 77–9, 152
Skara Brae   18–23, 25, 32
Solway Moss, Battle of   187
Somerset, Duke of   101
Spain   40, 60, 164, 167, 170–3, 183

St Andrews   103, 108, 136, 148, 158, 186, 187, 196, 197
St Aidan   66
St Augustine of Kent   66
St Benedict   108
St Bernard   108
St Columba   66–8, 71, 103
St Cuthbert   68
St Dominic   110
St Francis of Assissi   110
St Jerome   58
St Margaret   101–4, 108, 110, 132, 137, 150
St Ninian   67
St Patrick   66
St Paul   39, 65
St Peter   39, 65
Stamford Bridge, Battle of   95, 96
Standard, Battle of the   107
Stirling   109, 133, 137–9, 150, 175, 192, 196
Stirling Bridge, Battle of   132
Stone Age   2, 18
Strand loopers   18
Sutton Hoo   63
Synod of Whitby   66

Tacitus   51, 53–5
Tacksman   204
Tenochtitlan   171
Tetzel   181
Thor   66, 79
Timgad   46
Tollbooth   201
Tostig Godwinson   95
Trade   26, 37, 51, 55, 76, 78, 117–20, 122, 132, 158, 167, 170, 173, 186, 198, 201
Transport and Travel   10, 40, 41, 47, 60, 73, 76, 77, 79, 84, 94, 96, 112, 118, 123, 156, 158–60, 167–70, 196
Traprain Law   51, 60
Treasure trove   12
Tron   201
Turgot   102
Tutankhamen   12, 13, 27, 28

Up-Helly-A   74

Valhalla   74
Valkyries   74
Vandals   57, 60
Vespucci, Amerigo   170
Vikings   72–86, 89, 95, 117, 142
Villa   48, 63, 65
Vinci, Leonardo da   163
Vindolanda   15
Vinland   79

Wales   66, 130, 133
Wallace, William   132–5
Wars of the Roses   146, 152
Wessex   84, 85, 89, 93
William the Conqueror   6, 7, 92–6, 98, 99, 101
William the Lion   107, 117
Wishart, George   187, 188
Witan   87, 94
Wood, Sir Andrew   176

Xavier, Francis   183

York   55, 95, 112